WEDLOCKED

SEXUAL CULTURES

General Editors: Ann Pellegrini, Tavia Nyong'o, and Joshua Chambers-Letson
Founding Editors: José Esteban Muñoz and Ann Pellegrini
Titles in the series include:

For a complete list of books in the series, see www.nyupress.org

Wedlocked

THE PERILS OF MARRIAGE EQUALITY

How African Americans and Gays
Mistakenly Thought the Right to Marry
Would Set Them Free

KATHERINE FRANKE

NEW YORK UNIVERSITY PRESS

New York and London

NEW YORK UNIVERSITY PRESS
New York and London
www.nyupress.org

References to Internet websites (URLs) were accurate at the time of writing. Neither the author nor New York University Press is responsible for URLs that may have expired or changed since the manuscript was prepared.

Library of Congress Cataloging-in-Publication Data
Franke, Katherine.
Wedlocked : the perils of marriage equality / Katherine Franke.
pages cm. — (Sexual cultures)
Includes bibliographical references and index.
ISBN 978-1-4798-1574-6 (cloth : alk. paper)
1. Marriage—Government policy—United States. 2. Marriage law—United States.
3. Same-sex marriage—United States. 4. Equality—United States. I. Title.
HQ1001.F73 2015
306.810973—dc23 2015018556

New York University Press books are printed on acid-free paper, and their binding materials are chosen for strength and durability. We strive to use environmentally responsible suppliers and materials to the greatest extent possible in publishing our books.

Manufactured in the United States of America

10 9 8 7 6 5 4 3 2 1

Also available as an ebook

To Janlori Goldman, who helped me think through the most difficult parts of the argument, and to Paula Ettelbrick, who taught us all about how marriage was a precarious place from which to fight for justice.

CONTENTS

ACKNOWLEDGMENTS

This book is in so many ways a testament to my evolution as a scholar. I began research on slave marriages, war widow pensions, and post–Civil War meanings of marriage for newly freed people when I was teaching at Fordham Law School almost twenty years ago. I was instantly entranced by the stories the archives held and the tactile evidence they preserved: locks of hair from a husband killed fighting in a "colored regiment" in the Union army; dried pressed flowers from the wedding of two enslaved people; and thumb prints from ink spilled when a marriage license was signed in 1866 by a newly freed couple in North Carolina whose love and life together could be marked only with an X since learning how to write their own names could land them in prison.

Many people have helped me write this book. Megan McClintock's work on war widows' pensions gave me early inspiration for this project. Her article "Civil War Pensions and the Reconstruction of Union Families"[1] and discussions we had over dinner introduced me to the archives documenting the intimate lives of enslaved people. In fundamental ways she got me started down this path.

The research I subsequently did with the Freedmen's Bureau records, civil war pension files, and in state archives across the South were aided invaluably by archivists working in those locations who were willing to show me a special collection that only they knew of, sneak me in the back to look through unindexed boxes, and helped me think through the meanings of gaps in the records. These archivists included Reginald Washington at the National Archives, Debbie Cano at the Mississippi Department of Archives and History, Pamela Coleman at the Georgia

Department of Archives and History, Gordon Cotton, Blanche Terry, and Jeff Giambrone at the Vicksburg Courthouse Museum, and Ken Simpson at the North Carolina Division of Archives and History. Reference librarians at Columbia Law School's Diamond Law Library have been enormously generous with their time and ingenuity when asked to help track down an obscure citation. They include Dana Neacsu, Jody Armstrong, Jennifer Wertkin, Deborah Heller, and Patrick Flanagan.

The historical research was enabled by generous research support from Fordham Law School and Columbia Law School, and from the John Simon Guggenheim Memorial Foundation, which awarded me a fellowship to complete the research on this book.

Scholarly work always benefits from early engagement with colleagues who are willing to read the work and engage its premises and claims. This book is no exception as it has undergone numerous revisions based on generous and rigorous critique from Carol Buell, Naomi Cahn, Mary Anne Case, Nancy Cott, Adrienne Davis, Ariela Dubler, David Eng, Martha Ertman, Robert Ferguson, Sally Gordon, Ariela Gross, Frederick Hertz, Bob Kaczorowski, Michael J. McHugh, Naomi Mezey, Russell Robinson, Teemu Ruskola, Carol Sanger, Bill Singer, Judith Turkel, Urvashi Vaid, John Witt, and Ben Zipursky, and workshops at Columbia Law School, Duke Law School, University of Chicago Law School, USC Law School, Yale Law School, La Sapienza University Law School, UNC Law School, Vanderbilt Law School, UC Davis Law School, Oregon Law School, University of Michigan Law School, Yale Legal History Forum, the Chautauqua Institution, and the American Society for Legal History Annual Meeting.

Many students provided invaluable research assistance that made the book's arguments stronger. They include Ryan Mellon, Olena Ripnick, and Nikki Kumar.

Special thanks are due to Ann Pellegrini, who has been an enthusiastic supporter of this project since I first brought it to NYU Press. She has been a close, critical, and astute reader of drafts, pushing me to take the argument to another level, which deepened and rendered more complex the insights the book offers. Thanks are also due to Lisha Nadkarni and Eric Zinner at NYU Press for their work on the book's production.

Finally, Janlori Goldman's support and wisdom have been invaluable in moving the book to completion. She's been the manuscript's first and last reader, encouraging me to take risks, cautioning me when I may have stepped over a line, and reassuring me when the project and I found ourselves stuck in a wide range of scholarly *cul de sacs*. Thank you.

Introduction

When George Washington wrote his will on July 9, 1799, he put a price on his wife Martha's head—though that may not have been exactly what he thought he was doing. He and Martha owned 277 slaves—124 were his and 153 Martha had inherited from her first husband. In his will George gave Martha 123 of his 124 slaves, but with the proviso that they be freed upon her death. One has to wonder how much George cared for Martha, since the enslaved people at Mount Vernon learned shortly after George died in December 1799 that their freedom turned on Martha's death. Fearing that George's slaves were trying to poison her, Martha stopped eating and locked herself in the attic, not allowing anyone but close family members to visit her, and forbidding any of George's slaves to accompany them. While the end of the story is a bit murky, most likely a terrified Martha freed George's slaves a year after his death on the recommendation of George's nephew Bushrod Washington.

George's will, while complicated when it comes to Martha, is full of kindness toward his slaves. He expressed a strong desire to free them immediately, but recognized that to do so might cause them terrible hardship. "To emancipate them during her life," he wrote, "would, tho' earnestly wished by me, be attended with such insuperable difficulties on account of their intermixture by Marriages with the dower Negroes, as to excite the most painful sensations, if not disagreeable conse-quences from the latter."[1] By today's lights, it is hard to imagine how freedom would entail hardship, but in important respects Mr. Washing-ton was right. Given the complex laws of marriage and inheritance in the eighteenth century, neither George nor Martha was permitted to legally free her slaves. Since many of George's slaves had married and had children with Martha's slaves, to free George's slaves would likely result in the wrenching breakup of many families—her slaves would remain at Mount Vernon while his slaves, once freed, would be forced to leave the Commonwealth forever. At the time Washington died it was not uncommon that worried white Virginians would chase freed slaves out of the state. According to the 1800 census, there were 20,000 free Negroes living in Virginia. Most of these people had been freed either through a will or, like the Washington slaves, by their owner liberating them voluntarily. The presence of so many free blacks[2] made many white Virginians uneasy. Who knew what kind of uprisings they might organize or inspire in the enslaved people of Virginia simply by their very presence in the Commonwealth? In 1805 the legislature dealt with the problem by passing a law that required freed men and women to leave Virginia immediately after being set free. Once exiled from their homes and families many newly freed black people lived furtive lives, belonging nowhere and one step ahead of bounty hunters who sought to capture and return them to bondage. (Making exile the price of gaining new rights has a robust tradition in Virginia—recall that Richard and Mildred Loving, an interracial couple, were prosecuted in 1958 under a state law making it a crime for a white person to marry a person of another race, and the judge gave them the choice of either going to jail for a year or leaving the Commonwealth of Virginia for twenty-five years. They opted, quite reasonably, to leave.)

The story of George Washington's will lays bare two fundamental ironies lying at the core of many civil rights movements: First, the deeply gendered nature of marriage renders the "freedom to marry" a radically different experience for men than for women. And second, gaining rights—certainly a good thing—can sometimes make life *worse* for some of the people who "enjoy" those new rights. Freedom, in other words, shouldn't end the consideration of complex questions of justice and equality, but rather inaugurates a new set of hard questions about what it means to be liberated into a social institution that has its own complicated and durable values and preferences. Paradoxically, gaining rights can have the unintended effect of conscripting the beneficiaries of a civil rights movement into gendered roles they have little interest in inhabiting. Gaining rights can also, in some cases, even contribute to an intensification of societal hatred and resentment toward previously disenfranchised minorities.

We know well the stories of families torn apart by the ravages of slavery—husbands or wives being sold to other owners without any concern for the children and other family members they left behind. We have heard less about the families that were destroyed by freedom, as the story of the slaves at Mount Vernon so well illustrates. That George Washington believed he could best protect his slaves by prolonging their enslavement is a searing example of the complexities of freedom at that time. His will also gave his long-serving loyal "manservant" William Lee the option of being immediately freed or remaining, enslaved, at Mount Vernon with an annuity for his support—"this I give him as a testimony of my sense of his attachment to me, and for his faithful services during the Revolutionary War." Surprisingly, the former president considered ongoing enslavement as a gift or bequest he could leave his most trusted servant.

Yes, slavery was evil, but freedom was no easy matter either. Freedom had rules, and those rules were not always the ones the freed people might have chosen had they been in charge of their own independence. As many newly emancipated black people found in the nineteenth century, freedom meant that their lives transitioned from private control by their owners to public control through law. The experiences of black people emerging from slavery hold out lessons for other movements for freedom and equality today, particularly, as we'll see in this book, for those gay men and lesbians seeking to gain greater freedom and equality through a right to marry.

Exile from family and home was only one of the prices of emancipation that the Washington ex-slaves experienced in the antebellum South. As freed black people, even in the relatively progressive upper South,

Washington's former slaves learned firsthand that being *freed* was not the same thing as being *free*. Though no longer held in bondage, freed people enjoyed far fewer rights and liberties than did free white people. Instead, they lived in a netherworld between slave and citizen. Being freed did not erase the badge of inferiority that made black people enslavable in the first place, as the moral stain of race proved more durable than the sovereign endowment bestowed by their legal emancipation.

Throughout the South, numerous laws and customs structured the world of the freedmen, a world in so many respects better than the world of the enslaved, but certainly one inferior to the world of free white people. Blacks in the South were usually presumed to be slaves and had to carry passes, papers, or bills of sale to disprove this presumption. These documents quite often didn't protect them from horrible violence or re-enslavement. They were limited in the professions they could hold, in their ability to travel within their home state, and in their capacity to return should they leave the state. They paid higher taxes than did their white neighbors, and if they couldn't come up with the money to pay the tax bill they could be sold back into slavery. Some states required free blacks to have a white legal guardian through whom the free black person was required to conduct all his or her business. The guardian acted as a guarantor of all debts and other financial transactions his black charge might undertake, and thus had enormous power over him—a power that most guardians could not resist exploiting or abusing.[3] In some states, free black men and women who had been accused of crimes were tried in front of *ad hoc* tribunals rather than regular juries, they had no right of appeal, they were denied the right to self-defense against a white person, and they could not testify against a white person. Criminal penalties, including the death penalty, were much harsher for free blacks than for whites. Indeed, in many states the death penalty did not apply to a white person who murdered a black person. Social rules also regulated the behavior of free blacks in ways that reinforced their degraded status. For example, Charleston, South Carolina, adopted an ordinance prohibiting free blacks from "whooping or hallooing" anywhere in the city, making clamorous noises, singing aloud any indecent songs, or engaging in any loud or offensive conversations at street corners. They could not dance or engage in other merriment without prior permission from the city wardens, nor could they smoke pipes or carry walking canes in public.[4]

⌐

What drew my attention to this period and to the role of legal marriage in notions of safety, citizenship, and belonging was the complex way in which freedom could be both exhilarating and crushing for newly freed people. Standing alone, the unfolding of freedom for enslaved people by and through marriage was enough to sustain a book-length treatment of this complex social moment. Yet I could not resist looking at the ways in which many of the experiences of African Americans held out a message to the same-sex marriage movement today. It felt like a neglected resource for today's advocates who have thought hard about the merits and risks of elevating marriage equality to the top of the lesbian, gay, bisexual, transgender (LGBT) movement's "to do" list.

When I began research on this book over ten years ago I was drawn to the historical material as cautionary tales: gaining new rights in a society that still hates you can trigger a wide range of backlash, discipline, and punishment as the cost of civil citizenship. As I sat down to finish the book in 2015, however, this lesson seemed to no longer fit with the rapidly changing marriage landscape in the United States. The backlash against married same-sex couples that I expected has not taken place, or at least has been isolated to a few regions of the country. Instead, with speed unimaginable even five years ago, same-sex marriage fever has swept the nation and the predictable foes of marriage equality are revisiting their opposition to including same-sex couples in the domain of legal marriage.

This swiftly shifting political landscape forced me to reevaluate the thesis of this book and the lessons to be drawn from the experiences of freed people in the mid-nineteenth century who were newly able to marry. While I continue to believe that the "perils of rights" lesson has enduring salience for today's readers, what these stories more pressingly reveal to me now is a different set of insights—insights about both the continuities and discontinuities of the role of marriage in liberation movements for formerly enslaved people and same-sex couples. As more and more same-sex couples marry I have become acutely aware, in new ways, of the enduringly gendered nature of the institution of marriage. The stories in this book show how marriage produced gendered violence against black people in the nineteenth century, and same-sex couples experience its coercively gendered nature today. As for discontinuities between these two experiences of marriage, part of the success, stunning success really, of today's marriage equality movement lies in the capacity of homosexuals to cleave the sex out of homosexuality—a tactic unavailable to people of color, who are unable to separate themselves from the racial mark that underwrites their second-class social, legal, and political status.

While the conclusions of the book have shifted over time, the structure has remained the same. The book is made up of parables in which marriage figures at the core, parables that help us see connections between two fundamental struggles for human dignity, equality, and justice that have not yet been considered in relation to one another in the way I orient them in this project. They teach us important lessons about the possibilities and limits of rights. We can learn today from the experiences of newly freed people at the end of the Civil War: Once you set your sights on a right, the values of the right may overtake the values and aims of the people who seek it. These parables also show us that rights are complicated in the sense that each step forward brings with it new forms of vulnerability and even unfreedom, risks for which we should be prepared.

Much has been written about the failure of postwar reconstruction in the U.S. South. In this book I turn to that era not to retread familiar ground but for a different purpose: to offer a strange, some might say "queer," pairing of the experiences of freedom of newly emancipated people in the immediate post–Civil War period and that of lesbians and gay men today. I write these words just as same-sex couples in state after state are gaining the right to legally marry and are poised to gain a constitutional right to marry from the Supreme Court. I find it curious that marriage rights, rather than say, employment rights, educational opportunity, or political participation, have emerged as the preeminent vehicle through which the freedom, equality, and dignity of gay men and lesbians is being fought in the twenty-first century. Why marriage? In what ways are the values, aspirations, and even identity of an oppressed community shaped when they are articulated through the institution of marriage? What kind of freedom and what kind of equality does the capacity to marry mobilize?

What we are witnessing today with same-sex couples echoes the experience of new rights holders almost 150 years ago. To better understand how the gay rights movement today has collapsed into a marriage rights movement, and what the costs of this strategy might be, I look to an earlier time when marriage rights intersected with the rights of freedom, equality, and dignity of a marginalized population: newly emancipated black people in the mid-nineteenth century.

Since the birth of the same-sex marriage movement, advocates have argued that if miscegenation laws (laws prohibiting interracial marriage) were an unconstitutional form of race discrimination, then laws prohibiting same-sex marriage should amount to unconstitutional sex discrimination. This reasoning formed the basis of the first victory for the same-sex marriage movement in 1996 when the Supreme Court of Hawaii found that same-sex couples should have the same right to marry as different-sex couples.[5]

This analogy never sat well with me. I've long felt that before the gay and lesbian community committed to a civil rights strategy based on "if-they've-got-it-we-want-it-too," we ought to take a closer look at what "they" have before "we" insist on getting in on it. Don't get me wrong, I'm the first to admit that while what motivates some opponents of same-sex marriage is a hatred or intolerance of gay and lesbian people, otherwise known as homophobia, what underlies most same-sex couples' desire to walk down the aisle is love and an embrace of the structures of societal recognition, romance, and family creation with which marriage is so closely associated. Judith Kaye, the former chief justice of the New York Court of Appeals, summed it up best. "For most of us, leading a full life includes establishing a family. Indeed, most New Yorkers can look back on, or forward to, their wedding as among the most significant events of their lives," she wrote in *Hernández v. Robles*, the pivotal 2006 case in which five same-sex couples sought access to marriage rights. "They, like plaintiffs, grew up hoping to find that one person with whom they would share their future, eager to express their mutual lifetime pledge through civil marriage."

The whole nursery-rhyme conception of marriage ("First comes love, then comes marriage . . ."), despite being kind of trite, still holds true for most people—straight and gay. They marry for love, romance, commitment, and acknowledgement by their family, friends, and community. Yet for some same-sex couples who've been together for years, if not decades, and are now able to marry for the first time, they tie the knot not for romantic reasons but in order to take advantage of the legal rules, identities, economic benefits, safety, and structure that marriage makes available. They may not be proposing to each other like this: "Honey, let's get married so that if or when we break up the rules of divorce will determine how our stuff gets split up," or "Let's get married so that if you have an affair I can get your cheating ass arrested for adultery." (Adultery remains a crime in many states to this day.) But some of them are doing something pretty close: "If we get married and you give me HIV or hepatitis you'll have to pay me $100,000." Or "If we get married and you have an affair you have to pay me $50,000." (A lawyer friend of mine reported being asked to put these clauses in prenuptial agreements.) For these people, marriage brings with it a new sense of entitlement, or as some call it legal consciousness, that invites them to treat the rights and wrongs of a relationship as monetizable claims against one another. Interestingly enough, for some couples what before marriage amounted to the inevitable heartbreaks and betrayals of a relationship become opportunities to cash out the breach of an agreement once the relationship is framed by the legal structure of marriage.

For the most part, though, when couples say "I do" they are oblivious to the many legal rules that now govern their marriage, rules they can't just pick and choose (how many soon-to-be ex-husbands are shocked when they find out that they have to split all their assets with and pay alimony indefinitely to their soon-to-be ex-wives? "She's soaking me, and she's the one who wanted the divorce!").

If Judge Kaye is right that people think of marriage as part of what it means to live a full life, then they might want to have a wedding to solemnize their relationship in front of friends and family, but why a marriage license? State licensing means your relationship is now governed by law, and that you have to play by law's rules. An affair or a breakup now has legal in addition to emotional consequences. Put most bluntly, when you marry, the state acquires a legal interest in your relationship. Cloaking freedom in state regulation—as the freedom to marry surely does—is a curious freedom indeed, for this freedom comes with its own strict rules.

This has always struck me as sort of strange. Not very long ago lesbians and gay men found themselves harshly regulated by criminal law, subject to long prison terms for having sex with other persons of the same sex. Now we clamor to have the state regulate our romantic lives in a new way. You'd think that we might have wanted a bit of a break from the state. "Leave us alone while we figure out what it means to be free." But no, once the Supreme Court declared, in 2003, that we could not be criminalized for our private, consensual sexual conduct, we committed ourselves to the fight for marriage rights and the legal structure those rights entailed.

This odd yearning for state recognition is something we share with freed people in the nineteenth century. Just like today, marriage played a prominent role in the transition from enslavement to freedom. Freed people wanted to be free from control by their oppressors *and* to enjoy marriage rights for the first time. They found, as we might today, that you can't have both, or at least that having both creates new problems.

While I recognize why marriage matters so much to some members of the gay and lesbian community, I would have preferred if we, as a community, had paused before we invested so heavily in the blessing that the state can confer on relationships that it deems legitimate. A politics that turns on our being recognized by the state as worthy of its approval provides few tools with which to transform or render more just the fundamental underlying norms by which some ways of life are valued more highly than others. As Judith Butler has observed in another context: "The problem is not merely how to include more people within existing norms, but to consider how existing norms allocate recognition differentially. What new norms are possible, and how are they wrought? What might be done to produce a more egalitarian set of conditions for recognizability?"[6]

In the present moment we can learn something from the struggle for racial justice, not by analogizing today's marriage movement to the fight against miscegenation laws as many advocates do, but by looking at what happened last time a previously reviled and disadvantaged group won the right to legally marry for the first time. This is what led me to look into the immediate post–Civil War regulation of freed peoples' marriages. I suspected that this period might hold out some cautionary tales for us today. And it does.

Even as I urge this analogy, I'm aware that the racism experienced by the freedmen was very different from the homophobia or heterosexism gay and lesbian people experience today. The devastation of slavery and the durability of American racism have left an indelible mark on the U.S. Constitution and on our society that we have failed miserably to adequately address. Along with the conquest, massacre, and forced expulsion of native people in North America, the enslavement of black people is the original and founding sin of American society, and its history is looked to by virtually all subsequent social movements organized to secure the dignity, equality, and freedom of marginalized people, including women, immigrants, and the disabled. Advocates of race-based justice have built the constitutional scaffolding upon which all subsequent minority groups have hung their claims, sometimes uncomfortably. For instance, should the color-blind value that emerged from the race-based equality cases in the 1950s serve as a model for a sex-blind constitutional norm in the gender discrimination cases?[7]

Now comes the civil rights movement for LGBT equality and freedom. Today's marriage equality advocates have made explicit reference to the constitutional paradigms forged in race-based cases, typically claiming that if laws prohibiting interracial marriage violate the Constitution's equal protection clause, so too do laws prohibiting same-sex marriage. This analogy has been fiercely resisted in some quarters of the black community not only for homophobic or other bad reasons, but out of a concern that racism and homophobia are too different from one another to bear the comparison. My aim here is not to equate the two, but rather to associate the suffering and injustice endured by the gay community to the experiences of others. To this end the book offers a juxtaposition rather than an analogy between these two periods and civil rights movements in which marriage figured so prominently in the political conditions of belonging. The project is one of contextualization of the problem—as Edward Said put it: "to give greater human scope to what a particular race or nation suffered, to associate that experience with the sufferings of others."[8] What we can take away from this juxtaposition is a continuity and a discontinuity, both of which are important for the purposes of thinking across movements and within movements that focus their liberation strategies on formulations of freedom and equality that necessarily entail state regulation or governance.

As for the similarities, we can learn from this association something important about what it means to elaborate a new conception of freedom and equality through a form of state licensure. Like same-sex couples today, the freed men and women experienced a shift in status from *outlaws* to *inlaws*, from living outside the law to finding their private lives organized in both wonderful and perilous ways by law. Being subject to legal regulation is something to think carefully about. The experiences of the freedmen suggest some caution with respect to how rights—and specifically a right to marriage—can both burden you and set you free. A desire for rights should come with an awareness of the costs, constraints, and hidden agendas they bring with them.

But the dissimilarities are compelling and instructive as well; the recent successes of the drive for marriage equality illuminate how you can pull the sex out of homosexuality and thereby win major civil rights gains. The gay rights movement has rebranded itself as no longer about the right to non-normative sex and sexuality but rather about the dignity of gay families and kin who share a normative similarity to heterosexuals and the nuclear family. This rebranding campaign reached it nadir when the cause for same-sex marriage was taken up, if not taken over, by David Bois and Ted Olson, the mainstream, heterosexual, legal "dream team" who went all-in with a legal strategy that emphasized the dignity of marriage and of gay couples that deserved to be married. By contrast, people of color, particularly African Americans, have been unable to separate themselves from an indelible moral identity that licenses their subordinate social, legal and political status. In ways that few of us would have imagined only a dozen years ago, homosexuals have escaped the curse of Sodom much more readily and successfully than have African Americans the curse of Ham.

But more than this, the stories in this book aim to illuminate how the same-sex marriage movement is itself racialized, and that this racialization has redounded to the benefit of the gay rights movement while contributing to and reinforcing the ongoing subordination of people of color and the diminishing reproductive rights of women. Whether by deliberate strategy or unfortunate tragedy, a legal-political plot that rests on isolating sexual orientation as a singular characteristic of human identity that deserves special constitutional protection risks disaggregating sexualized from racialized subordination by equating homosexuality with whiteness. This is a troublesome consequence of modern gay rights politics not only for the way it erases people of color who may identify as lesbian, gay, or queer,[9] but also for the ways in which claims to rights for same-sex couples and families are based on appeals to their inherent dignity and decency, thereby distinguishing them from other undeserving, dysfunctional, or immoral sexual or kin formations that are almost always understood in racial terms. The book's association of today's same-sex marriage movement to the role of marriage in freedom for former slaves "does not mean a loss of historical specificity, but rather it guards against the possibility that a lesson learned about oppression in one place will be forgotten or violated in another place or time."[10] The stories in this book aim to unpack how the implicit whiteness of normative homosexuality has delivered a racial endowment to the same-sex marriage movement that has most certainly helped the cause of marriage equality, but sometimes at the expense of the rights and interests of both normative and non-normative families of color.

Gays and lesbians have celebrated the ways in which we have developed innovative families and relationships, combining friendship, kinship, love, and romance in ways that far exceed the narrow boundaries of the marital couple or nuclear biological family. Just as the black community has experienced acute societal, legal, and political judgment for maintaining families that are considered "dysfunctional," "unhealthy," or "pathological," so too the LGBT community should be ready to reap similar scorn for the non-traditional families we have forged. Gaining the right to marry risks bringing with it the expectation that all in the community conform to traditional notions of coupling, and can have the unintended consequence of making the lives of lesbian and gay people who aren't in traditional relationships more precarious, not less.

This book explores several contexts in which marriage figured centrally in the transition to greater freedom for formerly enslaved people in the nineteenth century. The parables of freedom herein are in many ways cautionary tales for today's marriage rights movements. Most of these stories contain versions of the message "be careful what you wish for," but they also teach us how rights-bearing subjects are almost inevitably shaped by the very rights they bear, most often in ways that reinforce stubbornly durable racialized gender norms and stereotypes. In fact, racial and gender norms are often braided together, deriving their meaning and force from each other, such that it often makes sense to speak of gender stereotypes as racialized, and vice versa.

Where possible I tell these stories through the voices of newly freed people themselves. In search of their words describing what it meant to be freed and why marriage was such an important part of their new lives, I spent months opening musty boxes containing old court records and other papers in Vicksburg and Jackson, Mississippi; Raleigh and Oxford, North Carolina; Nicholasville, Kentucky; Morrow, Georgia; and the National Archives in Washington, D.C. When I gently opened up the yellowed packets containing black women's petitions for war widow pensions after their husbands had been killed fighting for the Union, out would fall a lock of hair, or a faded scrap of cloth cut from a wedding quilt. Most were signed with a shaky X since few of these women could write their own names and they were no doubt nervous submitting such formal documents to a government official. Sometimes there'd be a faded fingerprint, left behind by an inky hand when a woman gave over the signed document testifying to her marriage to the now-dead soldier, her husband. Their stories moved me in their own right, while also making me think in new ways about what it means to be free and more equal today.

Chapter 1 tells the story of marriage as bounty. In 1864 President Lincoln was having a terrible time raising enough troops to fight the Civil War. Despite his early reluctance, he finally came around to the idea that the war would be lost without enlisting black soldiers. The Emancipation Proclamation freed enslaved people in the rebel states on January 1, 1863, and made black men available to join the Union cause. But the people held in bondage in the four slave states that had remained loyal to the Union (Kentucky, Missouri, Maryland, and Delaware) were not covered by Lincoln's freedom proclamation. To entice enslaved men in those states into running away from their owners and joining the Union cause, they were promised not only their freedom from enslavement, but that their wives and children would be freed as well. As a result, thousands of enslaved men ran away from their owners and volunteered for the Union army. The chapter explains how in Kentucky marriage was used as a kind of bounty that resulted in the wives and children of the men who took the deal being horribly abused by white Kentuckians who fervently clung to the slave system. Northern officials had little concern for the welfare of the families of the new black recruits—it was troops they wanted, and they used the promise of freedom for their families to lure them into military service. These women and children needed physical protection from their owners' lashes, but what they got were marriage rights—something that sounded noble and progressive on paper, but left them worse off than they'd been while enslaved. When these women's common law marriages rendered them subject to violent retribution for their "husbands'" enlistment in the Union army, the U.S. Congress decided that what they needed was more marriage rather than more protection from white violence. The enslaved men of Kentucky won their freedom as *soldiers*, while the women were liberated as *wives*. Neither would be allowed full citizenship rights until decades later. This story shows us how rights can be a cheap way to "do the right thing," buying the loyalty and sacrifice of an oppressed minority, but in ways that leave some members of that community more vulnerable than before they gained those new rights. The experiences of enslaved Kentuckians freed by marriage teach us something important about the durability of racial bigotry, but also illustrate how marriage can render women particularly vulnerable to public and private forms of violence when their subordinate racial and gender statuses amplify one another.

Chapter 2 tells the story of the intimate lives of enslaved people. While none of them could legally marry, many were married in "the eyes of god" and their community by clergy and other lay officials, and lived, while enslaved, as married couples. Others formed more fluid relations, "taking up" with each other—something more than dating and less than marriage—entering into trial marriages, or taking on more than one spouse. The many ways in which enslaved people formed intimate relationships may have been the result of the absence of formal legal marriage or the remnant of African customs, or perhaps were forged as an adaptation to the threat that at any moment their owners could break up their marriages and families by selling them away. Once they were freed, however, the multiplicity of their intimate relationships had to yield to one legal form: monogamous marriage, and those who "kept up the old ways" paid a dear price for doing so. In this sense, gaining the right to marry resulted in marriage "occupying the field," as we say in law, crowding out all other kinds of relationships as illegitimate, immoral, and unworthy of legal and social contempt. This chapter offers today's same-sex marriage movement a lesson in how gaining a legal right to marry may result in the marginalization of other non-marital kinds of relationships—many of which are quite common in both the African American and LGBT communities.

In chapter 3 the experiences of marriage rights for formerly enslaved people shows us, in ways that have a clear resonance today, how gaining a right to marry can quickly collapse into a compulsion to marry. While the Civil War was ongoing, many of the Northern military and civilian agents who were assigned to assist the black people fleeing enslavement felt strongly that marriage would help "civilize" their charges and would do much to repair the "degraded moral character" they found in them. "One great defect in the management of the negroes down there was, as I judged, the ignoring of the family relationship," observed a Freedmen's Bureau agent in late 1863. "My judgement is that one of the first things to be done with these people, to qualify them for citizenship, for self-protection and self-support, is to impress upon them the family obligations."[11]

Newly freed men and women quickly found that the importance of the marital relation was often "impressed" upon them through arrest and prosecution for violating the state's criminal laws prohibiting fornication, adultery, and bigamy. Many of them found themselves married without their knowledge, while others knew little of the laws of marriage. When their relationships ended and they separated from one another, they did so without going through formal divorce proceedings, unaware that they needed to do so. This often landed them in the county jail when they took up with another partner. Freed people learned the hard way that marriage rights were a mixed blessing insofar as marriage had strict rules and those rules could be—and were—used by unsympathetic whites to undermine the full emancipation of black people.

Today's same-sex marriage movement can learn much from these experiences given that contemporary laws automatically marry couples who were in civil unions, and many couples find themselves trapped in marriages they can't legally escape. So too, the perils of transgressing marriage's rules remain a threat since many states still criminalize adultery. Though such laws, like New York State's, are rarely enforced against heterosexuals even when they commit highly publicized acts of infidelity, as did New York governor Eliot Spitzer in 2008, there is a risk that they might spring back to life when law enforcement officials unsympathetic to same-sex couples' right to marry decide to make a few arrests to prove a point. Fornication laws criminalizing sex outside of marriage and laws making it illegal for a couple to live together in a "lewd and lascivious manner" also remain on the books in some states, and despite the common sense that these laws are outdated they are used from time to time by public officials who think this kind of conduct is sinful. Take Florida's law: "If any man and woman, not being married to each other, lewdly and lasciviously associate and cohabit together, or if any man or woman, married or unmarried, engages in open and gross lewdness and lascivious behavior, they shall be guilty of a misdemeanor of the second degree." Just as was the case for freed people in the nineteenth century, these arcane laws could be used to punish members of the gay community for pushing an agenda that local officials don't agree with: *You want marriage? We'll give you marriage!*

Chapter 4 takes a closer look at the prosecutions of black men for bigamy, adultery, or fornication in the nineteenth century. It turns out that in many cases it wasn't racist white sheriffs that arrested them for violating marriage's rules. To my great surprise when I dove into the archives in Mississippi and North Carolina, I found that many criminal cases were initiated by members of the black community against each other—by judgmental members of the community who wanted to punish their neighbors who were giving black people a bad name by "keeping up the old ways," or who wanted to get revenge on someone they disliked. "Good blacks" were policing the "bad blacks" this way. In other cases the complaint was brought to the local sheriff by a spurned lover, usually a wife, who wanted her husband back in the house or who simply wanted him to pay for leaving her. These sorts of vengeful or judgmental uses of the law have hardly gone out of style, and surely we can anticipate members of the gay and lesbian community dropping a dime to the local prosecutor when they don't like the person their spouses or neighbors have hooked up with. In this sense, the newly won freedom to marry may have a dark side; in the bad old days it was homophobes who called the cops on us, nowadays it may be our friends and family who do it.

The gay community today has already seen the use of marriage and criminal law to sort the good gays from the bad. The Supreme Court's *Lawrence v. Texas* case began when a spurned lover called the cops on his boyfriend when he took another man home with him. Several prominent conservative advocates within the gay community have urged that same-sex couples be able to legally marry so that this might civilize the unruly sexual practices that they abhor among gay men. To their minds, the reputation of the gay community in the eyes of heterosexuals will turn on the ability of same-sex couples to behave themselves and stick to the rules of marriage. On the other hand there is Dan Savage, a prominent gay journalist and political activist who has argued that marital infidelity is a virtue.[12] A culture war *within* the LGBT community about the role of marriage in the domestication and assimilation of gay rights into larger conservative agendas was declared at the very moment marriage equality was placed at the top of the gay rights agenda.

The book's central conceit, associating two eras and two civil rights movements with one another, is a risky one. The dissimilarities threaten to overwhelm the similarities. At no point does the book argue that an analogy can be drawn between African Americans' and same-sex couples' first experiences with marriage. They are not analogous and it would be foolish to insist that they are. Rather, as I argue in chapter 5, the aim in bringing these two periods together lies in what we can learn about the role of marriage in fundamental civil rights struggles in the United States. I come at this inquiry two ways: First, by appreciating how the experiences of African Americans may foretell for the gay community some of the perils of a politics of freedom and equality made real through marriage rights. Second, and perhaps more importantly, by plumbing the dissimilarities between these two experiences.

What can we learn about the badges of inferiority borne by people of color and by sexual minorities in this country by and through this juxtaposition and, crucially, by the differences it reveals? Remarkably and swiftly, same-sex couples have been able to deploy the fight for marriage equality to rebrand themselves as decent, loving people—just like everyone else. Marriage for gay people has been a site of reinvention and redemption. Yet for African Americans, whether in the nineteenth century or today, marriage has by and large served as a test they are doomed to fail. Through these failures the moral stain of race—as much moral as biologized—has been written and rewritten on black bodies. By contrast, for gay people marriage has proven a worthy vehicle for humanization and destigmatization. What can this difference tell us about racism, about homophobia, and about marriage more generally? Chapter 5 explores both these junctions and disjunctions when marriage is put to work as part of larger movements for freedom and equality.

The final chapter poses two last questions about the role of marriage in the gay rights movement, particularly when examined in comparison with the role it played in securing rights for African Americans. Newly freed women in the nineteenth century found marriage to be an institution that slotted them into roles of dependency and subservience to a male head of household, thus creating for them new forms of gender-based vulnerability at the same time as it promised new kinds of security.

In what ways might we expect same-sex couples to be gendered once their relationships assume the structure of legal marriage? Might the pre-scripted roles of marriage—husband and wife—be mapped onto gay men and lesbians in ways that reproduce hetero-gendered subject positions, or is marriage supple enough to accommodate a new cast of characters who promise to bust open marriage's essentially heterosexual form?

We can expect both intended and unintended consequences when same-sex couples are folded into the laws of marriage and divorce by which heterosexual couples have been governed for decades. For some lesbian and gay couples, the rules of marriage are exactly what they want: monogamy, mutual duties of economic support, comingling of finances, legal recognition as spouses for insurance and other benefits, and the rules of divorce, including fair distribution of property and obligations to pay alimony or other financial support after the couple legally separates. For others, not so much. What we're seeing in states where same-sex couples have married and then some of them break up and divorce is that many feel that the rules of divorce are ill suited to the structure, values, and needs of their relationships. Unlike with heterosexual couples, sex-based inequality does not structure same-sex couples' relationships. This is not to say that other forms of inequality are absent from these relationships, but rather that the basic inequality underwriting heterosexual marriage—a partnership between a man and a woman—is not relevant.

Chapter 6 concludes with one additional observation about the risks posed to the gay rights movement from the juggernaut that is marriage equality: how and where does sexual liberty figure in the movement? Have the arguments made in the marriage equality cases, arguments that domesticate the gay couple into the marital form, alienated sexual attachment or desire outside of kinship? Do non-marital forms of sexuality risk being dropped from—or more aggressively kicked out of—the gay rights agenda?

⌐

Wedlocked offers a way to understand today's movement for same-sex marriage rights in a larger context—one that echoes many of the complexities of what it meant for black people to marry for the first time at the close of the Civil War. Marriage then just as marriage now has been a potent vehicle for a subjugated minority to express a demand for full rights and belonging. Yet at the same time *being* married has been a mixed blessing, giving the enemies of equality new ways to express racist and homophobic intolerance. So too, marriage as a civil rights agenda has left behind large numbers of African American and lesbian and gay people whose personal insecurity cannot and will not be alleviated by gaining the right to marry.

The phenomenal success of the marriage equality movement provides an opportunity to think critically about the underlying nature of those successes. Are they best understood as victories for gay rights generally or for marriage rights specifically? That is to say, do they lie in the fact that the plea for dignity and equality is made by and through a demand for *marriage* as opposed to some other fundamental right? What is it about marriage that has made it a suitable vehicle for elevating the civil status of gay people?

Finally, why hasn't marriage played the same role for African American people in the United States? This, in the end, is the central question with which this book grapples: how does a right to marry help us better understand the stubborn, even indelible, nature of racial stigma, particularly when compared with the stigma of being gay? The dissimilarities that emerge when we hold next to one another the role of marriage rights in struggles for racial justice and for gay liberation illuminate how effective the gay community has been in using marriage to redefine what it means to be gay. A similar dignity of self-definition has never been made available to African American people. Not through the abolition of slavery, not through the passage of important civil rights laws, and certainly not through marriage. Understanding how gay men and lesbians have used the cause for marriage equality to rework the social and legal reputation of gayness helps us see even more clearly how, by contrast, the signature of race is a mark that African American people have had little hand in writing or rewriting.

1

Freedom by Marriage

Over the objections of almost every white politician in Kentucky, in April 1864 the Union army began to enlist black men enslaved in the state who were willing to run away from their masters and fight for the Northern cause. These new black recruits were paid by the federal government in two ways, one routine, the other beyond price. In exchange for their service they received $10 per month as salary, but they could be paid for their labor only if they were free men, so the first and most important "compensation" they received from the federal government was a certificate of freedom.

This new way of filling out the ranks of a dwindling Union army created a problem, one completely unanticipated by the U.S. military: when black men in Kentucky reported for duty—often running away from their owners to do so—their wives and children left back on the plantations were vulnerable to horribly cruel treatment by the plantation owners as retaliation for their enlistment. Once word of this racist and misogynist violence circulated among enslaved people in Kentucky it became much more difficult to recruit black men to fight for the Union cause.

In the spring of 1865 Congress got to work on the problem. They passed a law that promised that the federal government would free not only the black men of Kentucky who volunteered to fight for the Union army but also their wives and children. Secretary of War Edwin Stanton wrote President Lincoln offering his opinion of the measure as it sat on Lincoln's desk awaiting his signature. In Stanton's view:

the liberation of the wife and children from slavery, and placing them under the protection of the law as free persons, would relieve persons enlisting from great anxiety in respect to the condition of those whom they love and desire to protect, and would afford a strong inducement to encounter cheerfully every species of toil and danger to secure them the book of freedom, and therefore that such measure would promote the efficiency of the service.[1]

This chapter tells the story of how marriage became a "freedom ticket" for tens of thousands of enslaved women in Kentucky in 1864 and 1865, and how they, more than their husbands, suffered the violent backlash of Kentucky slave owners who loathed the idea of black people having greater, or for that matter any, rights. The reign of terror these women experienced could have been easily anticipated when federal officials issued new legal rules that recognized and encouraged their marriages, but the safety of these women and their children were of no one's concern. Or at least not of concern to officials who could have done something about it.

The experiences of marriage for black women in Kentucky in the 1860s teach us an important lesson today, as same-sex couples are marrying for the first time. Many newly married black women in Kentucky both celebrated their right to legally marry the men who were their husbands in the eyes of god but not the law, but this celebration was accompanied by new vulnerabilities created by the backlash their marriages unleashed. In fact, some of them ended up worse off married than they were before they enjoyed new recognition by law. The former slaves found themselves freed but not free, just as today many same-sex couples find themselves legally equal but practically inferior and vulnerable to homophobic discrimination and violence.

⌒

Kentucky played a key, yet curious, role in the enslavement and subsequent emancipation of black people in the 1860s. In many ways

Kentuckians were less committed to slavery than were their neighbors to the south. Kentucky was one of only two slave states that did not prohibit enslaved people from being taught to read, and Kentucky was the only slave state that required a jury trial for black defendants. Perhaps most importantly, Kentucky was one of only four slave-holding states that stayed loyal to the Union throughout the Civil War (along with Maryland, Missouri, and Delaware), resisting the pull from the south to join the Confederacy.

President Lincoln trod very carefully in his dealings with Kentucky, not wanting to risk alienating local political leaders who could easily tip in the Confederate direction if he pressed them too hard on the question of slavery. In August 1861 General John Fremont got out ahead of Lincoln politically and issued a proclamation freeing all of the enslaved people of Missouri. When Lincoln heard of it he promptly sent Fremont an admonishing telegram: "I think there is great danger . . . [in] liberating slaves of traitorous owners, [it] will alarm our Southern Union friends and turn them against us; perhaps ruin our rather fair prospect for Kentucky." Lincoln rescinded Fremont's proclamation when Fremont refused to do so himself. Shortly thereafter, Lincoln received a letter from Illinois senator Orville H. Browning supporting General Fremont's bold action, and Lincoln replied: "I think to lose Kentucky is nearly to lose the whole game. Kentucky gone, we cannot hold Missouri, nor as I think, Maryland. These all against us, and the job on our hands is too large for us."[2] While Lincoln held no love for Kentucky's stubborn attachment to slavery, keeping the state in the Union was a more pressing matter in the near term.

A policy of gradual, rather than wholesale, emancipation served both Lincoln's growing commitment to end slavery and the unrelenting need to raise new troops as the war progressed. By early 1862 he was getting enormous pressure from his top brass and from civilian politicians to enlist black troops. By mid-summer he relented, allowing the army to muster black men, but most of them served not in fighting roles, but rather as "military laborers" working as blacksmiths, carpenters, bakers, cooks, and launderers. The president, still worried about alienating the pro-slavery political leadership of Kentucky, was hesitant to allow black men to serve as true soldiers, bearing arms in the Union uniform. When a delegation of "Western Gentlemen," including two members of Congress, paid a visit to the president in the summer of 1862 ready to make available two regiments of black soldiers from Indiana, he refused their offer: "the nation could not afford to lose Kentucky at this crisis . . . to arm the negroes would turn 50,000 bayonets from the loyal Border States against us that were for us."[3]

Much of Lincoln's careful approach toward the abolition of slavery during the war was criticized by the likes of Frederick Douglass and other Northern abolitionists as appeasement of slavery interests. They issued strong rebukes of the president's hesitation to conscript black soldiers in the Union army, and the delay he took in emancipating enslaved people in areas under Union control. Part of what held Lincoln back on both scores was his desire to keep Kentucky in the Union. Eventually Lincoln came around to the notion that the abolition of slavery went hand in glove with defeat of the Confederacy. Not until late in 1862, just as the Emancipation Proclamation was to go into effect, did Lincoln relent on the issue of using black soldiers to fight the war for the North. The recruitment of black soldiers for real military service became an important and central aspect of Lincoln's emancipation policy from that point forward.[4]

While his policies, and those of the Congress, resulted in the gradual emancipation of enslaved people held by traitors to the Union, enslaved people in Kentucky found no relief. Even the Emancipation Proclamation, which took effect on January 1, 1863, and freed 3.1 million people held in Confederate states, held no promise for the slaves of Kentucky since by its own terms the Proclamation applied only to slaves in states in rebellion. As long as Kentucky stayed loyal to the Union the Emancipation Proclamation could not touch slavery in the state.

White Kentuckians bristled at the thought that their loyalty to the Union would be rewarded with a federal incentive for their male slaves to run away and be fitted out for a Union uniform and rifle. It was one thing for freed blacks in the North and former slaves in the Confederacy to be armed as Union soldiers. It was quite another to lure enslaved men away from their owners in the loyal slave states. Military officials met with the governor and other civic leaders, trying to convince them that it was in their interest to allow black enlistment—after all, Kentucky's draft quotas could be met by enlisting black soldiers, thus relieving the pressure on Kentucky's white men to serve. The governor was experiencing greater and greater difficulty meeting the state's federal draft quota, particularly given that a significant number of able-bodied white men were slipping into northern Tennessee to join the First Kentucky Brigade. The First Kentucky Brigade, also known as the Kentucky Orphan Brigade (those who joined these regiments were "civil orphans," traitors to Kentucky but sons of no other state), was made up of thousands of men from the Bluegrass State who deeply disagreed with the state political elite's decision to side with the Union, and thus formed several Kentucky regiments that mustered into Confederate service from camps in northern Tennessee starting in the fall of 1861.[5]

Notwithstanding the popularity of service with the Kentucky Orphan Brigade for many Kentuckians, by 1864 the majority of whites in Kentucky remained loyal to the Union while also hostile to the idea of watching regiments of armed black soldiers—their former slaves—drill in public view in Union uniforms. The governor of Kentucky, Thomas Bramlette, made it quite clear to military officials in Kentucky and political elites in Washington that he represented a sizeable majority of the white population when he vehemently opposed any federal regulation or law that would lure enslaved black men in his state into Union military service. Despite the thousands of black men who sought refuge behind the lines of the Army camps in Kentucky, eager to serve, the army of the North raised no black soldiers in Kentucky until the middle of 1864.[6]

Over Governor Bramlette's objections, Brigadier General Stephen Burbridge, who was in command of the District of Kentucky, issued an order in April 1864:

The recruiting of able-bodied slaves and free colored persons will be conducted within the limits of this State, under the following restrictions:

The assistant to the provost-marshal-general of the State, the provost-
marshals of districts, and the deputy provost-marshals in each county are
directed to receive and regularly enlist as soldiers in the service of the
United States all able-bodied negro slaves and free colored persons of
lawful age who may apply to them to be enlisted . . .[7]

The order provided that when a slave was enlisted, his owner would be
issued a certificate to be presented to the War Department for $300 in
compensation (or $4,590 in 2014 dollars). In effect, slave owners were
being paid by the federal government for releasing their slaves to military service. That the federal government was "buying" black men to
serve as soldiers in a war fought in part to abolish the very system that
permitted such sales was truly ironic, however the enlistment with compensation measure was intended to ease the fury of Kentucky whites.
Of course, it didn't, in no small measure due to the fact that the $300
promised by Washington fell far short of the going price for a healthy
black male, which was between $700 and $1,200 in Kentucky in 1864.[8]

The enlistment of black troops in Kentucky took some time to get up
and running, but by the end of July close to 10,000 black men had reported for duty—some of them free blacks, others enslaved, at the time
they signed up. In addition to the bounty paid to the owners of new
recruits, the black soldiers who had been enslaved at the time of their
enlistment were given their freedom, and all were paid $10 per month
(from which $3 per month was deducted for clothing). White soldiers,
by contrast, were paid $13 per month with no clothing deduction.

White Kentuckians responded maliciously and violently to the
groundswell of black enthusiasm to serve in the Union blue. One official
wrote Secretary of War Stanton: "Slaves escaping from their masters with
a view of entering the military service were waylaid, beaten, maimed,
and often murdered." Some men had their ears cut off by angry whites,
while others were "fastened to trees in the woods and flayed alive." John

Soldiers in the United States Colored Troops (USCT) at Camp Nelson, 1864. Courtesy of Kentucky Heritage Council/State Historic Preservation Office (http://heritage. kentucky.gov).

Gregg Fee, an abolitionist missionary who had founded Berea College, Kentucky's first racially integrated school, worked closely with black refugees seeking aid at Camp Nelson, a large quartermaster and commissary depot established in southern Kentucky's Jessamine County in 1863; he reported that of the first several thousand black volunteers who appeared at the camp "three out of five bore the marks of cruelty on their bodies."

Despite widespread violent attacks by angry white Kentuckians against black men in an effort to sabotage or deter their enlistment, by the end of the year the Union army had raised 25,000 black soldiers in the state. Within a year of black enlistment commencing in Kentucky more than half of the enslaved men who were eligible for military service had been emancipated through enlistment. Not infrequently, the wives, children, and other family members of the new recruits accompanied them to recruiting centers, flooding military installations such as Camp Nelson seeking protection, food, and shelter from the Northern troops stationed there. In fact, Camp Nelson, which served an important role in defending central and eastern Kentucky from Confederate attacks, became one of the nation's largest recruitment centers for black troops and a refugee camp for the families of the soldiers mustered into the Northern army—at one time housing over 3,000 people in flight from angry white Kentuckians.[9]

Unlike the millions of enslaved people covered by the Emancipation Proclamation who were set free on January 1, 1863, the black men of Kentucky earned their freedom based on their willingness to put their lives on the line in a Union uniform (for their valor they were famously given the worst guns, uniforms, and provisions, and deployed in the most perilous battles, suffering disproportionately high casualties as a result).

Not only did the recruitment of black soldiers give Lincoln something he sorely needed at this juncture in the war, a new source for fresh, able-bodied troops, but the new policy had the added advantage of accomplishing indirectly what Lincoln to this point had been unwilling to pull off directly, the emancipation of large numbers of enslaved men in Kentucky. Surely the abolition of slavery had become an acknowledged goal of the war by 1864. But most supporters of military abolition intended that the end of slavery would be the consequence of winning the war, not that winning the war would be the consequence of, and indeed dependent upon, abolishing slavery through the enlistment of black men.

The early enthusiasm of enslaved men to join the Union army soon cooled when they learned of the fate of their wives and children. When the families of the new recruits appeared at the gates of Camp Nelson seeking shelter they were not met as graciously as were the men signing up for service, and they often found themselves turned away only to be repossessed and brutally beaten by their owners. In other cases, where the families of recruits stayed put on the plantation, planters would re-

Barracks, cottages, tents, and huts at the Home for Colored Refugees at Camp Nelson, 1865. Special Collections, University of Kentucky. Courtesy of Kentucky Heritage Council/State Historic Preservation Office (http://heritage.ky.gov).

fuse to support them, casting them out of their homes and off the plantation without food, clothing, or shelter. While the men were compensated for their military service with a certificate of freedom and a wage, their wives and children remained enslaved and victim to retributive violence from angry white Kentucky slave owners. Many Northern military and political leaders were delighted at the swift course of military emancipation their policies had achieved. But the welfare of the enslaved women and children of Kentucky was not their project or their problem. Their most pressing need was to raise fresh troops. To expand the military campaign into a humanitarian relief effort would surely overstretch the already limited resources of the Union army. Again, to their minds attending to the mechanics of disestablishing slavery was a task to be left to civilian officials after the war was won, and could not, and should not, be taken up by the military as a part of the war effort itself.

The experience of Patsy Leach gives us a window into the kind of torture the wives of black recruits endured by virtue of their husbands' military service. Her husband, Julius Leach, joined the Union army at

Camp Nelson in the early fall of 1864 and was mustered into the 5th U.S. Colored Cavalry, which led an assault on October 2 on Saltville, Virginia, where the main salt works for the Army of Northern Virginia was located. The Confederates successfully repelled the Union attack, fueled in significant measure by their fury at the sight of armed black soldiers. The black troops impressed their white compatriots with their valor and fighting skills, but they suffered disproportionately large losses in the battle. The morning following the assault, Union soldiers awoke to what they thought was a new attack by the Confederates. "I heard a shot, then another and another until the firing swelled to the volume of skirmish line," reported one Union officer present at Saltville. What was taking place was not a general offensive against the Union troops, but a targeted massacre of black Union soldiers. The colored troops that had been either wounded on the battlefield and left lying there all night or had been taken captive by the Confederate troops were being systematically shot at close range by the rebel soldiers. The murder of black soldiers didn't end there. Two black soldiers who had been taken to a Virginia hospital that was treating both Union and Confederate wounded were shot in their hospital beds several days later. In the end, Confederates took not one black prisoner alive from the battle of Saltville. It is hard to be sure how many black soldiers were killed at what is now known as the Saltville Massacre, but Julius Leach was surely one of them.[10]

While Julius Leach paid for his service to the cause for black freedom with his life, his wife suffered horribly as a result of her husband's enlistment. Shortly after Julius ran away to sign up for military service, Patsy reported that her owner, Warren Wiley, "treated me more cruelly than ever, whipping me frequently without any cause and insulting me on every occasion." After Julius was killed in the battle of Saltville "my master whipped me severely saying my husband had gone into the army to fight against white folks as he my master would let me know that I was foolish to let my husband go he would 'take it out of my back,' he would 'kill me by piecemeal' and he hoped 'that the last one of the nigger soldiers would be killed.'" The violence culminated with a beating so bad it almost killed her: "he took me into the kitchen tied my hands tore all my clothes off until I was entirely naked, bent me down, placed my head between his knees, then whipped me most unmercifully until my back was lacerated all over, the blood oozing out in several places so that I could not wear my underclothes without them becoming saturated with blood. The marks are still visible on my back." The night of this last beating, bleeding and barely able to walk, Patsy grabbed her youngest child, a baby, and ran away to Camp Nelson, leaving five other children behind. In a written statement testifying to the violence she endured at her owner's hand as vengeance for her husband's enlistment, she pled for help in getting her other children away from this violent "Rebel sympathizer."[11]

Tragically, Patsy Leach's experience was more typical than exceptional when it came to the atrocities enslaved women suffered as a result of their husbands' military service. Martha Cooley, whose husband also served in the 5th U.S. Colored Cavalry and perished at Saltville, told of a beating she received from her owner when she informed him that she wanted to go to Camp Nelson:

> He said "I will give you Camp," and immediately took a large hickory stick with which he commenced beating me. He gave me more than thirty blows striking me on my head and shoulders and breaking one of the bones of my left arm. I have not the right use of it now. I told him I wanted my children. He said I could neither have my children or my clothes.[12]

She ran away with nothing, leaving her children behind, and once at Camp Nelson was very anxious for help in getting them to safety.

Clarissa Burdett also pled with Camp Nelson officials to help her rescue her four children from the grips of her owner, Smith Alford, who subjected her to horrible abuse after her husband, Elijah Burdett, enlisted. "He beat me over the head with an axe handle saying as he did so that he beat me for letting Elijah Burdett go off. He bruised my head so that I could not lay it against a pillow without the greatest pain." When Clarissa's niece, also owned by Alford, ran away to Camp Nelson, the beatings escalated. "He whipped me over the head and said he would give me two hundred lashes if I did not get the girl back before the next day." When she was unable to secure her niece's return, "he tied my hands . . . over a joist stripped me entirely naked and gave me about three hundred lashes. I cried out. He then caught me by the throat and almost choked me then continued to lash me with switches until my back was all cut up." She knew that he might kill her with the next whipping, so she ran away, leaving her children behind, knowing he would never let them follow her. "My master frequently said that he would be jailed before one of his niggers would go to Camp." Like Patsy Leach and Martha Cooley, she was desperate for help in getting her children away from this cruel man and to the safety of Camp Nelson.[13] The torture these women experienced forced them to choose between their children and their own lives—an unimaginably nightmarish "choice" that was the consequence of their husbands' freedom.

Black recruits were frequently well aware of the ill treatment their families were suffering as a result of their enlistment in the Union army. After an early rush of enthusiasm about service, it became more difficult to entice able-bodied black husbands and fathers to enlist because they understandably worried about the welfare of their families. While they were, almost to a man, enthusiastic about joining the fight for their people's freedom, they were incensed that doing so left their wives and children vulnerable to misery more intense than what they had already experienced as slaves.

As a result, recruiters had to find new measures to assure these men that their families would be safe after they entered military service. Congress raised the monthly pay for colored troops from $10 to $16 and threw in a $300 enlistment bounty (the same price that their owners were being paid to compensate them for the loss of their property). Most of the runaway slaves who joined the military took this bounty and gave it to their wives for their support in the event that their owners threw

Camp Nelson's "convalescent camp" for soldiers treated at its hospital, 1864. University of Kentucky/Camp Nelson Photographic Collection (http://kdl.kyvl.org/catalog/xt77sq8qcb8z_8).

them out without food, clothing, or shelter. This new money helped a little, but what the wives and children of these new recruits really needed was for the U.S. government to take responsibility for their care and safety. Three hundred dollars, while a substantial amount of money, would have provided little protection to the likes of Patsy Leach, Martha Cooley, or Clarissa Burdett.

In the opinion of the military officials running Camp Nelson, these refugees were distracting to their mission, brought illness and licentiousness with them, and ought better be sent back to their owners. General Lorenzo Thomas, Lincoln's man tasked with raising and organizing colored troops, was utterly insensitive to the repercussions of his policies on the black women and children of Kentucky. He issued the following order in response to concerns that it had become more difficult to raise black recruits on account of threats to the well-being of their families:

The law authorizing the enlistment of colored troops has only reference to the able-bodied negroes capable of bearing arms, and not to old men, the infirm, or women and children. Accordingly, none but able-bodied men will be received at the various camps designated for their reception. All others encouraged to remain at their respective homes, where, under the State laws, their masters are bound to take care of them, and those who may have been received at Camp Nelson will be sent to their homes. This latter is necessary, as many cases of disease have made their appearance among both sexes of such a nature as to require their removal beyond the limits of the camp. Furthermore, all of this class of persons are required to assist in securing the crops, now suffering in many cases for the want of labor.[14]

To military leaders, the men might make good soldiers, but the women and children were still slaves, and they were best put to work in the fields of hemp and tobacco, both very labor-intensive crops.

Not surprisingly, the welfare of their families remained the most important concern of the newly enlisted black soldiers in Kentucky. Despite military officials' efforts to discourage them from coming, Camp Nelson was overrun by the families of enlisted black men seeking refuge from their owners and proximity to their husbands and fathers. Ad hoc cabins and other rudimentary huts were built by the refugees within the camp lines with the help of sympathetic white soldiers and missionaries. Brigadier General Speed S. Fry, the commander of Camp Nelson, grew so frustrated by the burden these refugees imposed on his command that in late November 1864 he ordered that the 400 or so women and children at the camp be removed by wagons and carts and dropped in the woods about six miles away. John Vetter, a missionary working at Camp Nelson, described what happened:

> It was a bitter cold day, the wind was blowing quite hard and many of the women and children were driven from the Camp. I counted six or eight wagon loads. . . . When they were expelled their huts were destroyed and in some instance[s] before the inmates got out. . . . I found that one hundred or more had taken shelter in the woods having been driven from a meeting house in which they had taken refuge. . . . I found [another group] in an old shed, doorless and floorless sitting around a stack of burning wood with no food or bedding. One woman was apparently over come by exposure and another had given birth to a child in that place. Among those around the fire was a boy evidently near death whom on the following morning I found dead. . . . And upon evidence which I be-

lieve, I was assured that one woman had been so pressed with hunger as to offer her child for sale in the City to obtain bread. . . . As a Clergyman I believe the tendering of this measure was very demoralizing and highly prejudicial to the interest of enlistments of colored troops.[15]

Missionaries, such as Vetter, and compassionate white soldiers pled to no avail with General Fry not to expel the destitute women and children into the freezing cold. A number of the black soldiers stationed at Camp Nelson had to witness the expulsion and suffering of their own families. Joseph Miller had come to the camp in the summer of 1864 accompanied by his wife and children. They "came with me because my master said that if I enlisted he would not maintain them and I knew they would be abused by him when I left." When he signed up for a three-year term of service, his wife and children, ages ten, nine, seven, and four, were brought into the camp to live with him in a tent among other families of colored troops. His company was stationed at Camp Nelson on the night of November 22, when the refugees were forced out into the cold: "My little boy about seven years of age had been very sick and was slowly recovering." Joseph objected to his family's expulsion, given that they had no place to go and his son was so sick. They were allowed to remain in camp for the night, but the next morning they were told they had to leave.

"The morning was bitter cold. It was freezing hard. I was certain that it would kill my sick child to take him out in the cold. . . . I told the [man in charge] that I was a soldier of the United States. He told me that it did not make any difference. . . . He told my wife and family that if they did not get up into the wagon which he had he would shoot the last one of them." Thoroughly terrified, they departed, his wife carrying the sick boy in her arms. "When they left the tent the wind was blowing hard and cold and having had to leave much of our clothing when we left our master, my wife with her little one was poorly clad."

Joseph followed them as far as he could, to the camp's boundary, and then had to bid them goodbye not knowing where they would go or how they would protect themselves from the harsh elements and hostile white people outside the camp. As night fell, Joseph couldn't take it any longer:

> I went in search of my family. I found them . . . about six miles from Camp. They were in an old meeting house belonging to the colored people. The building was very cold having only one fire. My wife and children could not get near the fire because of the number of colored people huddled together by the soldiers. I found my wife and children shivering with cold and famished with hunger. They had not received a morsel of food during the whole day. My boy was dead. He died directly after getting down from the wagon; I know he was killed by exposure to the inclement weather. . . . I dug a grave myself and buried my own child.[16]

As if the death of his son weren't enough, within a month every member of Joseph Miller's family had died as a result of their exposure to the elements. Then, on January 6 Joseph died at Camp Nelson as well. The camp's death records read:

> Joseph Miller, Jr. (son of Joseph Miller, Sr.) died December 17th 1864.
> Isabella Miller (wife of Joseph Miller) died December 17th 1864.
> Maria Miller (daughter of Joseph Miller) died December 27th 1864.
> Calvin Miller (son of Joseph Miller) died January 2d 1865.
> Joseph Miller, Private, 124th C.S.C.I., died January 6th 1865.[17]

The November expulsion resulted in scores, if not hundreds, of deaths of black refugees. They sought aid and protection from Union troops at Camp Nelson but what they received from an army that was supposedly fighting on their behalf was at best indifference and at worst deadly hostility.

This incident gained attention almost immediately in the press in New York and Washington. A letter from an eyewitness to the events, calling himself "Humanitas," appeared in the *New York Tribune* on November 28 and was then reprinted in William Lloyd Garrison's *Libera-*

tor on December 9. (Humanitas was rumored to be Captain Theron E. Hall, an assistant quartermaster at Camp Nelson, who filed repeated reports with his superiors pleading for humane treatment of the families of black enlisted men.)[18] Humanitas described the Camp Nelson expulsion in passionate terms:

> Diabolical malignity could have desired no better day on which to perpetrate atrocious cruelty. The air was intensely chilly; the thermometer was below the freezing point all day, and strong men wrapped their overcoats close around them, when the provost guard turned four hundred women and children from their dwellings to face the wintery blast, with light and tattered garments, no food and no home! . . . Armed soldiers attack humble huts inhabited by poor negroes—helpless women and sick children— ordered the inmates out on the pain of instant death, and complete their valorous achievement by demolishing their dilapidated dwellings. The men who did all this were United States soldiers. . . . Four are already in their graves, one was frozen to death.[19]

When word of this treatment of the Camp Nelson refugees made its way to General Fry's superiors they were outraged. General Stephen Burbridge, still in command of the District of Kentucky, removed Fry from command of Camp Nelson and installed Captain Hall, the rumored Humanitas, as superintendent for the refugees. Hall immediately welcomed the outcast women and children back into Camp Nelson, and began building barracks to house them in the southwestern part of the camp (although the husbands serving in the army had to pay $25 for each cabin as "rent" for their families). With Fry gone, Captain Hall, with the help of Reverend John Gregg Fee, established Camp Nelson as an official Colored Refugee Home, at last treating the families of the new black soldiers not as the errant property of Kentucky planters, but as human beings.[20]

Word had quickly spread among Northern policy makers and abolitionist activists of the harsh treatment of the families of newly recruited black soldiers. Camp Nelson, a place few people outside of Kentucky had heard of before the November expulsion, became instantly famous, or rather, infamous. The event marked a turning point in the way enslaved people, running to the protection of Northern troops, were viewed by many Northern officials. No longer were they seen as the escaped property of Southern slave owners, or contraband as they were described most frequently, instead they were starting to be seen as refugees, with a fundamental dignity and entitlement to protection from the atrocities they were enduring as a consequence of enslavement.

That said, the transition in the way enslaved people were viewed by Northerners had not fully taken hold by the end of 1864. The sympathy garnered by the women and children of Camp Nelson was, in the end, derivative of larger interests in recruiting and retaining black soldiers, as the last lines of Humanitas's letter from Camp Nelson make clear: "No more efficacious plan could be devised for arresting the progress of negro enlistments than that which rests upon their families a merciless persecution compared with which Slavery, or even death itself, would be a positive blessing."[21]

Civilian missionaries who administered to the needs of the former slaves at Camp Nelson were frustrated by the disregard many military officials held for the welfare of the families of black soldiers. Abisha Scofield, one of the missionaries living there, was outraged by General Fry's expulsion of the families into the freezing November night and began to search for a way to better protect them. Since Kentucky still had not repealed its slavery laws, Scofield looked for a way to question the legal status of the refugees. "When a slave enlists, how does it affect his family? Are they free?" he wrote to William Goodell, a prominent Northern abolitionist, shortly after the November expulsion.[22]

The answer came quickly, but not from Goodell. On December 13, Massachusetts senator Henry Wilson, a strong abolitionist and later President Ulysses S. Grant's vice president, introduced a resolution into the Senate to address the legal status of the wives and children of formerly enslaved black soldiers. Entitled *A Resolution to Encourage Enlistments*

Cumberland Landing, Virginia. Group of "contrabands" at Foller's house. Photograph from the Peninsular Campaign, March–July 1862. James F. Gibson (b. 1828), photographer. Library of Congress Prints and Photographs Division, Washington, D.C.

and to Promote the Efficiency of the Military Forces, popularly known as the Enlistment Act, it declared the wife and children of any man who joined the Union army to be free as a matter of federal law. Many senators, both those who opposed and supported slavery, expressed concern: under what constitutional power could Congress deprive slave owners of their property without compensation? After a full-throated defense of the right of his state's citizens to own slaves, Kentucky senator Lazarus W. Powell offered an amendment: "That no slave shall be emancipated by virtue of this resolution until the owner of the slave or slaves so emancipated shall be paid a just compensation." The amendment was promptly defeated by a vote of seven for and thirty against.

More compelling was the speech of Senator Benjamin Franklin "Bluff" Wade of Ohio. During a visit to Camp Nelson the previous summer Wade had been horrified at what he found. No sooner had he stepped out of his carriage inside the camp than he was met by a female refugee and her child, pleading for federal assistance:

a colored woman, whom I should suppose to be thirty years of age, appeared before us, all bruised to pieces. Her face was all whipped to a jelly. She had a child with her which she said was twelve years old; one of whose eyes had been gouged out, and the other attempted to be, as they stated, by their mistress, the father being in the Army. Her head was all cut to pieces by what appeared to be a sharp instrument; her skull was laid bare almost, and her back perfectly mangled by the torture to which she had been subject. All this was done, as we were informed, because her husband had enlisted in the Army of the United States, and she and her child were compelled to flee to this camp the best way they could, in that condition.[23]

His exposure to the abuse and torture of the wives and children of black soldiers at Camp Nelson moved Senator Wade to introduce the measure that would legally free them. Wade's passionate argument on behalf of the black women and children of Kentucky was met, however, by a clever rejoinder from Kentucky senator Garrett Davis, who vehemently opposed the idea of wholesale freedom for enslaved people. If the measure's proponents were truly motivated by their concern for the welfare of the wives and children of black soldiers, "those who pass such a measure should in all humanity and justice make provision for the support of the beings that it will emancipate," he argued to his colleagues from the floor of the Senate. "This measure of justice and humanity in favor of which such a cry is raised, will just leave this helpless population without any means of support whatever . . . they would urge me to propose to the Senate that the cost of supporting these helpless beings should be undertaken by the Government itself."

Davis had a point. The measure, while purporting to come to the aid of the enslaved wives and children of black enlistees, was likely to leave them in a very precarious place. Davis's remarks exposed the ugly truth of the Enlistment Act: it's true aim was raising more black troops, not advancing the welfare of enslaved people in Kentucky generally.

Whatever the primary motivation for the measure, the drafters of the Enlistment Act had a serious legal problem that they were forced to solve creatively in the language of the bill: since the law would grant freedom to the wives and children of enslaved men who enlisted, it had to define what it meant for enslaved people to be married. Given that Kentucky was still a slave state, enslaved people could not legally marry. Only "persons" could enter into a civil contract of marriage. Slaves were treated legally as "property" and under the law had no more capacity to enter into a contract than would a horse or a plow. Nevertheless, as I discuss in chapter 2, many enslaved people lived as if they were husband and wife in the eyes of their god, their community, and often their owners, but not in the eyes of the law. The new law thus contained a complex definition of matrimony for Kentuckians who were unable to secure marriage licenses from the state:

> in determining who is or was the wife and who are the children of the enlisted person herein mentioned, evidence that he and the woman claimed to be his wife have cohabited together, or associated as husband and wife, and so continued to cohabit or associate at the time of the enlistment, or evidence that a form or ceremony of marriage, whether such marriage was or was not authorized or recognized by law, has been entered into or celebrated by them, and that the parties thereto thereafter lived together, or associated or cohabited as husband and wife, and so continued to live, cohabit, or associate at the time of the enlistment, shall be deemed sufficient proof of marriage for the purposes of this act, and the children born of any such marriage shall be deemed and taken to be the children embraced within the provisions of this act, whether such marriage shall or shall not have been dissolved at the time of such enlistment.[24]

After robust debate in the Senate, the Enlistment Act passed on January 9, by a vote of 27 yeas to 10 nays, with 12 abstentions. Both senators from Kentucky voted against. It passed the House on February 22 by an even closer margin: 74 in favor, 63 against, and 45 not voting (one congressman from Kentucky voted in favor, eight voted against, while almost all of the Maryland delegation abstained).

The president signed the bill into law on March 3, 1865, creating a new "freedom bounty" to lure new black recruits into military service with the Union. It was circulated through military channels and published in the press immediately.[25]

Lincoln's signature on the Enlistment Act had the effect of legally marrying tens, if not hundreds of thousands of enslaved people and instantly emancipating the wives and children of these marriages.[26] The new law accomplished indirectly what Lincoln had been unable to pull off directly: force the practical abolition of slavery in Kentucky. Colonel James Brisbin, the first commander of the 5th U.S. Colored Cavalry, stationed at Camp Nelson, reported in April that "Negro enlistment has bankrupted Slavery in Kentucky."[27]

As military officials hoped, the promise of freedom for the wives and children of enslaved black recruits had a very positive effect on the army's recruitment efforts. Colonel Brisbin reported, "From seventy to one hundred enlist daily, freeing, under the law of March 3, 1865, an average of five women and children per man. Thus from 300 to 500 black people are daily made free through the instrumentality of the army."[28]

Federal officials in Kentucky printed up "freedom certificates" "to be issued upon the application of the wives of colored men who entered the army, to facilitate them in procuring the necessary papers establishing their freedom."[29] Planters were told that they were obliged to pay wages, about $15 per month as second-class field hands, to the women and children freed by the Enlistment Act. Not surprisingly, Kentucky slave owners were disinclined to recognize the new legal identity of the women and children freed by act of Congress. Captain R. J. Hinton reported to his superiors in the fall of 1865 significant problems with slave owners refusing to recognize the new civil status of their former slaves:

A colored woman, proving herself the wife of one soldier in our army and the mother of another, complained that after working a year since her husband's and son's enlistment without pay other than food and part of a suit of clothes, she was driven from her home by her former master. She was a field hand, her son had also worked all the season without pay. Lt. Thing issued her the usual certificate of freedom, as a soldier's wife, on evidence of two witnesses that she had been recognized as the wife of the man for over twenty years; and thereon summoned the employer & certain witnesses to appear. He will report the result of the inquiry and his decision which will be of considerable importance, as there are many similar cases in Ky.[30]

Captain Hinton went on to predict that the woman's former owner would be required to pay her wages retroactive to the effective date of the act.

At the same time that white planters refused to pay wages to their former slaves, the "freedom certificates" did very little to stave off the violence black women suffered on account of their husbands' enlistment. In some districts the violence increased, fueled by white fury at the Enlistment Act's end run around Kentucky's slavery laws—emancipating hundreds of slaves a day without any compensation for lost "property."

Mary Wilson, a former slave freed by her husband's service in the U.S. Colored Cavalry, told Camp Nelson officials that in May 1865, when she was living in a house in Lexington, Kentucky, a local policeman arrested her for no reason and returned her to her former owner, William Adams. It seems that Adams had sought out the aid of the police officer in getting Mrs. Wilson returned to him as a slave. Once she was back in Adams's control on the farm, the police officer "tied her in a slaughterhouse to a rafter or beam and with a leather buggy trace inflicted upon her naked body a severe beating and bruising," as Adams stood by and watched approvingly. Wilson returned to her home in Lexington after the beating, but a few days later was seized again by the police and was beaten once more in Adams's slaughterhouse. Even worse, she testified,

Adams still had custody of her son who had also been freed by virtue of his father's enlistment. Mrs. Wilson had gone to military officials immediately after the beatings to seek help and gain her son's release, but nothing was done.[31]

Reading Mary Wilson's affidavit and others like it, the despair jumps off the page. The archival records of the refugees at Camp Nelson are full of stories like Wilson's, dictated to camp military officials and missionaries. Yet almost nothing was done to protect the welfare of the families of the black soldiers the U.S. government was so desperate to recruit. Yes, hundreds of paper certificates were issued, officially certifying their freedom according to federal law. But a piece of government paper—no matter how fancy the seals and ribbons—wasn't going to protect them from the backlash, literally lashes to the back, that they suffered when federal policy used their "freedom" as a way to entice their husbands into military service.

There's actually something perverse in how federal policy in Kentucky advanced national interests—raising black troops and punishing rebel sympathizers in the state for refusing to repeal their slavery laws—while at the same time rendering the families of those black troops more vulnerable to violent retribution by whites. With their husbands gone, and the Northern troops uninterested in their safety, there was no one left to protect them. Put the pieces together from the perspective of the wives of black soldiers: they were "deemed married" to men who had run away from slavery, enlisted in the military, been handed rifles, and told to shoot white Southerners, all of which made them prime targets for white fury. As such, marriage was a very dangerous business for the black women of Kentucky.

Recall Secretary of War Stanton's letter to President Lincoln, offering his strong endorsement of the Enlistment Act's main aim: "the liberation of the wife and children from slavery, and *placing them under the protection of the law* as free persons."[32] At precisely the moment when these women and children needed the protection of federal troops, they were given "the protection of the law." What law? As Mary Wilson's experience makes clear, the law was not on their side, but rather served as a tool for the violent hand of Kentucky slave owners. The apparently naïve belief that "law" could offer adequate protection for people making the transition from enslavement to freedom seems, in fact, willfully ignorant of the gravity of the situation. The words of Kentucky senator Garrett Davis suggesting that the federal government ought not only free the black soldiers' wives and children, but then take responsibility for their care and well-being once freed were prophetic about the precarious kind of freedom the black women and children of Kentucky were to enjoy by virtue of their husbands' and fathers' military service.

Considered a stroke of genius in Washington, the Enlistment Act may have had positive symbolic significance for abolitionists, but it had devastating practical consequences for the black women and children of Kentucky. While enslaved people living in states in rebellion were freed by the Emancipation Proclamation regardless of their sex or marital status, the enslaved people of Kentucky had to earn their freedom in deeply gendered ways. The price of freedom for men was military service, an "opportunity" made available only to men that reinforced a time-honored relation of masculinity to militarism. And a woman's entitlement to freedom was even more removed from her fundamental humanity insofar as it was made available to her only on the basis of her status as a wife. The gendering of freedom for enslaved women in Kentucky reflected the diminished legal status of women more generally during this era, insofar as a woman's legal identity was covered by or subsumed within the legal identity of her husband. Not only did this policy refuse to recognize fundamental liberty as something she possessed by virtue of her humanity, it made the gaining of freedom dependent upon the ability of a woman to find an able-bodied man to marry her or acknowledge her as his wife. While it was no small thing that the Enlistment Act transformed a woman's legal identity from that of property to person, it did so by locking her in the identity of a *femme covert*, a dependent who, like an underage child, had no independent legal identity that would entitle her to make individual claims to rights, protection, or dignity.[33] The best thing army officials thought to do when an unmarried black woman sought their help, according to one observer, was encourage her to find a black soldier to marry![34]

What can we learn from the enslaved Kentucky men and women in their first experiences of freedom? First, law can't be relied on to do all the work needed to make a subordinated people free and equal. It may be necessary to that project, but it isn't sufficient. As we saw from the resistance to the Enlistment Act, and later, the Thirteenth Amendment to the Constitution legally disestablishing slavery, law can deliver a title to one's humanity (and that's pretty much what the "freedom certificates" did). But for that title to be enforceable more is required, and this is where Northern officials fell short, leaving the women and children of Camp Nelson standing alone, armed only with a piece of paper. They needed something more than soaring speeches on the floors of Congress about the evils of slavery. They needed both words and deeds that would secure their freedom and protect their safety.

Nesting the freedom of the enslaved women of Kentucky inside their legal identity as wives meant that their well-being was managed and cared for within the domain of the private as spouses, rather than in a public identity as citizens. At least their husbands' military service, while admittedly deadly, signaled a kind of public citizenship that pointed toward other public rights and status. Not so for women, who emerged out of slavery as wives dependent upon their husbands and the kindness of strangers for the protection of their rights and interests. Hannah Arendt observed something similar of the Jews of Europe in the mid-twentieth century: as stateless refugees who had lost any claim to political citizenship, they had no recourse to human rights claims. To Arendt this was an abomination of the concept of human rights. Those who needed them most were least able to claim them. Without a legal personality that can make a claim to rights and a public place in society that others are obliged to respect, Arendt lamented, all they had left was a special kind of private pleading, more for the unpredictable hazards of friendship and sympathy as well as "the incalculable grace of love."[35]

These distinctly private and non-legal graces—friendship, sympathy, and love—were not something military officers were equipped to give to the enslaved women and children of Kentucky who flooded their encampments seeking aid and protection. But that was all that was left to them as wives, not soldiers, as freed, yet not truly free. Ironically, freedom was a "gift" that exposed them to greater risk of violence and torture. While law delivered sturdy legal status to enslaved men, all that was made available to enslaved women was a squishy, discretionary politics of sentiment. For the men, law imposed a duty between legal subjects, while for the women sentiment called up nothing more nor less than a plea for a kind of ethical identification with suffering.

The relationship between rights and freedom in this story shows us the kinds of unintended harms that can result when the law gets out, and in this case *way* out, ahead of the attitudes of society. To legally recognize the marriages of a group of people who were previously incapable of being legally wed, and then free them on the basis of that marriage, while not taking into account the underlying bigotry that caused their subordinate status, had the unfortunate result of leaving the newly favored group *worse off* than they were before they were recognized as rights holders.

Having said that, it's not as if I want the lesson of Camp Nelson to be that rights don't or shouldn't matter in a society that remains hostile to those very rights. Here's the interesting thing: even though the enslaved women of Kentucky knew that they would expose themselves to brutal violence if their marriages were legally recognized and they obtained "freedom certificates" as a result, they flooded Northern military and civilian officials with requests to exchange marital vows with their husbands. Despite the fact that the Enlistment Act had automatically married those couples who lived together, they wanted to stand before an authorized official, exchange vows, be pronounced husband and wife, and then be issued a formal marriage certificate. So great was the demand that one Kentucky military official wrote to his superiors begging for more blank marriage certificates: "I have the honor to state that the

Colored People of this place, who have been exercising the matrimonial relations under the old code or *practice*, wish to solemnize their relations in a legal manner during *Christmas*." He reported that "some seventy-five couples" had come to him, ready to wed over the holiday.[36]

For most, if not all of these couples—but particularly the women, as the men were taking oaths of loyalty as part of their military recruitment—this was the first time that their words could have legal effect. How incredible that must have been. No wonder it was in such demand.

By acknowledging both the symbolism and practical limits of marriage rights, it is understandable that the enslaved people of Kentucky wanted to have their relationships recognized by legal authorities. Rights are something we cannot not want, as others have noted,[37] and it was no small matter for the federal government to marry and declare free the enslaved people of Kentucky. But clearly the government relied too heavily on the rule of law to address the precarious, if not deadly, social, political, and legal status of the black people of Kentucky during this period of profound transition.

⌇

Sometimes new rights holders find themselves worse off in the aftermath of winning new freedoms. This tragic state of affairs can take place while the rest of the society catches up and gets used to the new legal regime. Other times, the steps backward that follow the steps forward lead to a permanent, sticky problem. Anticipating the pushback and planning for it can help minimize the costs of gaining rights. Yet what makes some civil rights revolutions take hold rather easily, appearing inevitable just as they begin to gain traction, while others advance in fits and starts, suffering setbacks, backlash, and the need to make the case for the rightness of their cause over and over and over?

As the story from Kentucky in this chapter makes clear, the experiences of black people who gained previously unimaginable rights and freedoms in the period just before the end of the Civil War show how some of them were left in worse shape by virtue of holding those new rights. Marriage played an important role in both the acquisition of new liberties and in the attendant violence that followed.

How is the experience of marriage and freedom by black people in Kentucky in 1864 and 1865 instructive to us today, when marriage is playing such a prominent role in the contemporary struggle for freedom and equality for lesbians and gay men?

The relationship of marriage to freedom and equality in Kentucky in the 1860s offers an important lesson, indeed a gendered lesson, about what it means to nest a civil rights struggle within marriage rights. For so long—forever, really—the private sphere has been the domain in which women have elaborated their fullest identities (as wives, mothers, caretakers) and in which, until quite recently, women's legal identity has taken form. In the nineteenth century, a woman's legal status merged with that of her husband; she had no independent legal "self". What economic and social benefits she derived came by virtue of her marriage to a man. Much of the modern women's movement has been devoted to reshaping this story and to granting women legal, economic, and social status independent of their husbands. Today women have their own public identities and need not rely exclusively upon the good graces of their husbands or, in the alternative, the unpredictable hazards of friendship, sympathy, and love of others. Still, too much of many women's well-being and flourishing remains tied up with their ability to marry well (economically, that is), and marry good (to a kind man, that is). Living outside of marriage (never marrying, divorcing, or living as a widow) continues to be a precarious place for too many women.

Yet the lesbian and gay community is investing great hope and enormous resources in the emotional and other riches that will flow from securing the right to marry. It is a curious thing to pursue a civil rights strategy that nests a fuller form of public citizenship within marriage, a distinctly private domain. Many members of the community will no doubt gain access to superior health insurance and other benefits now that they can legally marry, but they will do so as a consequence of their spouse's employment, not in their own right. They will lose those benefits should the relationship end, and may be hesitant to end a marriage or even address marital differences out of fear of losing those benefits. This is a familiar story to heterosexual women, but it is one the lesbian and gay community now faces for the first time. Winning for the members of our community the same questionable deal that many heterosexual women now have isn't such a great long-term political horizon.

Returning to the experiences of newly freed and newly married former slaves in Kentucky, have we seen a similar kind of backlash against married gay couples or evidence that gaining marriage rights rendered them more vulnerable? Well, in some ways yes and in other important ways no.

Now, as then, when a new group wins the right to marry, those who are offended by these new rights push back, and push back hard. The defenders of a traditional, heterosexual form of marriage believe deeply that the institution is god-given, not subject to radical reform, and that the law has no business messing with it. They see marriage as so deeply structuring their way of life that to change it would destroy their well-being and decimate the moral structure of their worlds. So too felt slave owners in the 1860s. They believed that they had a right to own slaves, and that this right was god-given. In 1857 the chief justice of the U.S. Supreme Court ratified this view, stating that it was a fixed and universal maxim that black people "had for more than a century . . . been regarded as beings of an inferior order, and altogether unfit to associate with the white race either in social or political relations, and so far inferior that they had no rights which the white man was bound to respect, and that the negro might justly and lawfully be reduced to slavery for his benefit."[38]

To a remarkable degree, the strategies pursued by those who oppose marriage rights for same-sex couples have come from the same playbook as that used by racists in the South who opposed the civil rights of African Americans. For instance, in 2009 as the marriage equality movement was beginning to gain steam, Watergate conspirator-turned-evangelist Charles Colson, along with prominent religious conservatives from the academy such as Princeton University professor Robert P. George and Beeson Divinity School dean Rev. Timothy George, drafted the *Manhattan Declaration: A Call to Christians of Conscience*.[39] The document, a kind of manifesto issued by Orthodox, Catholic, and evangelical Christian leaders, professed and affirmed support for the sanctity of life, traditional marriage, and religious liberty. In many respects the tone, form, and rhetoric of the Manhattan Declaration echoed the Southern Manifesto issued by white Southern Democrats in 1956 condemning the Supreme Court's *Brown v. Board of Education* decision mandating racial integration as a violation of states' rights and local governance. The Southern Manifesto appealed to the notion that the courts had overstepped in mandating a reordering of well-established and locally enforced racial relations in the South. The Manhattan Declaration similarly emphasized the illegitimacy of laws that violate foundational religious values: "Because we honor justice and the common good, we will fully and ungrudgingly render to Caesar what is Caesar's. But under no circumstances will we render to Caesar what is God's," the authors wrote, quoting the book of Matthew on the legitimate role of law in ordering public values.[40] While the Manhattan Declaration failed to gain the impressive number of signatories that its authors expected (one million signatures within ten days was their professed aim, but they attracted little over half a million in the end), it did mobilize a ready constituency that regarded law-based movements for racial and sexual justice as equally threatening to traditional values emanating from core religious principles.

As a tactic to oppose marriage rights for same-sex couples, the Manhattan Declaration's elegance of prose and deliberative, if not parliamentary, appeal to civil disobedience ("Because we honor justice and the common good, we will not comply with any edict . . . nor will we bend to any rule purporting to force us to bless immoral sexual partnerships, treat them as marriages or the equivalent, or refrain from proclaiming the truth, as we know it, about morality and immorality and marriage and the family") elide the racial pedigree of both its genre and underlying political commitments. Not so with other opponents of marriage equality who are more than happy to connect the dots between religious justifications for chattel slavery and racial segregation to the sanctity of marriage as an essentially heterosexual institution.

Take for instance the League of the South, a neo-Confederate group that aims to finish the project abandoned at the end of the Civil War: Southern secession and a society dominated by "European Americans." The league works on behalf of a "godly" nation made up of "Anglo-Celtic" (read: white) elites that would establish a Christian theocratic state and politically dominate blacks and other minorities. When Brad Griffin[41] joined the organization he prioritized street actions as a way to raise awareness about Southern nationalism and increase the League's membership. He also forged closer ties with the Council of Conservative Citizens (he sits on the group's board and is married to its president's daughter). The Council of Conservative Citizens is a white supremacist, nationalist, and separatist organization, a modern incarnation of the White Citizens' Councils that were formed in the 1950s and 1960s to combat racial desegregation. The group published the following illuminating justification for racial separation on its website in 2001: "God is the author of racism. God is the One who divided mankind into different types. . . . Mixing the races is rebelliousness against God."[42] According to the Southern Poverty Law Center, "Unlike the KKK, the CCA groups had a veneer of civic respectability, inspiring future Supreme Court Justice Thurgood Marshall to refer to it as the 'uptown Klan.'"[43]

Besides similar commitments to white supremacy, Southern succession, the idea of the U.S. as a Christian nation, and opposition to immigration and racial "mixing," the two groups share a visceral hatred of gay people and oppose marriage rights for same-sex couples. One of their first joint street actions, organized by Griffin, took place in Alabama in May 2014 when members of the League and the Council demonstrated against marriage equality. Michael Hill, chairman of the League of the South, explained that their protest was "a demonstration of support for the idea of

Christian marriage. . . . Just because people may have been, quote, married, doesn't necessarily mean the state has to recognize it."[44] Griffin told Council members: "This outrageous attack on Christian marriage and violation of states' rights cannot be allowed to pass without opposition."[45]

Protest organizers supplied the demonstrators with signs saying "Support Christian Marriage" and encouraged them to carry two flags: the Alabama state flag and the Kentucky Orphan Brigade flag. The Alabama state flag makes sense since the protest was in Alabama (though only ironically, given that the protesters sought to emphasize the priority of god's law over sinful manmade laws). But the Kentucky Orphan Brigade flag? A curious choice, particularly so given the importance of marriage to freedom for former Kentucky slaves as I recounted earlier in the chapter. The flag contains a solid red cross with thirteen white stars against a dark blue background. Presumably, for contemporary enthusiasts, the flag represents the marriage of three deeply held values: Christianity, white supremacy, and the sovereignty and power of individuals and local associations to resist federal power or control. It's hard not to sense the specter of the Klan when this flag is brought to protests, as its imagery is highly evocative of Klan symbols. Griffin's opposition to marriage rights for same-sex couples has also taken the form of frequent posts to his "Pro-White, Pro-South, Pro-Independence" blog, *Occidental Dissent*, supporting legislation that would create a religious exemption from recognition of same-sex marriages.

Many state legislatures have translated the Manhattan Declaration into legislation that would grant any person (defined to include not only natural persons/human beings but corporations, associations, and agencies, as well) the right to refuse to recognize a marriage between two people of the same sex, and would enable a business to refuse to provide services in connection with the wedding of a same-sex couple, such as photography, floral arrangements, or catering. As it became clear in 2014 that the Supreme Court was poised to rule on the constitutionality of laws that barred same-sex marriage, those who opposed same-sex marriage leapt into action, pushing religious liberty bills in state legislatures across the country. The bills, usually called Religious Freedom Restoration Acts, were introduced in the 2015 legislative sessions in more than ten states and reflected a well-coordinated effort to anticipate and undercut a Supreme Court ruling establishing marriage rights for same-sex couples as a national norm. As a preemptory maneuver, this form of backlash against the expansion of rights for gay men and lesbians was criticized for creating a "license to discriminate" in the name of religion.

The implicit violence lurking behind the rhetoric and protests by the opponents of marriage equality, including those whose opposition is grounded in appeals to religious liberty, has quite predictably inspired others to respond violently to same-sex couples who marry. One gay male couple told me this story: Once it became possible for same-sex couples to legally marry in Massachusetts they decided to do so, after having been together for many years already. When their wedding announcement appeared in a national newspaper, the parents of one of the men were called numerous times by a stranger who had read about their son's wedding. The caller made explicit and highly offensive remarks about their son's sexuality and made perverse suggestions about the parents' sexual practices. The parents called the local police, who were unable to trace the source of the calls, but suggested that a vehemently anti-gay religious organization, the Westboro Baptist Church, led by Fred Phelps, was likely behind them, based on the scripted nature of the harassing calls, and the fact that that they knew of other similar calls.

Backlash has taken other forms as well. Shortly after President Obama voiced support for the marriage rights of same-sex couples in the summer of 2012, Bryan Fischer, director of issues analysis for the American Family Association, a conservative advocacy group that opposes same-sex marriage, tweeted to his thousands of Twitter followers: "we need an Underground Railroad to deliver innocent children from same-sex households." In his radio talk show *Focal Point*, Fischer drove the message home. His kidnapping strategy was inspired by the case of "former lesbian" Lisa Miller, who entered into a civil union with her partner, Janet Jenkins, when they lived together in Vermont and had a child, Isabella, with her. Lisa later became an evangelical Christian, repudiated her "lesbian life," and moved to Virginia, taking Isabella with her. When a Vermont court ordered that Janet had a right to visitation and an ongoing parental relationship with her daughter, Lisa refused to honor the court's order and disappeared with Isabella, ultimately being secretly transported to Nicaragua by Lisa's radical Mennonite supporters. Janet did everything she possibly could to use the law to maintain her relationship with Isabella, while Lisa used extreme non-legal and illegal measures to keep Isabella from seeing Janet. This case stands out as an inspiration to religious radicals like Bryan Fischer, who tells his followers, "We must obey God's law, not man's law." When one of Lisa's Mennonite supporters went on trial for child kidnapping, Fischer tweeted: "Head of Underground Railroad to deliver innocent children from same-sex households goes on trial."[46]

A month after Fischer started urging his followers to kidnap the children of married lesbian and gay parents I received the following e-mail from a lesbian in upstate New York:

My partner and I have been in a same sex committed relationship for 15 years and have adopted 2 children. I am a teacher and my partner has health insurance through my employment for the past 7 years. I've paid taxes on this benefit even though she is a dependent.

I received notification that if we do not get married my partner will lose the benefit completely.

The only reason we do not want to get married is our fear for the safety of our family, especially our young special needs boys, ages 3 and 6.

We live in a very rural upstate county where we experienced many difficulties with the adoption due to our genders. I've read about an individual who advocates for the kidnapping of same sex couples' children. I've parked next to vehicles with derogatory bumper stickers.

This message shows the bind in which many same-sex couples now find themselves. Now that they *can* marry, they are being *forced* to do so in order to retain benefits they had gained in an era when marriage was not a legal option. Yet despite the change in the law, many still live in communities that are deeply homophobic, and they fear that exercising their new rights might provoke violent backlash from some of their less-enlightened neighbors. For this particular couple in upstate New York, the fear that getting married might result in violence or the kidnapping of their children is justified given the example of the Miller–Jenkins case and the hateful drumbeating of the likes of Bryan Fischer.

Other forms of retaliation against same-sex couples that have married are not hard to imagine. The plaintiffs in the Proposition 8 case described the awkwardness they experience when walking into a hotel or bank and referring to their boyfriend as a "partner" rather than "spouse." Jeff Zarrillo testified:

> [I]t's always an awkward situation at the front desk at the hotel . . . the individual working at the desk will look at us with a perplexed look on his face and say, "You ordered a king-size bed. Is that really what you want?" . . . It is always certainly an awkward situation walking to the bank and saying, "My partner and I want to open a joint bank account," and hearing, you know, "Is it a business account? A partnership?" It would just be a lot easier [to be able to say]: "My husband and I are here to check into a room. My husband and I are here to open a bank account."[47]

But being legally authorized to say, "My husband and I are here to check into a room or open a bank account," would not insulate Mr. Zarillo and his husband from the awkwardness that they might encounter in many parts of the U.S. in response to a man using the term "my husband." In fact, such language might result in something far worse than "awkward," such as ridicule, discrimination, and even violence from a hotel desk clerk or bank officer who is offended or outraged by the idea of two men marrying one another and referring to each other as "my husband." In this sense, Jeff Zarrillo and his new husband may be at *greater* physical peril in many places identifying as "husbands" than if they did so as "partners." The state may have issued them a license to use the word "husband," but that piece of paper affords them little protection from the responses they are likely to get when they refer to each other as spouses. Given that sexual orientation–based discrimination is legal in twenty-nine states, many Americans in same-sex relationships find themselves in the situation where they have a right to marry but exercising that right could result in losing their job once their employer learns of their marriage.

When I began writing this book I expected that this kind of backlash would continue to burn across the country and that the lesson to be drawn from the experiences of black people freed by military service and by marriage in Kentucky in the mid-1860s would be "be careful what you wish for." It seemed quite reasonable to expect that the new forms of vulnerability that I describe in the first half of this chapter would be echoed today in a reaction against newly married same-sex couples. And while I found some evidence of retaliation against or rejection of newly married gay and lesbian couples, a different story began to emerge in 2012 and really took hold after the Supreme Court's *United States v. Windsor* decision in June 2013. At that point a tipping point in the marriage equality movement was reached. Virtually everyone, from judges to elected officials to politicians to celebrities, took for granted the inevitability of marriage rights for same-sex couples. Wanting to be on the right side of history, a surprising number of public figures, religious leaders, and others who had previously voiced opposition to marriage equality jumped ship and identified themselves with the rights to dignity and equality entailed in the same-sex marriage movement. Even Republican attorneys general in the South pledged not to defend their states' laws banning gay marriage.[48]

How might we understand the widespread acceptance of same-sex couples into the dominion of civil marriage, particularly when compared with the way marriage provided new opportunities for white people to enact racist violence against former slaves in the nineteenth century? Put another way, why has marriage remained a deeply racialized, if not racist, form of governance for black Americans, while for gay and lesbian Americans marriage will be unlikely to offer either state or non-state actors a vehicle with which to enact sustained homophobic violence? In this sense, it is worth exploring both the junctions and disjunctions in the comparison of these two groups' first encounters with civil marriage. Both hold out the prospect of explaining something important about the powers and limits of law, and the riddle of gaining greater freedom through a form of state-run governance.

The contrasts between these two encounters with marriage, both situated critically in larger movements for social justice and freedom, illuminate important differences between racism and homophobia, between color and sexual orientation, and between race and sex.

For gays and lesbians, gaining the right to marry has marked a kind of emancipation from the burdens of social abjection in two key ways: First, the issuance of a marriage license to a same-sex couple marks a kind of social belonging and a recognition by the state of their legal equivalence to normative conjugal couples. Second, a marriage license works as a kind of credential, vouching for the legitimacy and quality of the couple's relationship and thereby entitling them to a wide range of social, legal, and economic benefits. The way in which a marriage license at once recognizes and confers a form of socio-legal personality on same-sex couples is, in no small measure, the effect of the arguments that gay rights advocates have made in courts, legislatures, and the media about why same-sex couples are entitled to the right to marry. They have emphasized again and again the injustice of same-sex couples not being recognized as equally deserving of the state's blessings as different-sex couples, and have rested their arguments on the similarities of same- and different-sex unions. So too, in order to make their case they have insisted on the inherent and critical dignity-conferring power of a marriage license along with the indignity of exclusion from the institution of marriage. By design or merely by implication, the gay rights advocacy on this issue has actually transformed the social meaning of marriage, rendering it a thicker and more meaningful form of state recognition of legitimate and deserving intimate adult commitment than it had been before the marriage equality advocates got their hands on it. Marriage, in the era of equal rights for same-sex couples, has been recharged as the most august holding environment for the elaboration of one's mature and authentic self, and one of the most fundamental institutions of a civilized society, thus echoing the account of marriage prevalent in an earlier era. As the Supreme Court put it in 1888, and gay rights advocates have repeated in their briefs: "marriage is one of the basic civil rights of man fundamental to our existence and survival and is the most important relation in life as the foundation of the family and society without which there would be neither civilization nor progress."[49]

Entitlement to the blessings of marriage was achieved by a conscious strategy of radically refiguring the meaning of homosexuality. This entailed carefully crafting a revised conception of gayness organized around a status or stable identity rather than sexual acts, and substituting love and familial devotion as the operative forms of affect that bound same-sex couples together rather than sodomy or sexual attraction. Put more bluntly, it meant reorienting the public's attention from the genitals to the heart, from the bushes to the hearth, from prurience to parenthood and from sin to sacrament.

Astonishingly, at least to me, it has worked. And worked rather quickly. Gayness has been successfully rebranded by cleaving the sex out of homosexuality. More radical precincts of the community are not so pleased with this remaking of gay and lesbian subjectivity and the turn toward respectability, but it surely has been an effective tactic that subsidized the incredible success of the marriage equality campaign.

African Americans, by contrast, have been unable to use marriage to rebrand blackness in such a way that sanitized racist stereotypes and coercive forms of racialized discipline. Unlike white gay men and lesbians who have successfully used law and rights-based advocacy to realize a new, more equal form of legal citizenship, freed from the burdens of stereotype and animus, African Americans remain tethered to an identity that both explains and justifies the many forms of inequality they endure. Their experience of newly won marriage rights did not originate in or even produce a new civil status as sovereign free subjects. Rather, marriage rights were more a tactic of governance that reinforced rather than erased a notion of racial difference for African Americans. That durable racial difference, an unshakable badge of inferiority, justified the emancipation of enslaved people into a state of freed-dom rather than freedom, and explains why marriage rights failed to provide security to the freed women and men of Kentucky, but rather left them worse off in many respects. The mistaken presumption that you could assert, as a black person, a kind of civil subjectivity implied by possession of a marriage license served as a provocation to white Kentucky planters who were prepared to beat, whip, or burn newly married freed people back into their proper place. Blackness, a stain indelibly marking inferiority, licensed all manner of racial terror, and marriage merely provided a new opportunity to elaborate that inferiority and terror rather than mitigate its violence.

In this sense, reading the success of today's marriage equality movement against the history of marriage for newly freed black people illuminates how the institution of marriage could accommodate, if not facilitate, racism, yet it does not seem to be a similarly friendly host for homophobia or heterosexism. Sadly, the success of today's marriage equality movement may even have benefited from this disjunction insofar as "gay marriage" has tended to be considered a "white issue," and has thus enjoyed a racial endowment that has helped its cause. In the next chapter I will dive more deeply into the ways in which some of the advocacy on behalf of same-sex marriage has had the unfortunate effect of off-loading stigma previously associated with gay families onto other non-normative families, thus collaborating in, if not contributing to, the ongoing racialization of marriage and pathologizing of African American families.

2

Fluid Families

"It Is Probable That the Soldier Had Two Wives"

"[W]e are deprived of every thing that hath a tendency to make life even tolerable, the endearing ties of husband and wife we are strangers to for we are no longer man and wife than our masters or mistresses thinkes proper marred or onmarred," wrote a group of enslaved men in a petition to the governor of Massachusetts in 1774.[1] Fast forward to 2001. The plaintiffs in a Massachusetts case challenging the state's ban on same-sex marriage petitioned the court: "This case concerns one of the most fundamental of all our human and civil rights: the right to marry the person you love, the person with whom you want to share your life. . . . The exclusion of same sex partners from free choice in marriage stigmatizes their relationships, and reinforces a caste supremacy of heterosexuality over homosexuality just as laws banning marriages across the color line exhibited and reinforced white supremacy."[2] Marriage then and marriage now remains central to our identities as free and equal people.

Like enslaved people in the antebellum south, until quite recently gay people in the United States were unable to legally marry. Slaves were not permitted to marry because the law treated them as property, not people; as property they could not enter into a civil contract. Same-sex couples have been barred from marrying because the institution of marriage has been traditionally understood as a bond between a man and a woman. Both groups have experienced their inability to marry as central to what it meant to be legally, socially, and politically oppressed.

Living in marriage's shadow—not being technically governed by the rules of marriage, but feeling its gravitational pull—enslaved and same-sex couples have had some interesting options. They could emulate marriage in the way they organized their intimate lives, mirroring and honoring the social value that the larger society places on the institution of marriage. But so too, they can "slip the knot," and experiment with forms of intimate, romantic, and sexual attachment quite different from traditional marriage's vows of life-long commitment, monogamy, exclusivity, and mutual economic and emotional support. What's interesting is that enslaved and gay people have done both; some members of the community construct relationships that are marital in form, while others have found that living outside marriage allowed for a kind of freedom to develop alternative forms of attachment, family, and love.

Some observers of these two communities have thought that the variety of relationships in enslaved communities and among gay men and lesbians was a symptom of their exclusion from marriage, a kind of deformed adaptation to their exclusion from "normal" and "healthy" social existence.[3] Others have taken a less generous view: that the nontraditional sexual and family lives of slaves and homosexuals were/are evidence of their essentially depraved natures, resulting in a licentious free-for-all that took place in the unregulated space outside marriage.[4]

Let me take a different view: could it be that the inability to marry creates a kind of freedom from the "bonds" of marriage? ("Why do you think they call it 'wedlock'?" my partner often asks.) On this view, while the exclusion from legal marriage may be motivated by a kind of discriminatory hatred of enslaved and gay people, the silver lining of this legal exile is that it allowed for a kind of intimate and sexual freedom and improvisation, liberated from the pressures of marriage and the marital form. Being barred from the marriage club pressed those who couldn't use legal marriage to organize and protect their relationships to find ways to work around this exclusion, and in so doing they developed forms of family, love, and care that aren't worth junking once marriage became an option. This chapter will look at the kinds of relationships, forms of kinship, and approaches to intimate connection that enslaved and gay people developed during the period when they could not legally marry. Only when we take it as given that marriage is the ideal structure for love and family do all alternatives appear to fall short. This chapter challenges us to unsettle, if only for a moment, the commonly held value we place on marriage as "the measure of all things," so that we might see the more fluid extended families more common in slave society, in African American society today, and in gay and lesbian communities in a better light.

In 1942 the U.S. Supreme Court famously observed that "marriage and procreation are fundamental to the very existence and survival of the race."[5] Again in 1978 the Court noted that marriage is "the most important relation in life . . . the foundation of the family and of society, without which there would be neither civilization nor progress."[6] The very existence and survival of the race? Both civilization and progress? Can marriage possibly do all this important work? Maybe, maybe not, but the experiences of enslaved and gay/lesbian people living and loving in social contexts where they could not marry offer a unique opportunity, almost a controlled experiment, to consider what society would look like in the absence of marriage. Would civilization as we know it end? Would the survival of the race (by this the Court likely meant "species") be in jeopardy? What other worlds are possible when marriage does not provide the basic structure of love, family, and kinship? What happens to those other worlds once marriage is made available to groups of people to whom marriage had been denied? Rather than characterize all of them as "fragile," "dysfunctional," "unhealthy," or worse "pathological," might some of the non-marital forms of attachment forged by communities of people excluded from marriage be worthy of acclaim and preservation as viable, if not preferable, alternatives to marriage?

⤺

Early historical accounts advanced a pathological view of slave families. These narratives generally portrayed enslaved people as culturally and essentially inferior to whites. Black men were considered either overly sexual, violent beasts or lazy, easily frightened, chronically idle, inarticulate buffoons or Sambos. Black women were seen as oversexed Jezebels or nurturing Mammys.[7] The American Freedman's Inquiry Commission, a body created by the War Department in 1863 to develop recommendations for dealing with freed people after emancipation, heard testimony that "[i]t is a very rare thing to find female virtue among [Negroes]."[8] In its preliminary report to the secretary of war, the commission stated that enslaved people spent "the night in huts of a single room, where all ages and both sexes herded promiscuously. Young girls of fifteen—some of an earlier age—became mothers, not only without marriage, but often without any pretence [sic] of fidelity to which even a slave could give that name."[9] The perceived sexual depravity of enslaved people seemed to fascinate nineteenth-century white observers, such as this Mississippi planter:

> As to their habits of amalgamation and intercourse, I know of no means whereby to regulate them, or to restrain them; I attempted it for many years, preaching virtue and decency, encouraging marriages, and by punishing, with some severity, departures from marital obligations; but it was all in vain.[10]

Those who judged the loose or low morals of enslaved people rarely acknowledged that their residential and domestic lives were hardly of their own choosing. Slaveholders throughout the South commonly shifted enslaved people around from quarters to quarters, motivated by economic necessity and cyclical labor needs over the course of a growing season, rarely giving a second thought to keeping family units together. George Washington, who was the largest slaveholder in Fairfax County, Virginia, at the end of the eighteenth century, never hesitated to move people around his five farms as production needs required—sometimes hiring out his own slaves to other planters in slow periods and renting slaves owned by neighbors when his own slave population wasn't big enough to do all the work needed. Work on the Washington farms was typically segregated by sex, with men and women doing different kinds of work. As a consequence, men's and women's jobs took place in different parts of the over 8,000 acres Washington owned. In the spring and summer, male field hands plowed, sowed, and weeded crops; cut hay, corn stalks, straw, and brush; netted fish; made baskets and horse collars; cut and mauled fence rails and posts; and performed other similar physical tasks. Meanwhile the women were digging post holes and making fences; heaping and burning trash; plowing, harrowing, and planting; gathering and spreading fish offal and dung; weeding and preparing meadows for oat and timothy grass; taking care of the cattle; picking apples; leveling ditches; cleaning hedgerows and fields; and filling gullies. Given that Washington didn't want working days shortened by the time it would take to travel great distances across his vast estates by foot, he had his slaves housed near where they were working. As a result, men and women who considered themselves married (in "the eyes of god") rarely lived together. For the most part, children lived and were cared for in the women's quarters, sometimes collectively, and their fathers saw them infrequently. In fact, nearly two thirds of the "married" couples at Mount Vernon lived separately and saw each other once a week on Sunday, if they were lucky.[11]

Even though these facts of slave life have been easily available to modern historians and offer a structural explanation for the form their family lives took, many, such as Kenneth Stampp in 1956, continued to express judgment about the "indifference with which most fathers and even some mothers regarded their children" and noted their "widespread sexual promiscuity."[12]

In the 1950s through the 1970s, prominent historians of African American life and culture such as E. Franklin Frazier and Stanley Elkins sought to counter these well-accepted images of black people living under slavery by telling a different story. By their account, the form of slave family life was not traceable to some intrinsic pathology, but to the annihilating effects that slavery had on black culture:

the Negro, stripped of his cultural heritage, acquired a new personality on American soil. . . . [T]he emergence of the slave as a human being was facilitated by his assimilation into the household of the master race. There he took over more or less the ideas and attitudes and morals and manners of his masters. His marriage and family relations reflected the different stages and aspects of this process.[13]

Thus, for the historians of this era, "the environment of the slave experience had been such as to exclude the development of black marriage and family norms."[14] Under this new view, by patterning their family lives upon those of their masters some enslaved people formed long-term, monogamous relationships and raised their children in nuclear-type families. By forming these kinds of kinship networks—networks remarkably similar to those of European Americans—black people were able to survive the devastation of slavery.[15] Nineteenth-century sources reinforce this view. The American Freedman's Inquiry Commission observed that "[the Negro] is found quite ready to copy whatever he believes are the rights and obligations of what he looks up to as the superior race."[16]

The views of Elkins, Stampp, and even Herbert Gutman are now being replaced by the careful research of younger historians who tell a more complex story about the family lives of enslaved people. The research of Laura Edwards, Brenda Stevenson, and Tera Hunter, to name only a few, approaches the domestic lives of enslaved people in ways that refuse an appeal to stock characters or totalizing stories that either cast negative judgment on or romanticize the agency of enslaved people.[17]

Rather than rehearse the arguments made by others in their own scholarly work, I sought out the voices of black people themselves. How did they portray their family and intimate lives? For several years I dug around in archives reading affidavits made out by black women seeking war widow pensions after the men they considered to be their husbands had died fighting in colored regiments in the Civil War. Since they could not legally marry, they could not produce marriage licenses to support their pension applications. Instead, pension bureau officers took oral testimony from these women and others in their communities as evidence of the "marital nature" of their relationships with the deceased soldiers. Of course, the veracity of these statements need be taken with a sizeable grain of salt, as they were made for the purpose of gaining a financial subsidy from the federal government, and thus the deponents had every reason to bend, shape, or invent their stories to satisfy the requirements of pension eligibility. Yet the stories they told drew from their lived experiences and were plausible narratives of matrimonial-like kinship in their communities. Regardless of their truthfulness in individual cases, they provide otherwise authentic snapshots of the range of kin relations formed by enslaved people. In this sense, they tell a story of the kinds of relationships enslaved people formed that were considered marital in nature by the community.

Stepping back for a moment, why war widow pension applications as an archive of family life for enslaved people? The Civil War resulted in enormously high casualty rates on both sides, which created an unplanned-for urgency for the federal government: the impoverishment of hundreds of thousands of surviving widows and children. In the summer of 1862, Congress took up the issue for the first time and enacted the nation's first pension law, creating a system of support for the bereaved families of deceased soldiers.[18] White widows and children were clearly the beneficiaries Congress had in mind when they passed the law.[19] Notwithstanding an overwhelming need to raise troops, and even after issuance of the preliminary version of the Emancipation Proclamation in July 1862, President Lincoln opposed the enlistment of black men into the Union army. At that point in the conflict he preferred the idea of colonizing blacks out of the country rather than integrating them into American life and making them soldiers.[20] Nevertheless, in the summer of 1862 War Department secretary Edwin Stanton approved the use of black troops in South Carolina, Louisiana, and Kansas without Lincoln's knowledge. Before too long Lincoln was forced to overcome his reluctance on the matter of conscripting black men to fight for the Union cause: "By spring [of 1863], the President was urging a massive recruitment of negro troops."[21]

Once black men were conscripted, their casualties were exceedingly high. In fact, the Confederate secretary of war declared that captured black Union soldiers were not to be treated as prisoners of war, but rather as "slaves in arms" who were to be turned over to local authorities whereupon they were executed as incendiaries or insurrectionists. To Confederate officials, "[t]he most efficient way to deal with the vexing issue of black prisoners was to take no prisoners."[22]

Then, in April 1864, Confederate soldiers massacred an estimated 800 Union troops, half of whom were black, at Fort Pillow, Tennessee. The Fort Pillow Massacre prompted Congress to contend with the problems of proof that had arisen in black women's pension claims.[23] Senator Lafayette Foster, a Republican from Connecticut who went on to be the acting vice president after President Lincoln was assassinated, sponsored a bill designed to address this issue:

> [T]here is this unfortunate distinction between the widows and children of white and black soldiers: the blacks who come from the slave States, and who probably were slaves before they entered the service, although they had wives and children, were not, according to the laws of the States within which they lived, legally married. [T]hey could not by law be recognized as the wives or widows and children of the persons thus killed.[24]

The Pension Statute was thus amended on July 4, 1864, entitling the widows and children of colored soldiers killed in the war to a pension "without other proof of marriage than that the parties had habitually recognized each other as man and wife, and lived together as such for a definite period next preceding the soldier's enlistment, not less than two years, to be shown by the affidavits of credible witnesses." An exception was made for those claimants who had "resided in any state in which their marriage may have been solemnized, the usual evidence shall be required."[25] The new law contained what is likely the first definition of marriage ever set out in federal law. If a petitioner was successful in proving that she was the surviving wife of a deceased soldier she would be entitled to an $8 monthly pension, increased by $2 per month for each dependent child.

This law was amended in 1866 after emancipation made it possible for freed men and women to marry. Under the new law, regardless of whether a black war widow pension claimant had been free or enslaved when she had married a deceased soldier, she was permitted to submit "proof, satisfactory to the Commissioner of Pensions, that the parties had habitually recognized each other as man and wife, and lived together as such."[26] The standard of proof required to demonstrate a valid African American marriage was amended one last time in 1873 when Congress required "satisfactory proof that the parties were joined in marriage by some ceremony deemed by them obligatory, or habitually recognized each other as man and wife and were so recognized by their neighbors, and lived together as such up to the date of enlistment."[27]

The commissioner of pensions was thus faced with evaluating claims by war widows for federal pensions in two different ways: white widows merely had to produce a marriage license to earn a pension, whereas black widows, in most cases, had to provide sworn testimony showing why they should be considered to be the wife of the deceased soldier and that they were recognized as married by their neighbors and other members of the communities in which they lived. As a result, the pension files of black widows are full of statements provided by the widows themselves, neighbors, black clergy, slave owners, and others attesting to the facts and forms of adult relationships between enslaved and freed black people.

Many of the files support the notion that relationships among enslaved adults in the antebellum period conformed to traditional norms of monogamous marriage, whether by "choice" or as a result of coercion (noting, of course, that the very notion of slaves "choosing" how to organize their lives is itself a problematic notion). Quite frequently enslaved men and women were married in ceremonies conducted by slave preachers. One pension claimant referred to her 1861 marriage by a black preacher as adhering to "slave rules."[28] Ellen Waters's application is typical in this regard. According to the testimony of two other slaves who were eyewitnesses to their marriage, Ellen Moore and Aaron Waters were married near Pine Bluff, Arkansas, on July 4, 1862. They testified that the marriage was officiated by Major Waters, "a colored Baptist preacher," who was "a slave and an illiterate colored man." (Presumably he was no relation to the couple he was marrying, but shared their last name because he was owned by the same man, a Dr. Waters. It was common for slaves to be given their owner's last name.) Aaron Waters enlisted in the army on September 15, 1863, and was mustered into Company G of the 54th Regiment of the U.S. Colored Troops. He suffered from chronic "diarrhoea contracted while in the line of duty" and died of dysentery on October 1, 1864, in a hospital in Little Rock, Arkansas. At the time of his death he held the rank of private. Ellen and Aaron Waters had no children. These statements were enough to establish a marriage under the 1864 pension act since Mr. and Mrs. Waters "were slaves at the time of the marriage and consequently there was no church or other public record of said event in existence." The hearing officer granted her petition for a monthly pension of $8.[29]

A similar story is to be found in the pension file of Elias Johnson, a free black man who enlisted in the 1st Regiment of the U.S. Colored Troops in Washington, D.C., on May 19, 1863, and died of diarrhea/dysentery on September 6, 1864. His wife, the former Nancy Gordon, was described in the 1846 court papers certifying her freedom as "a dark copper coloured woman . . . about five feet and half an inch high, rather handsome face, sharp pointed chin, and fine regular features, hair long and black and nearly straight and a scar from a burn on the front part of the neck." Beginning on September 6, 1864, Mrs. Johnson received a monthly widow's pension of $8 from the Bureau of Pensions. In order to secure the pension, Mrs. Johnson had produced the following two documents: a notarized marriage certificate issued by Reverend G. Brown, pastor of the First Colored Baptist Church in Washington City, D.C., dated March 6, 1850, and an affidavit of two long-time friends of the Johnsons who testified that Elias and Nancy Johnson had lived and cohabited together as husband and wife from the date of their marriage up until Mr. Johnson's enlistment in the army, that they had had a daughter, Eleanor, and that they had been regarded as married by their community.[30]

Margaret Johnson was found to have been the lawful wife of Elija Johnson, a colored soldier who was killed in action at the battle of Fussell's Mills, Virginia, on August 16, 1864. Affidavits supplied in support of Mrs. Johnson's pension claim showed that they had been married by the Reverend Abraham Freed, a minister in Somerset County, Maryland, on November 2, 1856. According to the documents, the Johnsons had lived together for eleven years prior to their marriage, during which time they had had two daughters, Leah Ann in 1851 and Eveline Frances in 1853. The file does not indicate why they chose to marry in 1856, having "lived together as man and wife for several years preceeding [sic] their marriage."[31]

On May 9, 1872, Milly Williams was awarded a pension due to the war-related death of her husband, George. In support of Mrs. Williams's claim, the couple's former owners Theodore and Martha Stanley supplied an affidavit stating that Millie "was married at our residence in the County of Cole & State of Missouri to George Williams colored man in 1859 by Isaac Handy a colored ex porter. . . . Milly and George Williams lived and cohabited together as man and wife from the day of marriage to the time of his entering the army as man and wife, were so regarded by the affiants and all their friends and neighbors then & until death." The couple had two children, Edward, born on October 31, 1860, and Terrel, born on August 17, 1863. George Williams enlisted on March 11, 1864, and was mustered into Company H of the 68th U.S. Colored Infantry and stationed at Camp Benton, just four miles outside of St. Louis. The winter of 1864 was "unparalleled for severe cold weather," and the colored troops were not allocated adequate clothing given the weather. Many had no hats or shoes and were given very little to eat. Between January 1 and May 1, 1864, 784 cases of pneumonia were documented among the colored troops at Camp Benton, and 130 deaths were recorded due to pneumonia or other pulmonary illnesses. Dr. Ira Russell, a volunteer doctor working in the winter of 1864 for the U.S. Sanitary Commission treating black soldiers at Camp Benton for pneumonia and other ailments, noted that "one hundred men were crowded into rooms that were originally meant but for fifty, necessarily rendering the air very impure; and this evil was rendered greater by the faulty construction of the barracks and the imperfect ventilation."[32] The following October a medical board was convened to investigate the horrific conditions the colored soldiers suffered at Camp Benton. It found that more than a third of those enlisted had died from various undiagnosed diseases and that colored regiments were most often bivouacked near swampy or poorly drained areas of the camp.[33] Over 100 of the new colored recruits died at Camp Benton before they were even deployed. George Williams was likely one of them. His wife's war widow pension application indicates that he died on May 1, 1864—less than two months after enlisting—at Benton Barracks from "inflammation of the lungs."[34]

Black preachers were not the only ones who presided over the marriages of enslaved people. Owners sometimes did so as well. It is remarkable that in states such as Missouri and Arkansas, border states that had been occupied by Union troops and that had had military governors appointed by Washington in 1862, former slave owners were willing to support the claims of their former slaves for pensions related to their husbands' service in the Union army.

Susan and Allen Alexander were both purchased as children by Charles Whitmore and taken from Virginia to his Mount Pleasant plantation in Mississippi. Allen worked as the Whitmores' coachman, and in 1838 he and Susan were married by their master in a ceremony that Susan described to a pension office agent as follows:

[T]hey stood up before him and he ask [sic] affiant if she was willing to take Allen as her husband and do for him all that a woman should and he asked Allen the same about affiant from that time until Allen was taken while in the army they lived together and cohabited as husband and wife.

While other slaves on the Mount Pleasant plantation regarded Mr. and Mrs. Alexander as living together as husband and wife, they were unaware that the Alexanders had undergone a formal marriage ceremony conducted by their owner. Louisa Woods, another slave owned by the Whitmores, testified that "they were not married at their owners just took up with each other and lived together for many years they were living together for at least 15 years." This fact did not negatively affect Susan Alexander's claim to a war widow's pension, yet it does reveal something interesting about marital norms among enslaved people at that time. Louisa Woods's testimony is evidence of the variety of slave relationships, which included "taking up," living together, and marriage. The community recognized these relationships as permanent, monogamous, and sacred without requiring formal legal sanction.[35]

Julia and Charles Alfred's marriage illustrates a different way in which owners involved themselves in the marriages of their slaves. Julia testified to an agent of the pension office that she and Charles had been born on the plantation of Gustave Le Gardeur, a prominent New Orleans lawyer whose family came from Normandy and boasted a direct line to French nobility (an interesting pedigree given that this last name evokes goat or sheep herding more than aristocratic origin). During the Civil War Gustave served as a captain in the "Le Gardeur Battery" and after the war he was one of the founding members of the Louisiana White League, a paramilitary association of former Confederates that worked to intimidate freedmen from voting and Republicans from holding office.[36] According to the pension agent, "About six years before the war (1861) affiant took up with Charles Alford and lived as his wife, on her said Master's premises in New Orleans, and with said Master's consent." Gustave Le Gardeur's son Leon supplied testimony in support of Julia's pension application and, according to the agent, noted that "at that time it was necessary that slaves should obtain the permission of their owners before being married, [and] that to his knowledge said permission was given." It does not appear that the Alfreds needed any religious or other ceremonial blessing in order to consider themselves married; evidence of their owner's permission was enough. They had two sons, Charles Jr. in 1858 and Lewis in 1861.[37]

Charles Alfred Sr. enlisted in the army in August 1862 at a pivotal moment in the war and in the role of black troops in the Union army. In May 1861 the governor of Louisiana created the first and only confederate regiment made up of free men of color, the 1st Louisiana Native Guards. When New Orleans surrendered to the Union in the spring of 1862 the Louisiana First offered itself to the Union army. General Benjamin Butler accepted their offer and mustered them into service on September 27, 1862, reorganizing them as the 73rd U.S. Colored Regiment, the first colored regiment to be enrolled into the Union Army. Thus Charles Sr. joined the regiment just as it was transitioning from a Confederate to a Union outfit. He was mustered into the unit on September 27, 1862, the day it was formally assembled as part of the Union army. He served until May 3, 1864, when he was killed aboard a Union transport boat, the *City Belle*, that came under fire from the Confederates as part of the Red River campaign.[38]

Some formerly enslaved people testified that it was not the custom to hold a wedding ceremony in order to establish a marriage between slaves. In January 1876, Dilly Bostick was granted a war widow's pension due to her husband Joseph's death from consumption at L'Ouverture Army Hospital in Alexandria, Virginia, in October 1864.[39] With respect to her marriage, Mrs. Bostick testified that she could "furnish no evidence of marriage, as no marriage ceremony took place she and her husband having been married by co-habitation." A close friend of the Bosticks testified that "it was not the custom for colored people to marry by regular ceremony."[40] This statement was echoed by Christianna Poole, who explained in her pension application that she and her husband Robert "went together in the days of slavery both being slaves, there was no marriage ceremony."[41]

These first-hand accounts document that a mix of "nonlegal ritual and ceremony accompanied most slave marriages."[42] These ceremonies, such as jumping over a broomstick, converted a slave union into a slave marriage. But the pension records reveal a more complex story, as unformalized slave unions were more common than some historians acknowledge. Instead, these records show that enslaved people's relationships took a number of forms in addition to monogamous marriage. Many formerly enslaved women described how they "took up" with a man, lived with him, even had children with him, but never sought out the services of a preacher to solemnize the relationship as a marriage.[43]

The pension files reveal another layer of complexity and intrigue: files that contained claims from two different women claiming to be the soldier's widow. It was not uncommon for an enslaved man to have more than one wife. Perhaps he'd have one wife living in one part of the plantation whom he was with during the planting season, and another living elsewhere whom he was with during the harvest season. Or when enslaved men were required to accompany their owners back and forth between their homes in the city and country, they'd have wives in both places. Take for example the pension application of Caroline Johnson, who claimed to be the widow of Collin Johnson. Caroline was born in 1842 on a plantation owned by Stephen Johnson located in the north-western corner of Mississippi, on the Tennessee/Arkansas border. The 1860 census shows Johnson to have owned 55 slaves, and local records indicate that he was one of the delegates who attended the state convention in January 1861 when Mississippi voted to secede from the Union. In the early 1850s Stephen Johnson bought Collin, then a young boy, at an auction in Memphis and brought him to live on the plantation in Mississippi. Caroline described Collin as "a farm laborer, he was about 5 ft. 9 in., brown black." She told the pension officer that they were married "under the slave rules" in the summer of 1861 by a Reverend Aaron Keys and that they had two children: Isaac, born in 1862, who died six months later; and Elizabeth, born in the early part of 1864, who died at about two years old. In June 1863 Collin ran away from the plantation and joined the 61st U.S. Colored Troops and later died in connection with his service. Her story of their marriage was backed up by testimony from Stephen Johnson's widow and son, both of whom said that Caroline was recognized on the plantation as Collin's wife. The pension office agent grew concerned when he noticed that a Harriet Johnson had also filed a claim for a pension as Collin's widow. Harriet maintained that she and Collin had been married in June 1862 by a colored preacher named Aaron Johnson, presumably another slave on the Johnson plantation. The testimony in the file indicates that all three of them were owned by Stephen Johnson and "it was very probable that the soldier lived with both Harriet and Caroline at the same time." Most likely these were "seasonal marriages," one wife for the planting season and another for the harvesting season, but ultimately both Caroline and Harriet Johnson abandoned their pension claims, and the records don't reveal why.[44]

Daniel Allen appeared to have maintained an even more complicated set of relationships. Two women claimed to be entitled to pensions as his widow; however, in this case, both women were successful. It appears from the record that Daniel Allen was enslaved by William Allen as his "body servant" and was brought to Mississippi when William Allen and his family moved there from Maryland in 1836. William Allen owned two properties in Mississippi: a plantation on the Mississippi River and a home in Vicksburg. Daniel frequently traveled back and forth between these two properties with his owner. Henrietta Allen had been sold to William Allen when she was seven or eight years old and when she grew up became the maid of William Allen's wife in Vicksburg. She came to know Daniel when he accompanied William Allen on his visits to the Vicksburg house. Henrietta told the pension officer that she secretly "had" Daniel without her owners' knowledge or consent. In 1862 when Daniel "got the maid [Henrietta] into trouble," Mrs. Williams became angry with her because, as Henrietta described it, "she tried to raise me as a white girl." Ultimately Mrs. Allen gave Henrietta permission to live with Daniel in "one of the servants' rooms."[45] According to Henrietta, from that point forward she and Daniel lived "as husband and wife" in Vicksburg. Henrietta and Daniel had two children while in the Allen house, but both of them died at a very young age. After they were freed by the Emancipation Proclamation Daniel and Henrietta moved to Natchez, Mississippi, and were married "under the flag," a commonly used term that meant they were married by Northern military officials.[46] Daniel enlisted in the army in September 1863 and served in Company D of the 58th U.S. Colored Infantry based in Natchez. A month later he contracted smallpox. Henrietta never left his bedside during his illness—"he was sick in the hospital for about ten days before he died, having received good medial care and attention, nursed by [me] until he died."

Asked whether she had remarried after Daniel's death (remarrying would disqualify her for a widow's pension), Henrietta told the agent: "I have not remarried but about 5 years ago I had Lewis Williams for a man for a number of months. He did not live with me but slept and stayed with me occasionally. I have nothing to do with any man before nor since. I have female disease from washing and ironing." The records revealed that Henrietta had a child with Lewis Williams, but the baby was stillborn. The Pension Bureau agent who worked on Henrietta's claim coldly noted in the file that there was no record of either the birth or burial of the child she had with Lewis Williams. He wrote: "A colored baby is of less account here to white people than a good dog." Whether he was expressing his own views or cynically editorializing views held by the larger community is not clear. But either way, he was giving voice to what surely was a widely held view among whites in Mississippi after the end of slavery about the value of free and freed black babies; to the former owners of slaves, black babies had less value as freed humans than they did as enslaved property.

As he was finalizing his work on Henrietta Allen's pension application the Pension Bureau agent discovered that another woman had already successfully filed for a pension as Collin Allen's widow. According to the earlier filing, it seems that when Daniel accompanied William Allen to the Mississippi River plantation, Diamond Bend, "he 'took up' with one Winnie Allen." When Daniel died Winnie successfully applied for a pension as his widow and received $8 per month until her death in February 1870. Only after Winnie's death did Henrietta get around to applying for a widow's pension herself. The investigator's notes indicate that "Henrietta, being a sleepy sort of woman with little energy, let it [Winnie's pension application] go without any serious contest. She [Henrietta] had no money or funds and the other woman [Winnie] had the pension. It seems true that the soldier did have two wives." Because the evidence demonstrated that Daniel cohabited with Henrietta at the time of enlistment, and because "Winnie Allen's case is settled by her death," Henrietta was awarded a pension.[47]

The distinction between marriage and "having a man" was significant for Mary Johnson as well. When asked whether her deceased husband was her first husband, she replied, "I never lived with any man as his wife before I lived with my husband but I now admit that I had one child by Jim Finley. . . . No, I never went under Finley's name. I never lived with Jim Finley. I simply had a child by him."[48]

But marriage and marriage-like arrangements were only one of the ways that enslaved adults got together. Some "sweethearted," "took up," and lived together in a wide range of non-marital relationships. "Sweethearting" was a common non-monogamous relationship, entered into primarily by young people—"a temporary tie that entailed more prerogatives than obligations and many new feelings and pleasures . . . many sweethearts had children together."[49] These children were often described as "sweetheart children," a term Susan Alexander used in describing her family in her application for a pension as the surviving widow of her husband Allen.[50]

Like "sweethearting," "taking up" was an open-ended and non-exclusive type of relationship. "Taking up" was a way to describe the non-exclusive relationships of older people, or sweethearts that had been together for some time. The relationships of couples who had "taken up" could mature into ones in which they were regarded by the community as living together or married. "Sweethearting" and "taking up" were distinguished from "living together" and marriage by two important factors: the nature of the commitment they represented, and the degree to which the relationships were recognized by other members of the community. Many slaves held the view that living together, like marriage, obliged a man and woman to stick together and be monogamous. The decision to marry or live together usually included the involvement of their fellow slaves or owners as witnesses to the commitment they were making to one another. If living together and marriage were relationships of a more public nature, "sweethearting" and "taking up" were more private arrangements. Often times, enslaved men and women, fearing retribution or punishment from their owners, had good reasons to keep their romantic lives secret. They may also have seen their commitment to one another as more short-lived or non-monogamous—perhaps due to the likelihood that they might be separated by their owners, or because they lived on different plantations, lived on different parts of large plantations, or simply didn't see a need for a public, long-term, and exclusive commitment.[51]

Community recognition was really what distinguished between levels of relationships. When a previously married member of the couple began to live openly with another person, the community treated the former marriage as dissolved. It was also common for enslaved people to enter "trial marriages" of several weeks or years, during which time the couple would check each other out. Harriet Beecher Stowe recounted a female slave's description of her relationship with a man as: "[W]e lib along two year—he watchin my ways and I watchin his ways."[52]

The prevalence of female-headed households, or matrifocal families, in many slave communities was pointed to as evidence of the dysfunction, or even pathology, of slave family life—absent fathers, single mothers, no signs of the structure that two parents make possible. But consider the context in which slave kinship structure emerged. It's clear that outside forces played as important a role in making enslaved mothers the heads of their households as did any "choices" they might have been making. The law of slavery established that the civil identity (free or slave, white or black) of all children followed the status of their mother, regardless of the identity of their father, thus tying black children to their mothers as a legal and social matter for generations. Of course, this also meant that white men could have sex, and children, with the black women they owned and could treat those children as property not progeny. But it also led slave owners to routinely consider all of the children born to female slaves as belonging only to their mothers, ignoring or denying any claim or role their fathers may have wanted. This made the breakup of families through sale or residential assignments that much easier, but also reinforced the matrifocal nature of the slave family.

In the end, the same evidence viewed from different vantage points leads to very different explanations for why enslaved people formed the families they did. As a preliminary matter, no generalization about the behavior of enslaved people would hold true for the entire system of chattel slavery, as the variations in the conditions of enslavement from one locality to another were often dramatic. In Louisiana, it was common for enslaved people to be housed in barracks, whereas in most other regions family cabins were the norm.[53] Evidence of a custom in many locations in favor of nuclear family groupings accompanied by informal marriages and monogamous coupling might lead one to conclude, as Gutman did, that this custom was an expression of the preferences of enslaved people. But it is equally true that planters consciously used housing policy, distribution of extra rations, marriage ceremonies, and work assignments to manipulate the birth rates among their enslaved workers.[54] Consider two very different plantations, one in Mississippi and the other in Georgia. On the Mississippi plantation, the planter determined that it would be more profitable to abandon growing cotton and instead engage in a "slave breeding" business, which led him to improve the domestic conditions in which the slaves lived. But a Georgia planter decided to maximize profits from his rice plantation by minimizing expenditures on the material needs of the slaves. Thus the first owner raised living conditions in order to "raise" people, whereas the second sacrificed the welfare of people in order to increase crop yield. In the first case the slave birthrate was 12%, whereas in the second, the child mortality rate was 90%.[55] This is not to argue that enslaved women were passively reacting to the market strategies of their masters, since enslaved women elsewhere were known to resist the tactics of owners designed to maximize fertility.[56] Rather, the formation of families under slavery must be understood as a complex synthesis of planter coercion and incentives, and slave resistance and accommodation.

⤶

"Slavery had a disastrous effect upon African-American families, yet sadly a child born into slavery in 1860 was more likely to be raised by his mother and father in a two-parent household than was an African-American baby born after the election of the USA's first African-American president."[57] This "insight" about the state of African American families formed part of the introduction to a fourteen-point pledge circulated by a conservative Iowa political organization in the summer of 2011. The Family Leader announced that it would not endorse any candidate for U.S. president who did not sign its "Marriage Vow." Conservative Republican presidential candidates such as representatives Michelle Bachman and Rick Santorum signed the pledge, while former representative Newt Gingrich and Texas governor Rick Perry agreed to sign only after the paragraph claiming that black children were better off during slavery was removed.[58]

By appealing to the notion that black people were better able to maintain stable, two-parent households when they were enslaved than they are today, the right-wing Family Leader injected a racialized form of "family values" into the 2012 presidential campaign. Oddly enough, their stance echoed the claims of left-wing historians and advocates in the 1960s and 1970s. In 1965 Assistant Secretary of Labor Daniel Patrick Moynihan set out to better understand the roots of black poverty and undereducation, and why the broad statement of racial equality issued by the U.S. Supreme Court in the *Brown v. Board of Education* decision in 1954 had failed to herald an era of greater racial equality. The Labor Department's Office of Policy Planning and Research published Moynihan's study, *The Negro Family: The Case for National Action*, in which he concluded that passing civil rights laws would not address the underlying problem that impeded racial equality and justice: the crumbling Negro family.[59] His report maintained that the "tangle of pathology" of contemporary black families could be traced to the manner in which slavery forced the formation of fatherless "matrifocal" families that were incapable of imparting the values necessary for successful and responsible adult life. The Moynihan Report was immediately criticized as racist by the black community and white liberals. Among those critics was Herbert Gutman, a well-respected labor historian who published a response to Moynihan's claims in his 1979 book, *The Black Family in Slavery and Freedom, 1750–1925.* Gutman aimed to debunk Moynihan's thesis by showing that enslaved people had formed viable nuclear families, notwithstanding many structural impediments. The book documented how "ordinary black men, women, and children . . . adapted to enslavement by developing distinctive domestic arrangements and kin networks that nurtured a new Afro-American culture."[60] Gutman offered up powerful evidence: enslaved people formed remarkably strong, stable, marriage-like family bonds despite overwhelming obstacles. His argument gave legitimacy to those who looked to larger social causes to explain the state of the modern black family (such as poverty, unemployment, overincarceration of black males, and racism) rather than something intrinsic in the black community itself. It is hard not to hear the echoes of Gutman in the Family Leader's "Marriage Vow."

In this sense, both conservatives and progressives have found it useful to advance the argument that enslaved blacks formed marital-like relationships—but surely not for the same reasons. Conservatives make the claim as a way to criticize the morals of black people today, while progressives do so to rebut the argument that there is something essentially immoral or pathological in black culture that impedes the ability to form healthy families.

War widow pension applications and other primary sources reveal that the kinds of families enslaved people created were incredibly diverse. That diversity could be explained several ways: old patterns of family formation they brought with them from Africa; adaptation to the reality that families could be broken up at any moment by an owner who decided to sell a husband, a wife, or the children; heeding the call of black clergy and the surrounding white communities that urged the moral superiority of the nuclear family; regional differences in the ways plantation owners set up slave housing and community structure; resourcefulness and innovation that grew in the absence of legal structure; and finally the pain, emotional devastation, and murder of the spirit that flowed from being enslaved. Nevertheless, the diversity of black families has been seen as something to celebrate or explore for its positive potential.

At turns labeled adaptive, resilient, pathological, immoral, deviant, damaged, or culturally distinctive, African American families, more than any other American families, have been subject to critical evaluation and diagnosis. The Moynihan Report was only one, albeit well-known, example of the negative portrayals of black families that provoked Gutman and others to counter the pathological view of black families with a more positive historical account.[61] To those who espouse the pathological view, every household headed by an unmarried black woman serves as evidence of a larger "truth" about the dysfunction of black families, traceable back to the immorality and disorder of the families of enslaved people. Whenever the black community is in crisis, as it was once again in the summer of 2014 in Ferguson, Missouri, after the police shooting of African American teenager Michael Brown, the "black family," and the delinquency of black fathers in particular, is trotted out to explain why black people are poor, undereducated, engage in disproportionate amounts of crime, or protest racist police violence.[62]

In the 150 years since the abolition of slavery, during which time black people have been able to legally marry, they have not had the same rates of marriage or formation of nuclear, two-parent households as other racial and ethnic groups in the United States. Even in recent years, as marriage rates have declined across American society, the rates of marriage in the black community have dropped even more precipitously, so much so that today black women are three times as likely as white women to have never married by age 45.[63] Black men are twice as likely as white men to never have married by age 45.[64] In fact, African Americans are the group least likely to marry, and when they do, they do so later and spend less time married than other Americans. They are also the least likely to stay married as compared with other groups. An African American child today is three times more likely to be born to parents who are unmarried than is a white child (75% of African American mothers are unmarried when they have children versus 27% of white mothers). In fact the percentage of African American children living with a single parent in 1960 was approximately 25%, and in 2012 it was over 60%.[65]

Through times of enslavement and freedom, low marriage rates have been a gnawing issue for the African American community. The non-traditional families and extended kin networks that black people formed while enslaved were seen by nineteenth-century racists as evidence of their savage natures, and since emancipation African Americans find their family lives still under enormous scrutiny, some pointing to the low marriage rates and high number of unmarried women bearing children as evidence of a kind of group-based depravity and pathology. The 1965 Moynihan Report's closing language expresses a view that remains widely held:

> At the heart of the deterioration of the fabric of Negro society is the deterioration of the Negro family. It is the fundamental source of the weakness of the Negro community at the present time. . . . [A]t the center of the tangle of pathology is the weakness of the family structure. Once or twice removed, it will be found to be the principal source of most of the aberrant, inadequate, or antisocial behavior that did not establish, but now serves to perpetuate the cycle of poverty and deprivation.[66]

Just as enslaved women were forming families under conditions that constrained their options in ways well beyond their control, so too are African American women today. Magazine articles, dissertations, and other academic research amply document how black women face a rather bleak "marriage market" in which it is extremely difficult to find eligible men who are financially and otherwise attractive partners. First of all, there is a gross imbalance in the ratio of black women and men wanting and able to marry, in no small measure due to the number of black men in prison. In fact, there are more African American men in the prison system today than there were enslaved in 1850. In thirty-two states more than one in ten young black men are in prison, and in ten states one in six young black men is behind bars.[67] With so few marriageable African American men, African American women are making other choices about love and family.

African American women's family and kinship choices are constrained by uncertainties in ways quite different from many white women's. High rates of violence in black communities and lower life expectancy due to poor health create incentives for living in the present rather than planning for a long future together as a married couple. "When both a woman and her partner believe that he will not live past the age of twenty five, the intensity of their relationship can escalate quickly, with coresidential living arrangements and a pregnancy ensuing before the couple has taken the time to really get to know one another," notes one study.[68] "Some African American women . . . anticipate the early demise of their partners," and "to reduce uncertainty and potential grief, women will severely limit their attachment and romantic commitment," the study continues. In such precarious circumstances, many African American women come to feel that having a child, even without the father's involvement, will create a more permanent form of attachment than would holding out hopes for romantic love and marriage. A child is also an investment in the future and a symbol of hope. For many women "having a child is the creation of a stable, enduring, perhaps lifelong, emotional and physical bond,"[69] that can be much more rewarding than searching for a suitable husband.

For many African American women today, opting out of the "marriage market" and having a child on their own makes sense given the complexities of their lives. These women rely on an extended network of family and close friends to help out and provide the love, support, and structure that they and their children need. But almost invariably, the media and policy makers portray these families as broken, fallen, fragile, and socially undesirable. Women whose circumstances leave them no alternative than to receive public benefits for their support find themselves vulnerable to being portrayed in stereotypic terms as "welfare queens" or as poor women who have more children to collect larger welfare checks (a pernicious myth since it has been shown that the average woman receiving public assistance in fact only has two children).[70] Social science research is full of studies attributing all kinds of social ills to these "dysfunctional" families—poverty, undereducation, drug abuse, crime, and general community degeneracy. Even if one were to accept the faulty causal connection between poor women's families and a host of social ills, marriage would be a poor solution to these problems. I don't want to minimize how hard it is to raise a child with only one wage coming in, but I do want to put on the table whether it's not being married to a black man that is the primary cause of the struggles a single black mother and her children face. If you look at the numbers, focusing on marriage deflects attention from the structural race-based impoverishment that single African American mothers suffer. For every dollar a white man makes (based on median weekly earnings), a white woman makes 81¢, a black man makes 74¢, and a black woman makes 66¢.[71] In this regard, getting a black man's wage in the house would be a far less advantageous strategy to increasing household wealth than would be getting the help of a white person's wage. Given the racialized structure of the wage-labor market, heterosexual marriage (to a black male) is not a great economic strategy for black women.

In addition, the condemnation of black families is amplified by the enduring stereotype of the absent black father and the belief that black men make bad fathers. These myths persist despite their repudiation in study after study. Most notably, in the summer of 2014 the Centers for Disease Control released a study that demonstrated unequivocally that black fathers are at least as, if not more, involved with their kids as other men in similar living situations. The report found that 70% of black dads said they bathed, diapered, or dressed their kids every day, compared with 60% of white fathers and 45% of Latino fathers.[72] Yet this kind of myth-busting data gets little traction in resetting the widespread view that black fathers are to blame for a wide range of dysfunction in African American communities.

Rather than jump immediately to the conclusion that non-traditional and extended families in the African American community are necessarily a symptom of larger cultural fragility, crisis, or dysfunction, perhaps we might consider how these alternative kinship networks grew out of the community, and whether their resilience and adaptability might offer a positive alternative to the nuclear family. Since slavery times, black parents and other adults have taught children to address older persons who were unrelated to them by either blood or marriage by the honorifics "Aunt" or "Uncle." Gutman's 1976 study argued that this practice created a structure of family, safety, and belonging among adults and children who were not necessarily related by blood or marriage, but who were nevertheless raising children together and were doing the kinds of care work we normally associate with kin. These patterns did not stop with the end of slavery. To this day, African Americans are much more likely than whites to rely upon "fictive kin" to help mitigate the impact of poverty. But research shows that extended kin networks not defined by marriage or blood are common among more affluent African Americans as well, creating a web of support, friendship, company, and care that can be drawn upon in illness, old age, or other times of need.[73]

Much has been written about the fragility of the nuclear family itself; created for the Industrial Age, it has been viewed in economic terms as a structure in which the husband's wages subsidized the unpaid support services provided by his wife. This model no longer works well for most families in today's economy where one wage—even if it's the wage of a white man—cannot maintain the family's basic needs in many cases. Given the cost of paid childcare, many women—even those who consider themselves middle class—are finding that they can't afford to work as the wages they are likely to earn are unlikely to exceed the cost of childcare.[74] Nevertheless, women in "traditional" families who stay home, care for their children, and are dependent upon their husbands' wages are in a profoundly isolated and vulnerable place, socially and economically. Oddly enough, we don't characterize the position of these women as fragile, at risk, weak, or unhealthy. Instead, we protect the ideal of the nuclear family by blaming their predicament on the cost of childcare, high taxes, and other external pressures such as gas prices that make commuting too expensive. The complete dependence upon a male partner's wages could be understood as a form of "private welfare" that enables stay-at-home moms' exit from the wage/labor market, just as "public welfare" enables other women to provide for the needs of their dependents independent of a wage. The parents receiving "private welfare" are not seen as collaborating in a dysfunctional family form, while recipients of "public welfare" surely are.

For African Americans, the nuclear family has never been the most common way they have arranged their family lives. Instead, black families have tended to be predominantly female-headed, and rather than relying upon on a single wage earner for financial stability and a single homemaker for domestic stability, they have drawn from a broad network of aunts, grandmothers, close friends, and others to provide support to both mothers and children.[75] In contrast to a conventional account of society in which the nuclear family is a distinctly private, well-bounded entity separate from other kin and the larger community in which it might be located, for many African Americans the family and the community are more porous. These kinship networks involve much more than the mother/father/minor-children constellation, and family/kin members feel and bear a sense of financial and emotional responsibility for one another. Extended families revolve around notions of interdependence and communal cooperation, rather than individualization and immediacy (in the sense of "immediate family" versus "others"). In effect, these family arrangements have been part of an effective strategy to help buffer the effects of labor market disadvantages that heads of black households face by virtue of structural and historical racism and other impediments. "Bloodmothers" and "othermothers"—women who share responsibility for childrearing with the legal parents of black children—have traditionally formed an important part of woman-centered kinship structure in the African American community.[76] A study in 2000 found that more than half a million African American grandparents aged forty-five and older were raising their grandchildren.[77]

Tasks that in "traditional" families are assigned to the legal parents of a child in one household, such as provider, disciplinarian, teacher, role model, comforter, and provider of moral guidance, get divvied up among a number of households and adults, each playing a different, yet complementary, role in a child's life. Along with this division of labor comes an understanding that the multiple adults who are "raising" a child have different "rights" and "responsibilities" to that child and to each other that are far more complex and nuanced than the approach family law typically takes to the relationship between parents and children: a child can have only two legal parents, both of whom owe the ultimate and full responsibility for the child, and all others (such as uncles, aunts, grandparents, neighbors, friends, caretakers, babysitters, nannies, teachers, etc.) are legal strangers to that child and can make no claim for visitation or input in important decisions relating to the child's upbringing.[78]

The 2010 census and other data reinforce the facts of how African Americans organize their adult lives: they are half as likely to live with a married spouse, their households are three times as likely to be headed by a single woman, and marriage is a much less common reality, or even ideal, way of "being together" in a romantic relationship. "Living apart together" or LAT relationships, relationships in which the couple does not expect monogamy, and fluid forms of attachment are much more the norm. African Americans have broken the tie between sexual or romantic attachment and parenting, insofar as whom you sleep with does not necessarily determine who helps you raise your kids.[79]

Of course "the family" figures centrally in the black community as a source of support, refuge, love, and care, as does family in any community, but so often black families' failure to conform to a nuclear model is regarded as a signal of instability or disorganization, a result of external stresses, pressures, and disadvantages. But the non-conventional form of black families is also a testament to resilience and resistance to generations of poverty, overincarceration, and racism. The ways in which the black family is less of a "unit" and more of body with tendrils reflect the protective mechanisms that have kept black families stronger and healthier than they are often portrayed in the media and by policy makers.[80] If black people had never suffered the catastrophe of enslavement, segregation, economic disadvantage, and race-based violence and hatred, would they have formed families that were more nuclear in nature? We'll never know. The precariousness and fragility of single-parent/single-mother households is amplified, if not distorted, by an insistence that we measure a family's health by its proximity to the ideal of a two-parent, nuclear household. In so doing, we notice what's missing rather than what's present and may be counterproductively venerating the familiar structures and supports of traditional Ozzie and Harriet–or, better yet, (The Cosby Show's) Cliff and Clair Huxtable–type families.[81]

Curiously, the forms of sexual, romantic, and kin-based attachment to be found in the heterosexual African American community share a great deal with the queer sorts of relationships and families that lesbian and gay people are making. Consider three examples of queer families. First: Sue and Linda have been a couple for twelve years and live in Philadelphia.[82] They are both African American, academics, and wanted to adopt a child. They looked into several different places that would allow adoption by a lesbian couple (many do not), and they chose one that allowed open adoptions. (With an open adoption both the identities of the birth parents and the adoptive parents are known to each other.) Linda was particularly interested in an open adoption given her own family history. At several points in her childhood she had lived with her aunt, and her grandmother had played an important parent-like role as well. She liked the idea of an open adoption for the way it allowed the birth mother to remain involved in the child's life, even though she knew there might be some risks in doing so.

The way this agency works, potential adopters provide photos and background information about their upbringing, education, and why they want to be parents. The birth mother then selects adoptive parents based on this information and an interview.

Gloria found herself pregnant for the second time with a man who was not the father of her first child. He was not on the scene and didn't intend to play any kind of fatherly role with the child he and Gloria had conceived. Gloria thought it best to put the child up for adoption, but wanted to have contact with her child as he or she grew up—thus she chose an open adoption. She flipped through the book of potential adoptive parents and settled on Sue and Linda; they were attractive, well-educated, had good jobs, and their being lesbians didn't bother her. Actually, given her experience with men she figured a two-mother household might be a more stable environment in which her child could grow up than one with a mom and a dad. As a black woman she also preferred having her child raised by black parents. She met Sue and Linda over coffee and they hit it off. Five months later she gave birth to a baby girl; Sue and Linda legally adopted her and named her Danielle.

Danielle is now six years old. She lives with Sue and Linda, whom she calls "Momma Sue" and "Momma Linda." Their house is about a ten-minute drive from Gloria's place, where she lives with her son, Reggie, her two sisters and their two children, and her mother, who lives upstairs in her own apartment. Danielle calls Gloria "Momma Gloria" and considers Reggie her brother. Sue, Linda, and Danielle are over at Gloria's house most Sundays for a family dinner. Danielle knows that Sue and Linda are her mothers, in a traditional sense. But she also has "Momma Gloria" and her aunts and grandmother, not to mention Sue and Linda's extended family, all of whom play roles in Danielle's life.

My second example is Howard and Darren, two gay men who live in New York City; after many years together decided that they wanted to be parents. They considered adopting, but knew of two couples whose attempts to adopt were thwarted when the birth mothers changed their minds, horribly disappointing the men who had wanted to be parents. Instead they decided to try having a child with a surrogate. Surrogacy is not legal in New York State, so the process they went through was pretty complicated. They used a surrogacy agency based in Boston, and began the search for an egg provider. In many states women who donate eggs are paid for their services just as are sperm donors. They struggled with what criteria to use in selecting a donor and at first agreed that they had a minor preference for someone who was attractive, on the tall side, and with light eyes. In the end they settled on an egg donor who was intelligent and healthy (though intelligence is a hard thing to objectively determine, they acknowledged). Darren and Howard are both white, and they discussed whether race should also be a criterion in their selection. After much hand wringing they decided that having two dads would be enough for the child to contend with, and adding the complexity of being racially different from them seemed unfair.

After they settled on an egg donor they then had to choose a "gestational surrogate"—a woman willing to carry and give birth to a child to whom she has no genetic relation. The agency matched them with Beth, a woman from Oklahoma who already had children of her own. She said she decided to be a surrogate because "[b]ecoming a surrogate provided a way for me to experience a planned pregnancy at a time in my life when I could enjoy the experience. There would be no lifelong commitment to raising another child, and it was one of the rare chances so few people receive to do something over."[83]

Forty-three eggs were "harvested" from the egg donor and they were fertilized with thirty million sperm, some from Howard and some from Darren all mixed together in a "fatherly cocktail." Nine months later a baby girl was born, whom they named Melina. She is the product of an egg from a woman living in Maine, sperm from one of the two dads living in New York, and gestation in Beth's womb in Oklahoma. After a number of complicated legal maneuvers, Darren and Howard became the two legal parents of Melina—one of them by virtue of biology (they flipped a coin to decide who to list on the birth certificate as the biological father), the other through a proceeding called a "second parent adoption." To get there they had to have lawyers in all three states terminate any legal claims to parentage that might be raised by the egg donor, the surrogate, and her husband (in many states the husband of a woman who has a child is presumed to be the child's father). Darren, Howard, and Melina have remained close to Beth and her family. After Melina was born Beth pumped her breast milk and shipped it to New York at her own cost—she refused to let Howard and Darren pay for the postage. She also came to New York with her two sons for Melina's naming ceremony when she was about a month old, and gave Melina a photo album she'd made with pictures from the whole experience—from egg implantation to Melina's birth. Beth's experience of being a surrogate was such a pleasure that eight months later she called Darren and Howard to tell them that she wanted to do it again, but they were still overwhelmed as new dads and decided they weren't ready for a second child. Beth described her experience as "babysitting for nine months," and the way she feels about Melina as "the same way I care for my nieces and nephews, and probably how I would care for a foreign exchange student."[84] After Beth visited New York, Darren asked Melina who Beth was and she answered: "my live in Beth's belly and my come out."

Surrogacy is becoming an increasingly popular way for gay men to have children, so long as they are sufficiently affluent: the fees paid to the agencies that triangulate the parties' contributions can run upward of $150,000.[85] The use of gestational surrogates raises new, previously unimaginable, opportunities for gay men to have children and families, yet it also raises ethical concerns that have been underexplored in the gay community. Some, including many feminists such as Gloria Steinem and Betty Friedan, find the practice a form of baby selling and argue that surrogacy contracts should be unenforceable.[86] Others push the feminist argument even further, pointing out that many gestational surrogates are low-income women of color and the overwhelming majority of intended parents who use surrogates are white. They liken the practice to white slave owners' "use" of their female slaves' wombs to harvest more slaves.[87]

My third example is of two of my gay male friends, Malcolm and Tom,[88] who bought a house in the suburbs of Maryland that turned out to be adjacent to the home of two lesbians, Sarah and Patricia. The two women really wanted to have children and after they'd been neighbors for five years approached the two guys about whether one of them would be willing to be a sperm donor. As it turned out, the guys were interested in more, and were open to being fathers, if in an uncle sort of way. Over the next several years each woman had a child, one with Tom as the biological father and the other with Malcolm. Sarah and Patricia are their primary parents, but the kids know the two men as their fathers, even though they agreed to relinquish legal paternity so that the kids could be legally adopted by their non-biological mothers (in Maryland, as in most states, a child can have only two legal parents, not three or more, although this is starting to change). Tom and Malcolm take the kids on vacations, go to parent-teacher conferences, and help out with homework, but they also live more independent lives than they would if they were primary parents as are the kids' moms. That said, they all go to church together on Sundays, where the congregation and the priest recognize them as one family. Things became a bit tense a couple of years ago when Sarah and Patricia approached Malcolm and Tom with the idea of having another child. The two children they have are ten and twelve years old and the men just couldn't imagine having parental responsibilities, even if on a less than full-time basis, for another eighteen, or more, years. They are both in their fifties and were looking forward to an empty nest in a few years. They bristled at the suggestion that one of them could just be a "donor" this time, not taking on any fathering role. They couldn't imagine having no relationship with a child they played a role in bringing into the world, and also didn't think it would be fair to that kid to treat him or her differently than the other two. After much talking and some counseling, the four of them were able to work it through, though Sarah and Patricia's disappointment was huge. They'd set their hearts on having another child. They all now live in suburban New Jersey: two homes, two same-sex couples, four parents, two kids, pretty queer.

These three stories are typical of the "queerness" of many families being formed by lesbians and gay men who want children in their lives. Rather than emulate a traditional, nuclear family they are creating complex families by design, motivated by the notion that a web of relations will strengthen the well-being of their children. When we compare these postmodern families to the non-traditional black families often termed dysfunctional that I described earlier in the chapter, many similarities emerge. While these lesbian and gay families are formed by choice, those choices were the result of constraints (biological and otherwise) that motivated them to innovate. They may have become legal and biological parents in non-traditional ways, but what's interesting is the way they have chosen to maintain a relationship with the other people who were intimately involved in the child's conception, even though those other people have no legal relationship to the child and the parents would have been legally entitled to cut them out of the child's life if they had wanted to. Sue and Linda value Danielle's birth mother, aunts, cousins, and grandmother as part of Danielle's larger extended family. So too, Darren and Howard view Beth and her family as part of Melina's larger network of kin.

It's also worth noting that marriage will do little to make these families more secure or responsible, nor will it "shore up" something now at risk or tenuous in their family structures. If Sue and Linda or Darren and Howard were married their children would be no more "theirs" for having done so. Marriage might be a way that these adults could express their love and commitment to each other, but it would be otherwise irrelevant to the integrity and well-being of their families. In fact, the nuclear family model that marriage presupposes may make these web-like families more precarious insofar as marriage ends up drawing bright lines between those who are to be treated as "real family" and those who are legal strangers. In New York State, for instance, if two lesbians decide to have a child together through donor insemination (where one is the biological mother and the non-biological mother does not legally adopt the child), and they raise that child together and later break up, the non-biological mother will have no rights to shared custody or visitation unless they have married or entered into a civil union in a state such as New Jersey or Vermont. If they have not legally formalized their relationship the non-biological mother has absolutely no rights as a parent and the biological mother can legally prevent her from any relationship with the child, regardless of how long the family was together and how close she and the child have become. Unlike some other states that take a more "functional" approach to who is a parent, balancing a number of factors including whether a person has acted like a parent "in fact," New York has chosen a more formalistic and rigid approach to family: unless you are the spouse of the legal parent or are biologically related to the child, you have no more rights to request a hearing on visitation than would a neighbor, teacher, or babysitter.[89] Lawyers who advise non-traditional families on their legal rights have noted that once states started to allow same-sex couples to marry, the rights of couples in non-marital families began evaporating. Whether it be relationship contracts between unmarried partners, de facto parental rights, or rights that might accrue between two partners as a matter of common law, little by little courts are saying: you could have married, and since you didn't we won't recognize you as having, or being able to create, any kind of alternative family relationship between or among you that is legally enforceable. The right to marry, thus, extinguishes a right to be anything else to one another.

Despite the attractiveness of marriage to many gay and lesbian couples, there remains a broad array of both improvised and well-planned alternative family forms in the gay and lesbian community where children have found themselves cared for and loved by a much larger group of adults than just two legal parents. The queer parents in such family structures are less likely to regard their children as their exclusive property, and their children are less likely to feel that they "belong" to only two adults. These parents have begun to push the legal system and society to stretch beyond a traditional, nuclear conception of family—challenging courts and schools, for instance, to acknowledge that children may have more than two significant adults in their lives, and retooling the way we think of a woman, such as Gloria, who doesn't have to stop having a role in her child's life after she is adopted by two other parents. Although many judges in the U.S. have ruled emphatically that a child cannot have three legal parents, courts around the country are becoming more open to recognizing three or more legal parents. One of the first such cases took place in Canada—a court in Ontario found in January 2007 that a young boy could have three legal parents: the boy's biological mother, the mother's lesbian partner, and the sperm donor. The boy lived with the two women, but they were unwilling to extinguish the parental rights of the donor—who played a meaningful role in the child's life—in order to make the non-biological mother a legal parent. What they wanted was that the boy have three legal parents, since this was how he viewed all three adults and the parents felt it would be a good thing for all three of them to have parental rights and authority, such as being able to sign consent forms should their son be hospitalized. The court agreed, recognizing that it was in the child's best interests to have his two mothers and his father legally recognized as parents.[90]

Courts in the U.S. have followed Ontario's lead, allowing a child to have three legal parents.[91] The privacy concerns that surround the legal proceedings in which legal parentage decisions are rendered make it difficult to assemble a complete inventory of the circumstances in which courts have been willing to recognize three legal parents, but the most common situation is when the third parent has a biological relationship to the child. This arises when the third party is a sperm donor,[92] or, as is the case in Louisiana, when a married woman becomes pregnant with a man who isn't her husband. As in most states, under Louisiana law the husband of the mother is presumed to be the father of a child born during the marriage. Louisiana courts will, however, allow recognition of both men, the husband and the biological father, as legal fathers of the child so that the mother or the state can come after the biological father for child support, and in order to allow the biological father to seek visitation with "his" child.[93]

Same-sex couples are in no way immune from the kind of messy parentage issues to which the law of Louisiana has responded. In 2008, a lesbian couple in a civil union in New Jersey underwent in vitro fertilization (IVF) using an anonymous donor. After their son was born the non-biological mother adopted the child so that both of them could be his legal parents. Three years later they broke up, and during the legal dissolution of their civil union and negotiation over custody of their son the birth mother revealed that the child was actually born of an affair that she had had with a man while undergoing IVF. After complex negotiations, the two women and the man successfully petitioned a court to have the biological father named as a third legal parent.

A Pennsylvania court in 2006 was faced with another complicated situation: two women who had been in a long-term relationship raising several children broke up and the biological mother sought child support from the non-biological mother (who had not legally adopted the children). The non-biological mother argued that if she was obliged to provide child support, so too should the sperm donor, who had been present at the children's births, had voluntarily provided ongoing financial support to the two mothers when they were together, and encouraged the kids to call him "Papa." In fact, at the time the suit was filed the children had only one legal parent: their biological mother. But the court determined that both the non-biological mother and the sperm donor must provide child support under theories of "fundamental fairness" and "equitable estoppel" (if you voluntarily behave like a parent for a period of time, you can't later deny being one in order to avoid the responsibilities of parenthood). The court didn't technically find that all three were legal parents of the children, but rather that all three had obligations to financially support them.[94]

What we're seeing in these cases where a third or fourth adult seeks legal recognition as a child's parent is the law trying desperately to catch up with a complicated reality, a reality made up of diverse family forms where notions of rights and responsibilities are being negotiated in complex ways. Both by example and through efforts to change law and policy, queer families such as the three I described earlier in the chapter are vanguards in the transformation of the modern family, creating positive alternatives to the traditional, nuclear two-parent household. Ideally, there would be positive spillover to other non-traditional families, such as those in the black community, that have suffered negative social judgments from many quarters. That is to say, African American families that fail to live up to an ideal nuclear form ought to be indirect beneficiaries of a shift in social norms in which queer families are now recognized as healthy families. But this hasn't really been the case. There has been little positive spillover. Why?

Some of this can be traced to arguments made in recent same-sex marriage cases. I gasped when I read the legal papers filed by the national gay rights groups challenging the Illinois marriage law in the summer of 2012. They made the argument that couples and families that must take form outside of marriage do so in a landscape in which they are regarded as missing out on the dignity and respect that comes with wedlock: "they are stigmatized by the creation of a separate, novel, and poorly understood legal status for them instead of marriage." The litigation in Iowa was even worse: during the oral argument before the state's supreme court the plaintiffs' attorney referred to a little girl in the courtroom who had lesbian parents and who had been told by a day care center that she couldn't talk about her family on "family day" because they weren't married. He told the court that this anecdote illustrated how important it was for her parents to be able to marry. But of course, what the anecdote reveals is the stupidity of the narrow conception of family at work at the day care center; the kids should be able to talk about their families, whatever form they take—marital, non-marital, or whatever (Grandma is in my family, Aunt Iphigenia is in my family . . .). It reminded me of the outrage a single-mom friend of mine felt when her kid came home from the first day of school after having to do the ice-breaking family tree exercise—the tree is already split into two main branches, and all the kids need to do is fill in the names of Mom, Dad, Grandma, Grandpa, etc. "Why not let them draw their own family trees with whatever branches they need, rather than have to fill one in that requires the kids to explain why some of the branches are empty or irrelevant?" she asked.

The marriage equality litigation in Illinois provides an interesting example of how the framing of the legal problem in these cases risks reinforcing the precariousness of non-marital relationships and families. Randy Walden and Bob Carey had been together for almost seven years when they decided to play a key role in challenging the Illinois law that barred same-sex couples from marrying. At the time they joined the ACLU's lawsuit in 2012, Randy was fifty-three years old; a decorated veteran of the U.S. Army, he was honorably discharged in 1983 from his job as a Russian translator because he was gay. He now works as a registered nurse case manager for the Illinois Army National Guard. Bob, then fifty, works as a performance manager for Ameren Illinois, a regional gas and electric company in Peoria.

Randy and Bob entered into a civil union on August 23, 2011, soon after this legal status became available in Illinois. Randy felt strongly about legally protecting his relationship with Bob. Before he met Bob he was in a nine-year committed relationship with Curt Sills, who died of cancer in February 2004. Randy went to doctor visits with Curt and helped to monitor his care and treatment. When Curt got sick they had a lawyer prepare legal documents that gave them "spousal-like" rights to make medical decisions for one another in the event that either was incapable to do so, expressed their wishes regarding what measures should be used if they became incapacitated, and indicated that they wanted each other to be able to visit should they be hospitalized. But when Curt was eventually hospitalized, hospital staff refused to talk to Randy about Curt's condition, repeatedly asking, "And who are you to him?" Not until he produced copies of the medical power of attorney would they acknowledge Randy. Even after they had the legal documents, the hospital staff asked Curt's parents to make medical decisions. Each time the hospital staff turned to Curt's parents they explained that Randy was the one in charge of Curt's care.

The power of attorney and living will that Randy first gave to the hospital was stamped "Permanent Chart Copy—Do Not Remove." However, in the three days that Curt was hospitalized, the documents disappeared twice and Randy was forced to provide additional copies. When Randy brought Curt to the hospital, he asked to be allowed to spend the night in his room. Although spouses were allowed to stay over, Randy was not.

Randy asked the hospital staff to call him immediately about any changes in Curt's condition, and that a note be placed on Curt's chart recording this request, listing Randy's home, cell, and work phone numbers. On the morning of Curt's third day in the hospital when Curt did not answer his room phone or his cell phone, Randy called the nurses' station and, after questioning once again whether he had any right to know about Curt's condition, the nurse told him, "He hasn't been doing well all night. You need to get here as soon as you can."

When Randy reached Curt's room, Curt awakened long enough to tell Randy he loved him, then lost consciousness and died. Moments after Curt's death, a nurse came into the room, ignored Randy, and asked, "Is there a spouse?"

Given this experience, it was imperative to Randy that he never encounter the same kinds of invisibility, rejection, and disrespect that he experienced as Curt's partner. Years after Curt's death when he began dating Bob, Randy wanted to take every measure he could to legally protect their relationship. "Although Bob and Randy acknowledge the additional legal protections provided them by civil unions, they know that nothing will provide them the security that comes from the understanding and respect that is only accorded marriage," the legal papers in the ACLU marriage case declare.[95]

Randy's story is an interesting, and in some ways curious, one to include in the Illinois same-sex marriage case. Although Randy and Curt were not married, the hospital staff was acting illegally and in violation of their own internal policy by ignoring Randy as the person to consult about Curt's care. Randy appeared at the hospital with documents that identified him as the person with legal authority to visit Curt and make medical decisions for him. Under the Illinois Power of Attorney Act hospital and medical personnel are required to recognize and respect the terms of these documents.

I am dubious that the discrimination Randy suffered when he was caring for Curt would have been solved by their being married. Most likely, the invisibility, exclusion, and bias Randy suffered were as much or more about Randy and Curt being a gay couple as it was about being an unmarried couple. Stories abound of bakeries refusing to provide cakes, florists refusing to sell flowers, and venues refusing to rent their spaces to same-sex couples who are marrying.[96] If Randy had shown up at the hospital with a marriage license, the hospital staff might have just as easily "misplaced" this document as they did the power of attorney form. Being married would have been unlikely to have inoculated Randy and Curt from the staff's discomfort or dislike of gay people. I'd wager that if a man had shown up in the same hospital to visit a woman he called his wife, he would not have been asked to produce a marriage license. Straight people don't carry their marriage licenses around with them because it doesn't occur to hospital staff to question the veracity of their marriages. Yet same-sex couples would be well advised to keep a copy of their marriage licenses in their wallets, ready to whip them out when confronted with the inevitable disbelief, or worse disdain, they'll encounter when they want to be treated as legal spouses. Even then, a paper license may not be enough to overcome the disdain with which some people view the marriages of same-sex couples and the underlying homophobia, if not revulsion, which underwrites that disdain in many cases.

If Randy had called a lawyer after enduring this horrible ordeal, his lawyer would have advised him that he could bring two different lawsuits. One approach would challenge the hospital's sexual orientation–based bias that motivated the refusal to recognize his legal right to visit Curt, spend the night with him, and make medical decisions on his behalf. Besides the fact that health care providers are legally obligated to respect medical powers of attorney and other similar documents, in 2006 Illinois governor Rod Blagojevich signed a gay rights law that added sexual orientation to the statewide law barring discrimination in employment, real estate, financial credit, and public accommodations. Hospitals fall under the "public accommodations" part of the law, which clearly includes hospital visitation and medical decision making. Had Randy brought this lawsuit he could have established an important principle challenging the nurse's question "Is there a spouse?" Not only would the case have exposed the latent homophobia motivating this question, but it would have likely reinforced the rights of a broad range of family and care providers who should be—and are—legally entitled to visit their loved ones in the hospital and make medical decisions for them. The aim of this kind of case would be a form of justice for the diverse forms of family to be found in most communities, not just the gay community. It would have done more than recognize the standing of the spouse or spouse-like person in the patient's life. Gay rights attorneys have brought these kinds of lawsuits across the country, demanding that hospitals and other institutions expand their policies to recognize not only family related by blood or marriage, but also extended families, friends, and caretakers.[97] The Obama administration issued new rules in 2011 requiring that hospitals respect patients' choices about visitation and decision making, and explicitly included a rule that hospitals respect a patient's right to choose who can visit them—a spouse, a domestic partner, another family member, or a friend.[98] Unfortunately, this new federal regulation was not in place when Randy was struggling to visit Curt in the hospital.

The second legal approach available to Randy—and the one he chose—was to bring a suit seeking marriage rights for same-sex couples. This suit, while certainly important, at best would secure rights for Randy and his partner equal to the rights that heterosexual married couples now enjoy. Practically speaking, its scope would be much more narrow than the first option, challenging the hospital's narrow definition of family member and disregard for the legal documents Randy had given them. That case would have been modeled on a notion of justice for a broad range of both traditional and non-traditional families, while the actual suit rests on a more constricted concept of equality: a demand that same-sex couples be treated in the exact same way that traditional straight couples are now treated. It takes marriage as a given, and merely asks that a new group of couples be eligible for the benefits that marriage promises. Marriage remains the only relationship that matters.

These marriage equality cases leave undisturbed policies that take it as given that only married people should be allowed to visit their loved ones in hospitals, share their health insurance with spouses and children, and gain other forms of legal, economic, and social recognition. Rather than seeing marriage as one of many ways a couple, household, or complex family unit might make their lives more secure, the insecurity of life outside marriage is reinforced when these lawsuits focus on a demand to be let into marriage's exclusive club. Perversely, it has not been in the interest of the marriage-rights movement to spend resources on strengthening the legal and social standing of civil unions, domestic partnerships, and other forms of legal recognition through private contract (such as powers of attorney and relationship agreements). The weaker and more "second class" those non-marital forms of relationships become, the better off the case for marriage equality becomes. As the lawyers argued in the Illinois marriage case: "Illinois reserves marriage for different-sex couples, while it has created a separate, novel, and inferior civil union status for lesbian and gay couples." (In fact this isn't exactly true, since Illinois is one of the few states to create civil unions that are open to both same-sex and different couples.[99] Hawaii and the District of Columbia have as well.)

Most states that have passed civil union laws or domestic partnership laws (Vermont, Connecticut, New Jersey, New Hampshire, Delaware, Rhode Island, California, Oregon, Washington, and Nevada) have limited them to same-sex couples. In these states, marriage is for heterosexuals and civil unions are for gay and lesbian people. In fact, the LGBT rights movement's lawyers and advocates drafted and lobbied for these laws specifically arguing that they should be limited to same-sex couples, sometimes over the objections of others who felt they should be open to both gay and straight couples. As soon as these new laws were enacted they were vilified from within the gay community as a meager step in the right direction, taken only because we hadn't yet achieved the political support for full marriage rights. Jackie Goldberg, a lesbian member of the California Assembly who drafted the state's domestic partnership law, wrote in the *Los Angeles Times*: "no one knows better than I do how it falls short of marriage. I've been in a state-registered domestic partnership for more than seven years and can attest to the inequality that remains, and is unavoidable, in that separate-from-marriage system."[100] Many advocates who wrote these laws insisted that they be limited to same-sex couples, and testified on their behalf in state legislatures with the view that they were crafting an institution "separate and not equal" to marriage. That inferiority could be pointed to later when they brought lawsuits arguing that only marriage could grant true equality and dignity to same-sex relationships.

The intentional "staging" of civil unions and domestic partnerships as inherently inferior undermines the work of some advocates of these laws who intended to create positive supplements to marriage. They may have denounced the discriminatory nature of marriage laws that were limited to "one woman and one man," but they also wanted to create viable, if not preferable, alternatives to marriage. Movement leader Paula Ettelbrick was one of the first and most vocal members of the

LGBT community to push for a domestic partnership law in New York City as a positive legal reform that would provide both same-sex and different couples another way for their relationships to be legally recognized, not as a stop-gap measure until marriage rights were achieved, but as a relationship form with its own integrity.[101] Ettelbrick often expressed a sense of betrayal when gay rights advocates premised their marriage equality lawsuits on the inferiority of domestic partnerships or civil unions. She resisted the claim that only through marriage would same-sex relationships gain the respect and dignity they deserved.[102]

Inadvertently or by design, the advocates in these cases accept the stigma and abnormality associated with life outside traditional marriage. Rather than address and try to ameliorate that stigma, they argue that their clients should be able to marry and thus escape the dishonor of life outside marriage. Winning the case thus leaves or, worse, reinforces the negative social and legal judgment assigned to non-traditional families. Letting same-sex couples into the club leaves in place the bias and shame suffered by those who can't or won't fulfill the criteria for membership.

Making arguments that trade in the value of respectability and the virtues of legal recognition seems a perverse strategy to me. It wasn't that long ago that all sexual contact between people of the same sex was subject to criminalization; we lived our sexual, romantic, and family lives under threat of arrest, strong social condemnation, if not disgust, and parental disapproval. While many heterosexual African Americans could take refuge from broader societal racism and violence by turning inward to their families and community, gay men and lesbians have, for the most part, had to construct their own safe spaces separate from their families of origin and the communities they grew up in. While this is changing as the society becomes more tolerant or accepting of homosexuality, it's worth thinking here, as in the context of African American families and relationships, about whether the growing acceptance of homosexuality, including the legalization of same-sex marriage in some states, will—or should—motivate same-sex couples to enter into monogamous, long-term, conventional relationships, including nuclear families, just like heterosexual people. Or are there distinctly queer forms of attachment, kinship, desire, and love that have developed in the gay community that are worth holding on to as viable, or even preferable, alternatives to marriage and the nuclear family, such as the three examples I offered earlier of Sue and Linda, Darren and Howard, and Malcolm and Tom?

Many in the legal community have argued that there are strong parallels between the civil rights struggles of African Americans and those of gay people—particularly when it comes to their sexual and relationship rights. The reasoning goes: if the U.S. Constitution's Equal Protection Clause was violated by laws that restricted whom one could marry based upon another person's race, then the Constitution should be similarly offended by laws that restrict whom one can marry based upon another person's sex. In 1967 the Supreme Court found in *Loving v. Virginia* that anti-miscegenation laws (laws prohibiting interracial marriage) were unconstitutional because they were grounded in notions of white supremacy. Advocates today claim that based on the same reasoning, laws prohibiting same-sex marriage are grounded in hetero-supremacy. Conservative judges, such as Richard Posner, have come to embrace the *Loving* analogy in their consideration of the merits of today's marriage equality cases.[103]

While I understand the appeal of using *Loving* as an analogy to advance the cause of same-sex marriage, I'm inclined to resist it, though not for the reasons that some people in the African American community recoil at attempts to analogize the claims of today's gay rights movement to earlier race-based civil rights claims.[104] To my mind, the turn to *Loving* risks reinforcing the supremacy of marriage as the ideal form of adult relationship, while strengthening the notion that non-marital, non-conventional relationships and forms of loving are nothing more than symptoms of an earlier more homophobic era, or deviant adaptations to criminalization. Real sexual freedom ought to entail viable alternatives to marriage and the nuclear family, and so we ought to feel some discomfort with the longing for our *Loving*.

The turn to *Loving* as the proper analogy through which to understand the civil rights stakes today is one that already comes at some cost. On June 11, 1967, Richard and Mildred Loving—he was white, she was black—were criminals in the Commonwealth of Virginia, but on June 12, 1967 (the day the Supreme Court issued the decision in their favor), they were not. On June 11, the Lovings were not legally married in the Commonwealth of Virginia, but on June 12, they were. In this circumstance, there is no social or legal daylight between being subject to the regulation of criminal laws and being subject to the regulation of civil laws. The effect of winning the constitutional challenge to a status-based disadvantage of this kind is that the district attorney walks a file containing your criminal case over to the clerk in the marriage license office. You and your relationship never leave the building. But then, in cases brought under a *Loving*-like paradigm, the civil rights plaintiffs never look for the exit sign to get out from under the direct control of government and governance. Being shown, or finding, the door, so to speak, gets framed as a setback for equality rather than as a viable, indeed progressive, remedy to a constitutional violation.

What's the alternative? Well, in a sense, in 2003 the gay community found itself and its forms of loving in a unique spot of being un- or under-regulated by the state. No longer subject to criminal law after the Supreme Court found state sodomy laws unconstitutional in the *Lawrence v. Texas* case, and not yet subject to the governance of state marriage laws, for a few years our relationships occupied a kind of gap in the regulatory reach of the state until they got swept into the bin of legal marriage.

How might we understand the relative absence of regulation of homo-sexualities as an opportunity rather than an injury? The challenge we faced in making the case for marriage equality was arguing for marriage rights for same-sex couples who wanted them, while not denigrating or shrinking sexual liberty for those who choose or were forced to live outside of marriage. Couples who want to marry surely should be able to do so, but winning the right to marry should not result in making non-traditional families, such as my three earlier examples, even more vulnerable for their failure to take a nuclear form. What is more, gaining the right to marry should not result in pressure to marry. The debate within the gay community has largely been framed as between those who favor marriage rights and those who regard the marriage equality movement as regressive, unenlightened, and far too traditional. I happen to think we can argue that same-sex couples be allowed to marry while also offering strong critiques of the institution of marriage itself.

Why not see the gap between marriage and non-marriage as both permitting and germinating new, more expansive forms of sexual liberty rather than pursuing a movement strategy that puts all our eggs in the marriage basket? Marriage offers certain rights and responsibilities to those who are willing to conform their sexual lives to its constrictive demands: only two adults, not married to anyone else, who pledge to be monogamous, are financially interdependent in a particular way, and will be bound by a set of default rules when one or both parties seek to terminate the marriage. Thus the institution of marriage demands the surrender of a great deal of the liberty acknowledged in *Lawrence*, such as a right to a sexual partner of your choosing free from governmental regulation. In this sense the rules of marriage supersede any "side agreements" a couple might make about what they expect from one another while married (such as non-monogamy, let's give it a try for ten years and then see how we feel, let's keep all our property separate, the kids are really your responsibility, not mine, for instance).

If the institution of marriage compromised only the sexual liberty of those people who choose to marry, I would be less concerned about the terms of the commitment it demands. But its influence extends well beyond the boundary of its official territory, to its shadow as some have argued.[105] There exists a rich literature, to which I have made only a marginal contribution,[106] that explains how the legitimacy and respectability that law confers on married couples reinforces the illegitimacy and deviance of those whose sexual, intimate, and affective commitments lie in non-marital contexts.[107] But we can say more. The importance society places on the institution of marriage establishes it as the standard by which all other forms of kinship, family, friendship, temporary alliance, and love are both made legible and assigned value. In this society, as in most, marriage is "the measure of all things." Thus loving and/or sexual associations that lie outside the formal paling of marriage are evaluated and understood by virtue of their likeness to, or dissimilarity from, marriage. A euphemistic term such as "significant other" finds its meaning in reference to marriage; it is meant to come as close to "spouse" as possible—e.g., "spouses and significant others are invited to the office holiday party." In so doing, it crowds out the plausibility of alternative kinds of "significance" and "otherness" that do not nod to the ideal of the marital form.

As we celebrate winning the right to marry for same-sex couples we need to notice that this right has been won, in part, as a result of arguments made in court that portray families with unmarried lesbian or gay parents as missing a "special something" that only marriage can confer. In a way that should be familiar to the African American community, some lawyers in the same-sex marriage cases have argued that our inability to marry harms our children, and that the most stable and healthy families are ones where the parents can—and do—marry. Ironically, the central injury described in the cases conjures up what we might call a "gay Moynihan moment." In a brief submitted in the case challenging New Jersey's ban on same-sex marriage, the American Psychological Association and New Jersey Psychological Association declared that:

> marriage can be expected to benefit the children of gay and lesbian couples by reducing the stigma currently associated with those children's status. Such stigma can derive from various sources. When same-sex partners cannot marry, their biological children are born "out-of-wedlock," conferring a status that historically has been stigmatized as "illegitimacy" and "bastardy." Although the social stigma attached to illegitimacy has declined in many parts of society, being born to unmarried parents is still widely considered undesirable. As a result, children of parents who are

not married may be stigmatized by others, such as peers or school staff members. This stigma of illegitimacy will not be visited upon the children of same-sex couples when those couples can legally marry.[108]

The Moynihan-esque flavor of some of the arguments made by the proponents of same-sex marriage is troubling for a number of reasons. Not only have some advocates of same-sex marriage abandoned any effort to promote respect, non-discrimination, and recognition of diverse family forms, but they have veered in the direction of portraying families with non-married parents as a site of pathology, stigma, and injury to children. Marriage is figured in the briefs and testimony in some same-sex marriage cases as the ideal social formation in which responsible reproduction can and should take place—unfortunately, in increasingly racialized terms.

At the same time, the opponents of same-sex marriage have not been shy in racializing their defense of conventional heterosexual marriage. Maggie Gallagher, the president of the Institute for Marriage and Public Policy, whose motto is "strengthening marriage for a new generation," has offered unabashedly white supremacist justifications for her opposition to same-sex marriage. Her argument runs like this: low fertility rates among Europeans and people of European descent threaten the continued viability of these cultures. Society needs an institution that will encourage white people to have children. Marriage is that institution. Low fertility rates are linked to the movement away from marriage. Thus if white people in developed countries are not to become extinct, they must marry and have children.[109] This sentiment was echoed by the wife of a North Carolina legislator who was the chief sponsor of a successful amendment to the state's constitution limiting marriage to one man and one woman. She was quoted as saying, "The reason my husband wrote Amendment 1 was because the Caucasian race is diminishing and we need to uh, reproduce."[110]

In early 2012 a set of strategic memos developed by Maggie Gallagher's other group, the National Organization for Marriage (a conservative political organization devoted to defeating marriage rights for same-sex couples), were made public. They included such statements as the following: "The strategic goal of this project is to drive a wedge between gays and blacks—two key Democratic constituencies"; "Find, equip, energize and connect African-American spokespeople for marriage; develop a media campaign around their objections to gay marriage as a civil right; provoke the gay marriage base into responding by denouncing these spokesmen and women as bigots. No politician wants to take up and push an issue that splits the base of the party." This strategy was deployed in the campaign to pass Proposition 8 in California—the ballot measure that defined marriage as between a man and a woman—though it is unclear how successful it was. Dan Savage and other prominent voices in the gay community "blamed" the African American community for the passage of Proposition 8 and thus the loss of marriage rights for same-sex couples,[111] but this claim has been roundly contested if not entirely disproved.[112] Once the memos became public, the NAACP and other civil rights organizations immediately denounced the strategy as a cynical attempt to drive a wedge between the gay and black communities (as if there weren't black people who were gay or lesbian), and some held the view that publicity about the memos played an important role in President Barack Obama's decision to publically support the marriage rights of same-sex couples in the spring of 2012.

The marriage equality movement faces a set of challenging questions about the short-term strategic choices it made that have reinforced the negative reputation of non-normative families in communities of color as degenerate or failures. The relative success that same-sex couples have had in persuading the courts and the broader public of the decency of gay families, thus entitling them to the blessings of marriage as a constitutional matter, can be attributed in some measure to a racial endowment enjoyed by the marriage equality movement. This endowment has been earned, legitimately or otherwise, on account of the reputation of the gay rights movement as a white movement. How might the fight for marriage equality have taken more seriously the racial implications of its organizing strategies? Are there ways in which it might have adjusted its normative claims so as to minimize collateral damage to non-normative families, including families of color? Are there better strategies that could have been deployed that would both dismantle the homophobia that underwrites the exclusion of same-sex couples from marriage without shifting that stigma to other stigmatized groups and individuals?

What I also lament is a failure of the gay rights movement's leaders to appreciate the creative political possibilities that the middle ground between criminalization and assimilation might offer. Cultural/literary theorist Leo Bersani has expressed sadness at the thought that homosexuals would quickly and easily settle for a notion of ourselves cleansed of all fantasmatic curiosity,[113] a curiosity that is drawn to a kind of unruliness that is antithetical to being organized within the marital form. We have for now lost the opportunity to explore the possibilities of a "lawless homosexuality" that is neither regulated by criminal sodomy laws nor licensed by civil marriage laws. What would that look like? How would we know ourselves? What might be the costs of refusing the political and psychic certainty of being able to articulate and legally nail down what it means to be gay? New kinds of fantasmatic curiosities might both be foreclosed or wither as our curiosity gets channeled or tamed in the direction of the familiar, the safe, and the respectable nuclear family. Of course, as a matter of fact the nuclear family is not always familiar, safe, and comfortable, but it is as an ideal that shapes our fantasies, dreams, and desires.

One way to meet this challenge is to consider how marriage equality might be won without sacrificing a robust sense of sexual liberty. This is a very tough question, for liberty is often lost in the pursuit of equality and vice versa. There are ways to demand access to the legal institution of marriage while at the same time unsettling marriage as the institutional "measure of all things." I explain how to do this in the next chapter, but this is the hard work that I think lies ahead of us. It requires us to think more and differently about the domain of love, care, and sexual attachments that live outside marriage, in the domain of queer culture.

What the history of African American families in this chapter is designed to show is that the gay community and the black community, rather than being ideological opponents, actually have stakes in each others' efforts to combat Moynihan-izing judgment about the fragility, dysfunction, or pathology of their families and lives. The tactics and vitriol of the National Organization for Marriage help us clearly see the evil siblings, racism and homophobia, that underlie the movement to elevate marriage above all other forms of family or romantic relationship. It's in the interest of both the black and lesbian/gay communities to take a hiatus from vilifying or marginalizing those within our midst who cannot or will not conform their lives to a marital, nuclear form. Once we've welcomed them into the tent, we might be better able to appreciate what life on marriage's outside has to offer in the way of more love, support, security, flexibility, and freedom. So too we may recognize that some of the struggles that unmarried people face are a consequence not of the dysfunction of their family forms but rather of the hurdles and judgment that society's pro-marriage values impress on them.

Boots next to the Bed

Getting Caught in Marriage's Web

One evening in late March 1892 Sam Means was spotted entering the home of Frances Slaton, a single woman who lived on the edge of town in Oxford, Georgia, just east of Atlanta. Means was immediately arrested and then tried for violating Georgia's criminal fornication law: "voluntary sexual intercourse by an unmarried person with another person." Frances Slaton was never arrested for "keeping company" with Sam Means, even though she was equally guilty of violating the fornication law. Census data tells us that Means was a sixty-two-year-old black man, a blacksmith by profession, and a father of a twenty-three-year-old son named Frank. Neither Sam nor his son could read or write. Slaton was likely in her mid-forties, worked as a domestic servant, was also illiterate, and was identified by some census agents as white and by others as mulatto.

Who was watching Means and Slaton and then ratted them out to the local police? Why would anyone care that they were keeping each other's company? Turns out it was William Landers, a forty-one-year-old local white man who was the acting town marshal at the time. He'd been spying on Frances Slaton for a couple of months before he turned her and Means into the local sheriff. Called as the state's first witness in Means's fornication prosecution, he told the jury, a panel of twelve white men, "About February or March of 1892 I saw Sam Means enter Mrs. Slaton's house two or three times with a bucket on his arm, he would stay a few minutes and come out." Then he got to the heart of the matter: "About the last of March 1892 I think it was I was watching her house one night and about nine o'clock. I saw Sam Means enter the front door and go in," Landers testified. "Soon after I went up to the front door and asked to be let in, Mrs. Slaton refused to let me in," he continued, referring to Slaton as "Mrs." as he did throughout the trial, perhaps as a term of respect for an adult woman or because she was a widow. Two hours later, around 11:00 p.m., Landers returned to Slaton's home, accompanied by Rigdon McCoy McIntosh, a fifty-six-year-old white professor in the music department of nearby Emory College who was well known for writing and publishing Sunday school tunes and religious hymnals. "The lights were out in the house, and I broke the front door down and went in the front room of the house. . . . Mrs. Slayton was standing in the middle of the room in her night clothes," testified Landers. "There was but one bed in the house . . . the bed looked like someone had been sleeping in it. There were two pillows and it seemed like both of them had been used," he continued. When Professor McIntosh was called as a witness for the prosecution he told the court, "The bed looked like two persons had been sleeping in it. Both of the pillows were pressed as if a person's head had been lying on them. . . . There were the prints of two bodies that had lain lengthwise of the bed. I saw a pair of boots near the bed and also a pair of pants." Landers testified that he saw Sam Means running out the back door of Mrs. Slaton's house when he and Professor McIntosh entered through the front door, and with that the prosecution rested its case.[1]

Sam Means's lawyer, Ellijay "Elijah" Flournoy Edwards, stood up and began his defense. Edwards was one of the most prominent lawyers in the county. He had fought for the Confederacy with the famous Troup Artillery and had been one of the founders of the Newton County Confederate Veterans Association. He later went on to serve a term as the town mayor, as a judge in the Newton County Court of Ordinary (probate court), and as a state senator.[2] How he came to represent a poor black man arrested for violating the state's fornication law is a mystery. Edwards offered a smart, though ultimately unsuccessful defense on Means's behalf. He presented a witness who offered an alibi for the boots, putting on the stand George Robinson, a black man, who claimed that "Sam Means had sold them [the boots] to me several days before this, for what he owed me for work I had done for him." Robinson then had to explain why the boots were in Mrs. Slaton's house: "I was doing some ditching for Mrs. Slaton and some other work around her lot at the time these men came down there at night and I had left my boots in her house that night and had worn my shoes home. . . . I know nothing about the pants."

Edwards made no attempt to discredit the identification of Means at Frances Slaton's home that night—although it was dark and the suspect was seen only from the back as he fled out the rear of the house. Maybe he felt that in Newton County a black man charged with this kind of crime was assumed to have done it, and trying to convince a white jury otherwise was a waste of time. Instead of trying to win on the facts, Edwards's strategy was to attack the prosecutor's case on the law. The bulk of his defense turned on a legal technicality: since the crime of fornication was defined as voluntary intercourse between an unmarried person and another person, Sam could not be found guilty, Edwards argued, if he were married. (Of course if he were successful with this defense Means might be guilty of adultery, but that is not what he was charged with. So too, Georgia's miscegenation law only criminalized a black person marrying a white person, not a black person having sex with a white person.) Thus Edwards focused his defense strategy on proving that Means was married to Ellen Johnson at the time he was charged with having sex with Frances Slaton. He introduced evidence showing that Sam Means and Ellen Johnson were living together as a couple in March 1866. This date was key because Georgia, like many other states reentering the Union after the end of the Civil War, enacted a law in the immediate postwar period that automatically married freed men and women who were living together as husband and wife on the effective date of the law, in this case, March 1866. Several black members of the community testified to Sam and Ellen's cohabitation and marriage, as did the son of Means's former owner, who had known Sam his entire life. If they had been automatically married by law in 1866, then it would have been technically impossible for him to commit fornication some twenty-six years later. The prosecution countered this strategy by offering other witnesses who testified that Sam was known to have lived with Louisa Stone, that Louisa often went by "Louisa Means," and that she had passed away seven or eight years earlier. The prosecution argued that if Sam had cohabitated with two different women and had not formally elected one of them as his wife, then he was legally unmarried and would be in violation of the fornication law when he was found in, or at least near, Frances Slaton's bed.

The 1870 and 1880 census records from the county (the 1890 records had been destroyed in a fire so are unavailable) would have sunk Sam's case had they been introduced as evidence. The 1870 census recorded Sam as living with Louisa, a thirty-eight-year-old illiterate black woman who was "keeping house." In 1880 and 1900 he told the census taker that he was widowed.

Even though the census data wasn't introduced at trial the jury didn't go for Sam's defense and returned a verdict of "guilty" after deliberating only two and a half hours. Judge George Gober not only accepted the jury's verdict, he also ordered Sam to pay the costs of the state's attorney's fees, something he surely couldn't afford (recall his friend George Robinson's testimony that Sam didn't have enough cash to pay him for work he'd done, compensating him instead with his leather boots). Inability to pay the court fees would almost certainly result in an extension of his sentence while he worked off those fees on a chain gang. Elijah Edwards appealed Means's conviction to the Georgia Supreme Court on the theory that he was married at the time he was charged with fornication, but the high court took little interest in the case despite the notoriety of the lawyer handling it and issued a two-word opinion: "Judgment affirmed."

For Sam Means marriage played a pivotal role in his struggle to navigate the complex demands of freedom in the late-nineteenth-century South. Means probably wasn't aware of the Georgia law passed in 1866 automatically marrying ex-slaves who had lived together "as husband

and wife" when he moved in with Ellen Ferguson or when he told the census taker in 1870 that he was living with Louisa Stone. Ignorance of the legal consequences of their domestic living arrangements got quite a few freed men and women into trouble when they left those relationships and took up with other partners. In Means's case, however, marriage law provided his lawyer with a clever defense—maybe too clever for a Georgia jury. But his case does illustrate the incredibly complex way in which marriage laws regulated the lives and freedom of black people in the post–Civil War South.

↤

Marriage, it turns out, is one way a society signals new acceptance of a previously outcast group—whether it be formally enslaved people in the nineteenth century or same-sex couples today. Marriage was and remains a curious vehicle through which newly freed or equal people can elaborate their freer and more equal selves, since marriage comes with a passel of non-negotiable terms and conditions. Getting married means that your relationship is no longer a private affair since a marriage license converts it into a contract with three parties: two spouses and the state. Once you're in it you have to get the permission of a judge to let you out. And what you learn when you seek judicial permission to end a marriage is that it's a lot easier to get married than it is to get divorced.

Freed people in the nineteenth century encountered the beneficial and burdensome consequences of marriage through their lived experience with the law. While many of them correctly saw the inability to marry as one of the most important ways the society treated enslaved people as less than human, few understood that marriage laws would govern their lives so uncompromisingly and harshly. This chapter tells the story of how they discovered that the freedom to marry did not mean the freedom to organize their intimate lives as they saw fit. Instead, granting the right to marry to former slaves gave white people a wide range of new ways to meddle in the lives of newly freed people:

coercing them to marry in many cases, punishing them if they didn't, and bringing the criminal law to bear when they didn't follow the rules that being married entailed.

⌒

In 1862, John Eaton was appointed by General Ulysses S. Grant to set up "contraband camps" for black refugees in Tennessee and northern Mississippi (rather than call them "refugees" the Yankees called them "contrabands," still treating enslaved people as the enemy's illegal property instead of persons fleeing enslavement). Edward Pierce, a young lawyer from Boston who had been assigned the task of overseeing the first contraband camp at Fortress Monroe, Virginia in 1861, was met by his charges with disbelief that they were still being treated like chattel. When they learned that they were being held in contraband camps they asked Pierce "Why d'ye call us that for?"[3]

Eaton, a Presbyterian minister born in New Hampshire in 1829, described in his memoir his first encounters with the fleeing slaves in Mississippi: "Imagine, if you will, a slave population, springing from antecedent barbarism, rising up and leaving its ancient bondage . . . coming garbed in rags or in silks, with feet shot or bleeding, individually or in families and larger groups . . . a blind terror stung them, an equally blind hope allured them, and to us they came." He continued: "Their condition was appalling. There were men, women, and children in every stage of disease and decrepitude, often nearly naked, with flesh torn by the terrible experiences of their escapes."[4]

The destitution, disease, and need of people freed by law or circumstance were overwhelming. Henry Rowntree, a civilian missionary who had come south to help address the needs of indigent black people with the Contraband Relief Society of Cincinnati, described the living conditions of the people he found living on Jefferson Davis's plantation in Vicksburg, Mississippi, after Davis had been driven away by Northern troops:

I called at a cattle shed without any siding, there huddled together were 35 poor wretchedly helpless negros, one man who had lost one eye entirely, and the sight of the other fast going, he could do nothing.

Five women all Mothers, and the residue of 29 children, all small and under 12 years of age. One of the Women had the small pox, her face a perfect mass of Scabs, her children were left uncared for except for what they incidentally [received]. Another woman was nursing a little boy about 7 whose earthly life was fast ebbing away, she could pay but little attention to the rest of her family. Another was scarcely able to crawl about.

They had no bedding. Two old quilts and a soldiers old worn out blanket comprised the whole for 35 human beings. I enquired how they slept, they collect together to keep one another warm and then throw the quilts over them. There is no wood for them nearer than half a mile which these poor children have to toat as they could carry, hence they have a poor supply and the same with water, this has [to] be carried the same distance and the only vessel they had to carry it in was a heavy 2 gallon stone jug, a load for a child when empty.

They owned One Pan, and one Iron kettle amongst them, they had no tin cup, no crockery of any kind, no knives or forks, and certainly were the poorest off, of any I have met with being litterally and truthfully destitute in every sense of the word.

All of them were homeless, and most of them had almost no possessions and were sick, hungry and had no means of work.[5]

Given the desperation, illness, and injury that drove the slaves to seek refuge with Union troops, it may come as a surprise what the Northern officials who were charged with their care prioritized as among the fleeing slaves' most pressing needs: the rites of marriage.

In its reports to the secretary of war, the American Freedmen's Inquiry Commission reflected the view dominant among whites that black people were uncivilized, undisciplined, and lived in wholly "unchristian" ways. Their solution: the rule of law as well as patient guidance from whites would tame and civilize them. The commission observed that "[t]he law, in the shape of military rule, takes for him the place of his master, with this difference—that he submits to it more heartily and cheerfully, without any sense of degradation."[6] Urging an active role for the federal government in the moral cultivation of black character, the commission's final report concluded on an optimistic note: "[T]hey will learn much and gain much from us. They will gain in force of character, in mental cultivation, in self-reliance, in enterprise, in breadth of views and habits of generalization. Our influence over them, if we treat them well, will be powerful for good." In support of this argument, the commission referred to a Canadian high school principal who maintained that proximity to whites could even "whiten" black people's "unattractive" physical features: "[c]olored people brought up among whites look better than others. Their rougher, harsher features disappear. I think that colored children brought up among white people look better than their parents."[7]

In March 1864, the secretary of war made Eaton's regulation official United States policy, and ordered Freedmen's Bureau[8] agents to "solemnize the rite of marriage among Freedmen." Thereafter, superintendents of the contraband camps uniformly reported that "the introduction of the rite of christian marriage and requiring its strict observance, exerted a most wholesome influence upon the order of the camps and the conduct of the people."[9] The necessary relationship between morality and citizenship framed the approach that federal officers took to managing black peoples' transition from slavery to safety.

So important was marriage to the overall humanitarian and civilizing mission of the Northerners who came to the aid of the slaves who flocked to hastily set up contraband camps that some officials insisted that the couples marry as a condition of entry into certain camps. John Eaton boasted that "all entering our camps who have been living or desire to live together as husband and wife are required to be married in the proper manner. . . . This regulation has done much to promote the good order of the camp."[10] In his instructions to the officials running the contraband camps he ordered: "Among the things to be done, to fit the freed people for a life of happiness and usefulness, it was obvious that the inculcation of right principles and practices in regard to the social relations ought to find a place."[11]

In hearings before the American Freedmen's Inquiry Commission—the federal commission created in 1863 to suggest methods for dealing with the emancipated slaves—one of Eaton's chief administrators, keeping on message, testified that

> [o]ne great defect in the management of the negroes down there was, as I judged, the ignoring of the family relationship. . . . My judgement is that one of the first things to be done with these people, to qualify them for citizenship, for self-protection and self-support, is to impress upon them the family obligations.[12]

Federal officials acted as the guardians and supervisors of the moral practices of black people in order to qualify them for freedom and citizenship. The enforcement of marriage laws was widely regarded as the most useful lever to accomplish these ends as it was seen as the perfect "remedy for the widespread immorality and promiscuity that whites believed to prevail among blacks."[13]

The desperate physical state of the enslaved people when they reached the gates of the contraband camps renders it all the more shocking that the officials running the camps highlighted the moral degradation of their charges and prioritized marriage over basic human needs like shelter, clothing, water, food, and medical care. To the extent that the freed people were described as living in a subhuman state, the reports filed by federal officials noted their failure to adhere to marriage norms, rather than starvation, illness, and a lack of basic sanitation as the cause of their desperate circumstances.

Much of the rhetoric by key actors working with the newly freed men and women related to the need to civilize them. White officials informed the freed people that "[t]he loose ideas which have prevailed among you on this subject must cease," and that "no race of mankind can be expected to become exalted in the scale of humanity, whose sexes, without any binding obligation, cohabit promiscuously together."[14] The refugees' hunger, illness, and wounds from years suffering the whip were not enough to justify aid from Northern troops and other "agents of benevolence." Rather, the refugees also had to prove that they were morally deserving of help. Today it is taken as a given that all humans, by virtue of their humanity, are entitled to a basic level of care and safety. Yet for the ex-slaves it was almost as if their humanity needed to be proven through a social institution such as marriage before they would be regarded as deserving aid.

↬

Once the war was over the federal government established an agency that fanned out through the South to attend to the needs of newly freed people. The Bureau of Refugees, Freedmen, and Abandoned Lands, more commonly referred to as the Freedmen's Bureau, set up district offices in all eleven of the rebel states as well as Washington, D.C., and the border states of Maryland, Kentucky, and West Virginia. The Bureau fed millions of people, built hospitals, set up schools, negotiated labor contracts for ex-slaves, and settled labor disputes. Bureau agents were charged with looking after the welfare of the former slaves and many saw themselves as stewards of the freedmen's physical and moral well being.

The violence that formerly enslaved people suffered at the hands of Southern white planters did not cease when the war ended; in fact for many it got worse. The Ku Klux Klan was founded during the period ostensibly to keep the peace in a period of enormous social chaos, but instead devoted itself to terrorizing the newly freed black members of Southern society with the aim of "keeping them in their place." In the months immediately following the end of the war, civilian Freedmen's Bureau agents had their hands full dealing with the pervasive violence suffered by the freed people, including lynchings, rapes, beatings, and other brutal assaults—"outrages," as they called them at the time. Across the South there was overwhelming white resistance to the idea that black people should and could demand a wage for their labor, and much of the Freedmen's Bureau's work involved getting the plantation owners and farmers to honor labor contracts with their former slaves.

Faced with the overwhelming violence of white resistance to black freedom it may seem surprising that Freedmen's Bureau officers would have had time to worry about much else. But just like their military counterparts during the war, the postwar civilian staff voiced inordinate concern about the freed people's reticence to conform to the strict rules of marriage. Their weekly and monthly reports to Washington were replete with exasperation regarding the manner in which freed men and women were flouting the institution of marriage. Agents complained that the freed men and women persisted in "the disgusting practice of living together as man and wife without proper marriage," "living together and calling themselves man and wife as long as it conveniently suits them," and maintaining bigamous or adulterous relationships.[15] In "many instances," wrote one agent, "where after being legally and lawfully married they live together but a short time. Separate and marry again or live together without any obligation at all."[16] Time and again, the agents complained that blacks continued to "act as they did in time of slavery,"[17] clinging to "old habits of an immoral character."[18] "It is no uncommon thing for the husband and wife to [illegible] and live in adultery on the same plantation," one wrote. "[T]he planters say they do not sanction it but they are powerless to remedy the evil. Some severe laws will have to be passed and [illegible] executed before these conditions in this respect will be improved."[19] They were particularly outraged by the habit of a couple "taking up,"[20] and then separating when they tired of one another.[21] "It would appear to be more difficult to change their ideas in this matter than on any other affecting their welfare," wrote Alvan Gillem, commander of U.S. troops in Mississippi in the postwar period.[22]

Gillem was perhaps the most strident critic of the freed people's tendency to flout the "marriage relation." In fact it might be said it was his obsession. Not a minister or missionary, as was the case with many of the men who assumed posts with the Freedmen's Bureau after the war, Alvan Cullem Gillem was a native of Tennessee, a graduate of West Point, staunchly loyal to the Union, and served valiantly in the war commanding the 10th Tennessee Volunteer Infantry. After the war ended he commanded the U.S. troops in Mississippi and served as a Bureau agent in the state staring in 1867, only to be relieved of his command and sent to Texas in 1868 on account of his vocal criticism of the Radical Republicans in Congress, who he felt were too lenient toward the former confederates.

Gillem's obsession with the freed people's family lives comes through loud and clear in his monthly reports to Washington in which he righteously expressed increasing frustration at their refusal to take marriage seriously. In June 1867 he wrote,

> It seems almost impossible to make the more ignorant class of freedpeople understand their Marriage relations—Husbands leave their wives and wives leave their husbands . . . they marry and afterwards abandon one another without the least cause, especially in the rural districts.[23]

Gillem noted some progress, however, when he "had some of them arrested and after explaining to them their duties and obligations in this respect induced them to return to their homes and live together amicably."[24]

Every one of Gillem's monthly reports to Washington displayed similar exasperation. In July 1867 he wrote, "[T]he greatest immorality exists in the vicinity of the larger towns where the freedpeople congregated during or immediately at the conclusion of the war."[25] Then in August 1867: "No improvement has been reported or observed [with respect to marital relations]. Instances where men change their wives just as their pleasure or convenience prompts them and women their husbands are frequently reported."[26]

Many Bureau agents felt that moral suasion was insufficient to gain freed peoples' compliance with marriage laws and determined that the law should step in to impose discipline. Gillem was chief among the advocates of bringing local law enforcement officials into the project of addressing the freed people's "immoral" ways: "It is no uncommon thing for the husband and wife to . . . live in adultery on the same plantation," he wrote in one of his reports to headquarters. "Some severe laws will have to be passed and . . . executed before these conditions in this respect will be improved . . . laws are required to remedy this evil."[27] His frustration led him to observe that Bureau agents' efforts "to suppress immorality among the freedpeople would be greatly assisted by the civil authorities if they enforced the State laws on this subject." As part of this effort, he turned adulterers, bigamists, and fornicators over to the local authorities for prosecution under local criminal laws. Agent Gillem informed the Washington Bureau office that "I have caused the proper steps to be taken to bring this matter before the Civil Courts and shall urge that offenders be brought to trial and punished." He continued, "It is to be hoped that the civil authorities of the State will soon recognize the necessity of taking action in a matter in which all good citizens should feel an interest and by a few proper examples exert a salutary effect upon the masses." "The courts alone can establish a radical cure," wrote Gillem.[28]

Southern legislatures stepped into this cause as well. Shortly after the end of the war Southern states acted quickly to amend their constitutions or enact statutes validating marriages begun under slavery. Quite often laws were passed that simply legitimized "slave marriages" if the couple was cohabiting as husband and wife when the law went into effect. Mississippi's 1865 civil rights law was typical: "All freedmen, free negroes and mulattoes, who do now and have heretofore lived and cohabited together as husband and wife shall be taken and held in law as legally married."[29] Georgia, North Carolina, South Carolina, and Virginia passed similar laws during this period.[30]

Some states, such as Florida, took a different approach to the marriage of former slaves, giving "all colored inhabitants of this State claiming to be living together in the relation of husband and wife . . . and who shall mutually desire to continue in that relation" nine months to formally marry one another before a minister or civil authority.[31] These laws further required a newly married couple to file a marriage license with the county circuit court, a bureaucratic detail that carried a prohibitively high price for many freed people.[32] In every state with such laws, failure to comply with these requirements while continuing to cohabit would render the offenders subject to criminal prosecution for adultery and fornication.[33] North Carolina gave the freed people just under six months to register their marriages with the county clerk. Each month they failed to do so constituted a distinct and separately prosecutable criminal offense.[34]

Agent Gillem's campaign to persuade the freed people to observe the sanctity of the marriage relation was greatly aided by these new laws. In Tupelo, Mississippi, George Hall's wife went to the local Bureau agent and reported that her husband had been cohabiting with another woman. The agent turned him over to the local justice of the peace, who had him arrested. Law enforcement officials explained to him "the evils of such a course of conduct and the punishment that would be visited on him by law if he still persisted in such actions." He was released from custody only after he promised to return to his wife and conduct himself in a proper manner.[35]

As cultural background we should remember that the tendency to have multiple wives or husbands was in no small measure the product of slavery itself. It was not uncommon for an enslaved man and woman to marry one another, only to experience the eventual sale of one spouse to another planter. Subsequently, they would marry other people, believing, reasonably, that they would never see their first spouse again. James Massie, a British minister and abolitionist, visited Mississippi in 1863 and observed, "The laws of most of the slave states withhold all legal protection to the chastity of female slaves, and authorize masters to sell husbands and wives, parents and children from each other; and when a husband or a wife is sold, a second marriage may take place while the parties are all living."[36]

Christianna Poole testified to exactly this set of circumstances in her war widow pension application: "My first husband and I went together in the days of slavery, both being slaves, there was no marriage ceremony, and him being sold away, it is impossible for me or anyone else to say anything about him."[37] After emancipation, when formerly enslaved people struggled to reunify relationships shattered by slavery, the first husband might reappear and expect his wife to live with him as his spouse. Thus many formerly enslaved people found themselves with two or more spouses at the end of the war. In some cases women who emerged from slavery with more than one husband would choose a legal husband based upon factors such as the man's wealth or his willingness to provide for all of her children, even those fathered by other men. Other women chose to reunite with their first husbands to whom they felt a special moral connection because their marriages had ended due only to their forced separation. Ex-slave Jane Ferguson chose her first husband, Martin Barnwell, even though she had married a man named Ferguson after her owner had sold Barnwell away: "I told [Ferguson] I never 'spects Martin could come back, but if he did he would be my husband above all others."[38]

After the war, marriage started to permeate the public and private lives of freed men and women in ways they never would have anticipated. Given that bigamy and fornication were crimes in every state, persons with multiple spouses were forced to choose one and only one legal spouse and to cease intimate relations and/or cohabitation with others. The Georgia legislature tried to put a stop to what they perceived to be widespread bigamous practices in the black community in an 1866 law relating to "persons of color":

[P]ersons of color, now living together as husband and wife, are hereby declared to sustain that legal relation to each other, unless a man shall

have two or more reputed wives, or a woman two or more reputed husbands. In such an event, the man, immediately after the passage of this
Act by the General Assembly, shall select one of his reputed wives, with
her consent; or the woman one of her reputed husbands, with his consent;
and the ceremony of marriage between these two shall be performed.[39]

The statute then warned that persons who failed or refused to comply
with these requirements would be prosecuted for fornication, adultery,
or both. South Carolina imposed a similar statutory duty to choose one
and only one spouse.[40]

Even though some state's laws were silent on the question of multiple
spouses, state and federal officials saw it as their job to force freed men
and women to choose one and only one spouse as a matter of practice.
In some cases where a freed man or woman was unwilling or unable
to choose, Bureau agents felt free to do so for them. An agent in North
Carolina reported that "[w]henever a negro appears before me with two
or three wives who have equal claim upon him . . . I marry him to the
woman who had the greatest number of helpless children who otherwise
would become a charge on the Bureau."[41]

Although reluctant at first, state law enforcement officials did, after
a time, heed the pleas of Gillem and others to prosecute and jail freed
men and women who persisted in maintaining "deplorable" extramarital
relationships. However, the new marriage laws' automatic legalization
of slave marriages was a double-edged sword for many freed men and
women. Because the laws did not require them to "remarry" one another
or register their existing marriages with the state, the freedmen were
able to have their relationships automatically sanctioned and legitimized
without the additional expense of a wedding or licensing fees. This sav-
ings was not trivial, as many of them were unable to afford the $4 mar-
riage license fee charged in states such as Mississippi. One Bureau agent
observed: "Many of the colored people are, as your Excellency need not
be told, very poor; and they can ill afford to pay four dollars for a marriage license. I am not aware whether this is the sum charged in all the

counties, but it is in Vicksburg."[42] In Mississippi as in many parts of the South, freedmen were paid at the end of the growing season, earning a proportional share of the profits from the sale of the crops (typically a quarter share). As a result, for most of the year they were cash poor, since at best they had an equitable share in the crops they worked, and planters were notorious for failing to make good on paying their workers at the end of the season the share they had been promised in their labor contracts.

The full implications of being automatically married were quite devastating for many black people. More than a few of them found they bore the responsibilities that accompanied marriage without enjoying many of the rights that came with it (such as being able to protect their children from being seized by white planters under the apprenticeship system, which I discuss in chapter 4). The provisions in many states' automatic marriage statutes requiring the choice of one and only one spouse produced tragic circumstances for many ex-slaves as the reunion of fractured families often left people married to more than one person. If a man, for instance, failed to make such a selection and continued to cohabit with two women he would be considered married to neither, while at the same time vulnerable to a fornication prosecution. This is exactly what happened to Sam Means, whose story opened this chapter. A Georgia jury convicted him of fornication upon a finding that Means, "a negro man, was living with two women as his reputed wives, and had never selected either and made her his lawful wife, as required by the [1866] act."[43]

The automaticity of the marriage laws meant that many couples found themselves legally married when they had never intended to be; many were unaware at all that they were legally wed. Gillem acknowledged this problem in his correspondence to Washington in 1868:

This act was doubtless based upon the best of motives. Its effect was to enforce matrimony between tens of thousands of freedpeople who were ignorant of the passage of the act. A large proportion of them is today still ignorant of the purport of that law. It is safe to say that one half of the adult freedmen of this state are by this law married to those with whom they cohabit on the 25th of November, 1865, and are ignorant of their legal marital relations.[44]

An Alabama judge echoed this observation when he wrote the "the only witness [to the alleged wedding] was an ignorant negro woman, who probably was unable to understand the meaning of what was actually said and done."[45]

Southern judges stepped in after a period to rectify this unhappy situation, and, as the following cases demonstrate, the technical requirements of marriage laws were enforced uncompromisingly against black people regardless of whether they understood how the new laws worked "on them." In *Williams v. Georgia*, the male defendant, whose first name is never mentioned by the court, was married to Elizabeth Williams when they were both enslaved. They were separated by their master and sold to different owners but were reunited sometime near the end of the war—they couldn't exactly state when. A witness testified at trial that he remembered the couple's reunion was two months after Sherman's army occupied Savannah, and the court noted that the army of General Sherman came to Savannah on December 21, 1864. (It was not uncommon in this era for enslaved people to date events by reference to important personal or cultural events. Time and dates in general, were something enslaved people were unable to keep account of; they certainly did not have watches, and many did not know their own ages because they had been separated from their parents when very young—their births were rarely recorded anywhere.) After her reunion with Mr. Williams, Elizabeth "associated immorally with another, and the defendant quit her and married another woman." Since Williams had reunited with Elizabeth before March 9, 1866 (the effective date of the act legitimizing pre-existing slave marriages), and did not "quit" her until after that date, the court found that he was legally married to Elizabeth when he married his second wife. The judge rejected the defendant's argument that he did not intend his cohabitation with Elizabeth in 1866 to amount to a legal marriage. Instead the court ruled that the 1866 act married the couple and that "[h]is wife was unfaithful; he got mad and married again without divorce. Being a free citizen, he must act like one, carrying the burdens, if he so considers them, as well as enjoying the privileges of his new condition."[46]

Allen Melton met a similar fate in North Carolina, where he was criminally prosecuted for bigamy. The trial court found that Mr. Melton had been married to Harriett Melton when both of them were enslaved and that they had continued to cohabit as husband and wife after emancipation. By operation of North Carolina's 1866 marriage law, they were "ipso facto married and no acknowledgment before an officer was essential."[47] Melton subsequently married Delia Ann Teel in 1894 without having divorced his first wife. Most likely he did not know that he was legally married to Harriett when he married Delia. On these facts, Melton was convicted of bigamy.[48]

Stephen King was a bit luckier. As with Melton, a local prosecutor went out after King for violating the Georgia criminal bigamy law. Seems that before the war while they were enslaved King had represented to the community that Nancy Moreland was his wife. At the end of the war he left her, but returned in January 1866 for a year during which they lived together and had "sexual relations"—facts that convinced the local prosecutor that under Georgia law they had become automatically married. In 1868, while still "married" to Nancy he married Henrietta Grubbs, thus triggering the bigamy prosecution. At trial he argued that he did not know that he could be punished if he married a second time without divorcing Nancy. The trial court didn't buy this argument and convicted him. On appeal, however, he found a more friendly audience. The Georgia Supreme Court reversed King's conviction, ruling that while enslaved persons might have called their relationships "marriages," they may not have comprehended the sacredness of the marriage tie:

[T]here were also a large number of cases among slaves where the marriage tie was very loose. It had not the sanction of law; and circumstances, inevitable in in [sic] their character, made it liable to many interruptions, and when freedom was cast suddenly upon the race, it is not strange that for some time both men and women should cohabit under circumstances where it was very doubtful what was the true relation which they proposed to occupy to each other. They might be man and wife, they might be living together immorally.[49]

Ignorance of the law served as no defense for a black man named Kirk who was convicted of bigamy under almost the exact same scenario as Stephen King. The court found that Kirk had lived with Tiney Burke from December 1865 until sometime in 1879 when he married another woman. Since the Georgia automatic marriage statute "operated to make them married people" in 1866, his second marriage was found to be bigamous. The Georgia Supreme Court was unwilling to reverse his conviction as it had with Stephen King, finding instead that "even if a marriage between persons of color in December, 1865, was illegal, which is by no means apparent, yet if they were living together as man and wife at the date of the act of 1866, the marriage relation was thereby established, and bigamy could be predicated thereon."[50]

In the Williams, Melton, King, and Kirk cases, newly freed men got into trouble when the laws "operated to make them married people" without their affirmative consent or knowledge. In these cases newly freed men had no idea that they were married in the eyes of the law, and had even less of an idea of what being married obliged them to: monogamy, financial support of their wives and children, and formal legal divorce proceedings to end the marriage. The way they mistakenly figured it, if the law could automatically marry them because they were cohabitating "as husband and wife" then the law could automatically unmarry them when they stopped living together. Many black people found themselves ensnared in "marriage traps" that resulted in prosecutions for bigamy, adultery, or fornication when they thought they could get out of their marriages as easily as they had gotten into them.

In 1867, Celia McConico married David Hartwell. After two and a half years of marriage, they "mutually agreed to separate and did then separate from each other as husband and wife." A year later McConico married Edom Jacobs and was thereafter prosecuted for bigamy. At trial McConico argued that since Alabama's 1867 law automatically solemnized pre-existing slave marriages without legal formalities, she reasonably assumed she was able to dissolve her marriage without legal formality. A jury convicted her of bigamy and the court sentenced her to two years in the state penitentiary. Her conviction and sentence were affirmed by the Alabama Supreme Court.[51]

Freedmen's Bureau agents, like the judge in the McConico case, held little sway with freed people who ignored the requirements of divorce law, even when they were fully aware of its technical demands. A local agent in Tupelo, Mississippi, wrote in his monthly report to Washington in August 1867 that he would

> hear of men leaving their wives and running away with other women to parts unknown and some women leaving their husbands, taking up with other men. I feel confident these acts are not done through ignorance of the law in such cases, but more from the want of a will to comply with the law. I have explained the law to them with reference to adultery etc. but without much avail.

He picked this issue up again in a report to Washington three months later: "There is much need of a reform with reference to the marriage relations of the freed people in this Sub District, they either do not understand the law in this particular, or disregard its teachings. I am inclined to think the latter."[52]

Thus freed people who "took up" or were "sweethearts" but who failed to formalize their relationships in accordance with the law were prosecuted for adultery, fornication, or both. Others who neglected or chose not to comply with the technical requirements for obtaining a divorce and began a sexual relationship with another person not their lawful spouse were prosecuted for adultery, bigamy, or both.

Marital infidelity or immorality also formed the basis for the denial of pension benefits for black war widows who had lawfully married after 1866 but behaved in what was considered an unseemly manner after the death of their husbands. When Congress amended the pension laws in 1866, it included a provision denying pension rights to a widow who was shown to have engaged in "immoral conduct." The 1882 amendments required the termination of a widow's pension where she was shown to live in an "open and notorious adulterous cohabitation." Mary Johnson fell victim to these provisions when her pension claim was rejected because she was found to have "cohabitated with other men from within two or three months after the death of her husband." Similarly, Elizabeth Johnson lost her claim for a pension when the investigator concluded that "for more than twenty years she was mistress of one of the most disreputable houses of prostitution" in New Orleans.[53]

It is easy to understand how freed people may have misunderstood or underappreciated the legal consequences of having their relationships solemnized by the laws of marriage. Yet even those who were aware that their marriages could be legally dissolved only by complying with the formal rules of divorce may have opted to end their marriages less formally. Not only did a divorce require hiring a lawyer and paying court fees—expenses that most freed people could not afford—but divorces were much more difficult to obtain in the nineteenth century than they are today. Unlike modern no-fault divorce rules that make it possible for a couple to end a marriage without having to prove the fault of one of the parties, in the mid-nineteenth century marriage was a much more durable bond. A divorce could not be granted unless you could prove, for example, your spouse's adultery, impotency, abandonment, cruel treatment, or drunkenness. North Carolina would allow a divorce only in extreme circumstances: adultery together with abandonment by either party, adultery on the part of the wife, or impotence. If a spouse could show abandonment and extreme cruelty she could get divorce only from "bed and board"—meaning that the couple would be legally separated but not fully divorced, and thus unable to remarry. South Carolina had the most conservative divorce laws in the country. Having completely barred divorce in the antebellum period, the state's 1868 constitution included a clause allowing divorce in very limited circumstances. The state repealed all its divorce laws again in 1878, and in the ten years between 1868 and 1878 not one divorce was granted by the South Carolina courts. Interestingly enough, the state's marriage laws formally prohibited adultery, yet at the same time its inheritance laws anticipated and provided for the widespread practice of concubinage, permitting a husband to leave up to one quarter of his estate to his mistress. (Not surprisingly, wives were not similarly allowed the power to leave some of their estates to their paramours.) South Carolina's laws of divorce during this period applied only to white people, while black people sought the assistance of black church courts to dissolve their marriages and handle their domestic affairs.[54]

The Freedmen's Bureau, working in tandem with local law enforcement authorities, undertook an aggressive campaign to force freed men and women to comply with the requirements of local marriage laws. Freedmen thus found themselves locked into matrimony with few options available to them should they want a way out of those marriages. As such, the "right to marry," so celebrated in many quarters, was experienced by many freed people of this era as an unwelcome and punitive responsibility that resulted in the incarceration of many people—particularly men.

I have a strong suspicion that black men were prosecuted for bigamy, fornication, and adultery—serious crimes, often felonies, in many states in the postbellum period—in part to achieve their disenfranchisement. This was accomplished either explicitly through statutes or constitutional provisions that denied the vote to certain convicted criminals, or implicitly by binding convicted black men to work in circumstances that made voting a practical impossibility.

In this regard, it also seems clear that the prosecution of black men for these crimes was related to the evolution of "a labor-market cartel among white employers" in the postbellum period. In an effort to maintain the viability of the plantation system in the absence of slave labor, Southern planters enlisted the aid of local governments to accomplish what race prejudice could no longer pull off on its own. Many postwar Southern legislatures resisted the full emancipation of former slaves by enacting laws that intentionally denied their basic civil rights in a range of ways. Called "Black Codes," these laws criminalized vagrancy, poverty, disrespect for white people, and a wide array of other racially inflected conduct. Black men were selectively and falsely prosecuted under these laws and their incarceration made their labor available to private employers at cut-rate prices through the use of convict leasing and criminal surety policies.[55] These policies assured an abundant and cheap source of labor in the postbellum era in a manner that perpetuated a new kind of pseudo–slave labor for black men.

Under the convict lease system, which was particularly popular in Southern states in the 1880s, convicted criminals were leased from the state by private employers to work at extremely low wages and under working conditions that exceeded those of the antebellum slave system in their barbarism. Criminal surety laws worked a similar expropriation of labor. Under these laws, a person convicted of a crime for which a financial penalty was assessed could enter into a peonage contract with a bondsman who would pay the convict's fine in exchange for allowing the surety to hire him out until he had worked off his debt. In Mississippi, for instance, the law provided that any black person who failed to pay within five days all fines or costs levied in connection with the conviction of a misdemeanor "shall be hired out by the sheriff or other officer, at public outcry, to any white person who will pay said fine and all costs."[56]

The working conditions of criminal surety peons were even worse than those of leased criminals, and both were often worse than the working conditions of slaves. The mortality rate among convict-workers was extremely high because the system created incentives for the leaseholder to work the people he had leased to death. The person leasing the convict "had no interest in keeping the convicts alive past the end of their sentence or contract period, since the convict has no 'scrap' or 'resale' value"—"a slaveholder receives the full capitalized value of the slave's output for his entire working life, [so] he has an incentive to maintain the slave's health." In some cases the death rate on chain gangs was as high as 45%.[57]

In 1919, Alabama governor Thomas E. Kilby declared his state's chain gangs and convict lease system "a relic of barbarism [and] a form of human slavery." Mississippi abandoned the convict lease system in 1890, Tennessee in 1895, Georgia in 1908, Florida in 1924, and North Carolina in 1933. In 1914, the United States Supreme Court invalidated criminal surety systems as violations of the Thirteenth Amendment's prohibition of slavery and involuntary servitude, but convict leasing programs remained in effect up to and through the turn of the twentieth century in Virginia, Georgia, Florida, Tennessee, Alabama, and Louisiana. Although these laws were racially neutral on their faces, virtually "all the convicts caught in this lethal system were blacks."[58]

Thus the aggressive enforcement of bigamy, fornication, and adultery laws against black people played an important role in serving the needs of white planters to restaff the plantations with cheap, fungible labor while at the same time denying these newly enfranchised citizens the right or opportunity to vote.

Many newly freed people made a big error when it came to understanding what it meant to gain the right to marry: they naïvely thought that the freedom to marry meant the freedom to organize their family and intimate lives on their own, free from governmental intrusion. "The men contended that they had a right to have as many women as they could support, cohabitation without marriage is quite common," wrote a Freedmen's Bureau agent in Greenville, Mississippi, in September 1867.[59] For a group of people who had just emerged from the tyranny of having every aspect of their lives subject to upheaval, disruption, and rule by white people, many of them reasonably expected that the freedom to marry as freed people meant that whites would no longer have any say about how to organize their family lives. "Living together in a state of concubinage they have come to look upon as a privilege, in fact, a right which no one has a right to interfere with," observed a Bureau agent.[60]

They couldn't have been more mistaken. The historical record shows that once they were able to legally marry they were forced to do so by the white people who came south to offer them aid and comfort. Whether it was at the gates of contraband or refugee camps as a condition of entry, or by military and Freedmen's Bureau officers who would pick a spouse for you if you were unwilling to settle on just one, the freed people of the South found marriage to be as much a compulsion as a right. Being able to legally marry quickly collapsed into a requirement that they do so, either by automatic operation of law or by other more obviously coercive means.

Marriage was experienced by freed people as a curious right indeed. Imagine having a right to free speech that entailed a requirement that you exercise that right by saying something, or desegregating lunch counters and then requiring that you eat at them, or winning the right to vote and then jailing those who didn't show up to cast a ballot. Hard to imagine, since in the U.S. we cherish the liberty right to keep the government out of our business as fiercely as the equality right to be treated fairly. Yet with marriage, winning the right transformed immediately into a state-sponsored demand that freed people exercise the right, or worse, that the right be exercised "on them" automatically.

Once married, many freed people learned the hard way that marriage had rules, and that breaking those rules could be very costly, if not deadly. They learned how the law of wedlock created a set of trip wires that could easily set off arrest by local sheriffs and criminal prosecution by local prosecutors. To fully understand how marriage figured in the lives of newly freed people we have to appreciate the way in which it gave white law enforcement officials a new way to regulate and harass black people. It became a very effective vehicle to limit what it meant to be black and freed in the postwar South.

Unlike other contexts that have provided the setting for important civil rights struggles, such as lunch counters or public transportation, marriage is a particularly value-laden institution within which to lodge claims for full citizenship. The same might be said of military service and even equal educational opportunity. But for present purposes, when claims for full citizenship are articulated though a demand for marriage rights, the disenfranchised group's interest in equality and freedom must contend with the values of dignity, discipline, respectability, and security, which are entailed in the institution of marriage itself. Surely, exclusion from the institution of marriage inflicts a subordinating harm on those excluded. Yet a demand that the exclusion be lifted in the name of equality and freedom must take account of the fact that marriage has its own well-entrenched agenda that can sometimes become a bitter foe of new rights holders. In this sense, marriage can quickly become a tragic way to be free since it is at once a place of love, comfort, intimacy, and kin, and fraught with danger, discipline, and even death.

⟿

What can gay and lesbian people today learn from the experiences of newly freed people at the end of the Civil War when it comes to elaborating free and more equal selves through the institution of marriage? Do we risk being automatically married just as were newly emancipated people? Is it crazy to worry that lesbian and gay people risk criminal prosecution as a consequence of being married? Are there ways in which the right to marry might collapse into a compulsion to do so today, as it did 150 years ago?

Yes to all these questions. In fact it's already happening. In the enthusiasm to recognize the marriage rights of same-sex couples, some states are marrying them automatically without their knowledge and without their consent. As a result, these new "beneficiaries" of a civil rights revolution find themselves unwittingly bound up in legal twine for which they never signed up, which has left them in legal knots very similar to those of African Americans who were automatically married in the nineteenth century.

The evolution of marriage rights for same-sex couples in California presents the most interesting example. Starting in 1999, the state began to create a set of rights for same-sex couples under a domestic partnership registry. At first it included only hospital visitation rights and health benefits for the partners of state employees. Subsequent amendments to the domestic partnership law expanded these rights to include the ability to make medical decisions for one another, and stepparent adoption rights. Yet even as California enlarged the rights and responsibilities included in domestic partnerships, this legal status never included the broad range of financial and other rights that marriage entailed. Most importantly, entering a domestic partnership did not include the merger of two people's financial lives, nor did it create marital kinds of rights to financial support, such as an equitable share of the couple's assets or alimony after divorce. To end a domestic partnership all you needed to do was either send your partner a termination letter ("I'm breaking up with you and ending our partnership"), or stop living together and file a form with the state indicating that the partnership had ended. That was it—no court proceeding, no "grounds" for divorce, no alimony, and no complicated entanglements that a judge or a set of rules would govern.

In a sense, domestic partnership remained a legal status that signaled to others a kind of commitment between two parties to one another and a set of reciprocal rights *during* the relationship, but entailed very little in terms of obligations once the relationship ended. It included a bundle of rights one could assert against third parties, but did not entail any obligations owed to one another, particularly in the event that the partnership ended. This made domestic partnership a very different legal status from marriage. For better or for worse.

For better: some gay and lesbian couples thought of domestic partnership as a positive alternative to marriage, a way of gaining some of the benefits of being in a committed relationship without necessarily assuming all of the rules or obligations of marriage or having the state set the terms of the relationship. In this sense, domestic partnership offered a kind of freedom to queer couples who did not want to conform to traditional marriage norms. They entered into domestic partnerships precisely because it didn't look exactly like marriage.

For worse: other gay and lesbian people yearned for a legal status with their partners equivalent to marriage, and regarded domestic partnership as a kind of second-class consolation prize provided to same-sex couples in lieu of marriage. Some worried that the more economically powerful person in the couple could just walk away from the relationship with no legally enforceable obligation to provide financial support of any kind to their former partner. In this sense, some members of the gay community looked to marriage laws as a way to create economic security for the less affluent person in the couple, just as women in heterosexual relationships had fought for decades to reform the laws of divorce.

In 2003 the California legislature changed everything by radically overhauling the domestic partnership law. With the California Domestic Partner Rights and Responsibilities Act of 2003, domestic partnership was declared the functional equivalent of marriage: "Registered domestic partners shall have the same rights . . . and . . . responsibilities . . . as . . . spouses."[61] This included all the rights of state law while married *and* the requirement that the couple go through a formal divorce proceeding when they broke up, including the division of the couple's marital assets according to community property rules and a duty to provide ongoing support after the marriage had ended. Widely regarded as a huge victory for the gay community, the authors of the bill were faced with a difficult decision: What effect would the change in the law have on people who had entered into domestic partnerships before 2003? Would the law apply retroactively? Would it, in effect, automatically marry them?

The answer was yes. The new law not only "upgraded" the status of domestic partnerships prospectively, but it also converted all existing domestic partnerships into marriages retroactively and abolished the legal status of "domestic partnership" as something different from marriage, thus substantially changing the nature of the rights and responsibilities of people who had become domestic partners under the old rules. The only way to avoid having one's domestic partnership turned into a marriage was to terminate the domestic partnership before the law went into effect, which was a year from the date it was signed by the governor. In that year's time the state was required to send out three notices to all people in domestic partnerships giving them notice of the impeding change in the law and instructing them the only way to opt out of the change was to terminate their domestic partnership before January 1, 2005. The notice told them: "If you do not terminate your domestic partnership before January 1, 2005 . . . you will be subject to these new rights and responsibilities and . . . you will only be able to terminate your domestic partnership, other than as a result of your domestic partner's death, by the filing of a court action [aka a legal divorce action]."[62]

In the book's last chapter I'll plumb further the meaning of the decision to sweep all existing domestic partnerships into the rules of marriage, particularly attending to the ways in which the underlying hetero-gender norms and assumptions of marriage map onto same-sex couples. But for now I want to stress the similarities between what happened in the nineteenth century when it was thought to be a good thing from a civil rights standpoint to automatically marry African Americans, and the impulse to do the same with same-sex couples in California in 2005.

In both instances it was assumed that cohabitating couples that couldn't wed would surely want to marry when given the chance to do so. For newly freed black people in the nineteenth century this presumption resulted in a kind of domestic evulsion whereby couples were unwittingly swept up into the regulatory grasp of marriage. California's changes to the domestic partnership law in 2003 did the same thing, impelling into marriage all couples that had entered domestic partnerships on the assumption that if they didn't want to upgrade their relationships they would terminate their partnerships before the effective date of the law. Of course, California could have adopted an "opt in" rather than an "opt out" regime, leaving on the books the status of "domestic partnership" as something different from marriage, and then giving people in domestic partnerships the option to upgrade the legal status of their relationship. If domestic partners didn't opt in, they would remain governed by the law in place at the time they entered the partnership. In fact, this option was considered ("allow these already-registered domestic partners to simply re-register without terminating their partnership, at a reduced registration fee")[63] but was rejected in favor of an opt-out approach. Same-sex couples in California were offered a more stark choice: marriage or nothing. The opt-out regime was defended by the bill's drafters as sensitive to the less educated, less affluent, or less sophisticated partner, whose interests were supposed to be better protected by marriage than by the "inferior" rules of domestic partnership. Yet if the opt-out approach to the change was designed to protect domestic partners with fewer assets or education, it turns out that the rules of automatic marriage may have made them more, not less, vulnerable.

The consequences of the automatic marriage of domestic partners are legally and economically both wide reaching and very complex. The new status meant that your domestic partner's income would be taken into account when calculating eligibility for some public assistance, thus raising the possibility of being rendered ineligible for state Medicaid and food stamps, educational grants and scholarships, and other needs-based benefits; you would assume full legal responsibility for your partner's debts, thus rendering you and your assets vulnerable to seizure by your partner's creditors; your assets would come under community property laws, subject to equitable distribution upon divorce; and if you willfully abandoned your partner in a destitute condition or neglected or refused to provide your partner with necessary food, clothing, shelter, or medical attention you could be found guilty of a misdemeanor. It should come as no surprise that the California automatic marriage regime siphoned into marriage some couples that had not received any of the notices about the change in law, received the notices but ignored them, or were otherwise oblivious of the ways in which the law acted upon them without their affirmative consent. The legal consequences of automatic marriage in California have arisen most frequently when a couple in a domestic partnership breaks up—one partner assuming he or she can walk away under the old rules and the other asserting rights to court-supervised divorce, division of their assets under community property rules, and alimony. Most often this problem arises in one of the following scenarios:

- The couple broke up and stopped living together before the effective date of the automatic marriage law but forgot to or weren't aware that they needed to file the official "termination of domestic partnership" form with the state.
- The couple broke up and stopped living together before the effective date of the automatic marriage law but one partner (perhaps the one who didn't really want to break up) lied to the other about having filed the official "termination of domestic partnership" form with the state.
- The couple broke up after their domestic partnership had been automatically converted into a marriage but were unaware of the change in the law governing their relationship (perhaps they had moved and never received the notices in the mail, or simply disregarded them) and mistakenly followed the "old law" rules to terminate their domestic partnership.

Lawyers in California who handle family law cases in the gay community have encountered all of these scenarios, and they raise thorny problems of what courts should do. Is it fair, indeed is it constitutional, to retroactively alter the legal terms of a domestic partnership without the couple's actual consent? Some scholars have argued that it isn't, that automatically granting one partner rights to the other partner's assets while also collectivizing their individual debt amounts to a denial of due process and a taking of property without due process of law.[64]

The retroactive effect of the California law has created a mess for many couples. Consider a lesbian couple that lived in Oakland and entered a registered domestic partnership in August 2001. One of them got a job in Chicago and they moved in July 2002. Three notices from the California secretary of state required by law were mailed to their Oakland address, alerting them that their relationship was now governed by the laws of marriage, but they never received them. When they broke up in 2006 the less affluent woman consulted a lawyer who advised her to file for divorce in California and to ask for half of her partner's assets as well as alimony. Her partner consulted her own attorney, who urged her to challenge the constitutionality of the retroactive application of the law, automatically marrying them without their knowledge. She considered this option, but was hesitant: Did she want to be the person who was known for invalidating a law that many people in the lesbian and gay community regarded as a huge step forward in advancing the rights and recognition of same-sex relationships? A kind of evil twin sister of Edie Windsor? Surely, she thought, her name would appear in all the gay community papers as someone who was not only unwilling to support her partner but would take the law down with her, threatening the security of hundreds of other couples. What is more, the cost of bringing a constitutional challenge to the law, including appeals, would be in the hundreds of thousands of dollars. She might as well settle out of court with her partner and put this all behind her. And so she did.

No one has yet brought a lawsuit to challenge the constitutionality of the retroactive application of the law of marriage to couples in domestic partnerships. For the same-sex couples today that were married without their knowledge or consent the likely impact of automatic marriage will be largely economic in nature. Some may be saddled with their partner's debts and find themselves sued by creditors to discharge those debts with assets that they thought were "their own" funds, separate from their partner's. Others may find themselves suddenly ineligible for public benefits otherwise available on account of HIV disease, or student loans, or food stamps. In almost every case, breaking up will be more costly to the richer partner in the couple than it would have been under the old rules.

For same-sex couples in registered domestic partnerships in California the consequences of being swept up into the law of marriage will less likely result in an encounter with the criminal law. But it's not unthinkable. Consider a scenario that hasn't yet taken place but certainly could in the not-too-distant future: Bob and Steve, two men who live in a small town in southeastern Massachusetts and have been together for over ten years, decide to get married to express their love for one another and to better protect their finances. Luckily for them, Massachusetts is one of the states that allows same-sex couples to marry. Unluckily for them, Massachusetts is one of the states that still criminalizes adultery; in fact it's a felony, though not subject to the state's sex offender registration law.[65] Bob and Steve have agreed to have an open relationship, meaning that they consider each other their primary partner, are committed to each other for the long run, but are okay with each other having sex with other men, so long as it doesn't turn into a "serious thing." Let's say Bob and Steve's arrangement worked well for them for almost a decade and they considered it would still be their "deal" after they were married. A year later Bob confessed to Steve that he had been sleeping with another man for a few months and was in love with him. When they file for divorce, Bob might admit the affair in court and the judge, who could easily be a social conservative and had never supported the idea of same-sex marriage, could have him arrested for adultery. He might tell Bob: "If you people want the right to marry you better live by its rules. I don't care what 'deal' you had with Steve, when you said 'I do' you agreed to 'forsake all others.' Period."

If Bob were to challenge the Massachusetts adultery statute as unconstitutional he would probably lose. The court would likely point to the 2003 state high court decision finding that it was unconstitutional to deny same-sex couples the right to marry, noting that in that decision the court had referred three times to its own 1983 decision upholding the criminal adultery law. You want marriage, we'll give you marriage.

People who are married have affairs all the time. Many do so publicly. South Carolina governor Mark Sanford, New York governor Elliot Spitzer, and presidential candidate Newt Gingrich all admitted to having affairs while married in states that criminalized adultery. In June 2010 former vice president Al Gore and his wife, Tipper, announced that they had decided to separate, but not divorce. Mr. Gore began openly dating other women, even though adultery is a serious crime in Tennessee, his home state. Bear in mind that the state can bring charges even if the cuckolded spouse doesn't press for them, yet not one of these adulterers has been prosecuted.[66] Adultery is a crime in twenty-five states, a felony in five of those and a misdemeanor in the other twenty-one. It's easy to say that the adultery laws are outdated, rarely prosecuted, and the state legislatures simply aren't getting around to repealing them. While this is likely true in many states, it isn't true in all of them.

In fact, the campaign for marriage rights for same-sex couples has fueled efforts to reinvigorate adultery and bigamy laws. In several states conservative legislators have rejected efforts to repeal existing adultery laws and have advocated far stronger laws in reaction to the notion that same-sex couples were marrying and might undermine the sanctity of the marriage relation. For instance, for several years in the 2010s the New Hampshire House of Representatives passed a bill that would repeal its 200-year-old criminal adultery law, but the Senate could not muster the votes to do as well, responding, in part, to pressure from Cornerstone Action, a local conservative organization that sees same-sex couples marrying as one step on a slippery slope toward the total erosion of the institution of marriage. (Oddly enough, married same-sex couples may be exempt from the state's criminal adultery law. In 2003 the New Hampshire Supreme Court decided that the state's adultery law does not cover a married person who has an affair with another person of the same sex, reading the state statute's requirement of "sexual intercourse" to mean heterosexual intercourse.[67]) Finally, in the spring of 2014 both houses of the New Hampshire legislature passed the bill repealing the state's misdemeanor adultery law, but only after a competing measure intended to expand the definition of intercourse in the adultery law to include acts between adults of the same sex was defeated.[68] The same kind of repeal efforts in other states have similarly failed to garner enough votes.[69]

Gay men and lesbians have long been accustomed to having otherwise ignored laws applied to them on account of their homosexuality. In 1991, when sodomy was still a felony in Georgia, Robin Shahar lost her job as a lawyer in the state attorney general's office when her boss found out that she had planned a commitment ceremony with her female partner. The attorney general argued that it was unethical for him to employ an assistant attorney general who had admitted to being a lesbian when it was the job of lawyers in his office to enforce the state's sodomy law. Of course, the attorney general's office didn't refuse to employ people who had cheated on their wives and husbands, even though adultery was also a crime in Georgia. Everyone understood that Shahar's treatment was about the kind of sexual crime she was accused of, not a neutral policy that disfavored unconvicted criminals working for the state.

Ironically, the attorney general himself, Michael Bowers, later confessed that at the time that he revoked the job offer to Robin Shahar he had been conducting an adulterous affair with a female employee for ten years, thereby admitting to hundreds of criminal acts since adultery was a misdemeanor in Georgia and each sexual act likely amounted to a separate violation of the law.[70] Given this history, it is possible that in states where gays and lesbians are able to legally marry, adultery and fornication laws might be enforced against them both directly and indirectly with greater vigor than they are against heterosexual people. Ample historical evidence justifies some level of concern. Studies have shown that same-sex couples, especially male couples, are more tolerant, if not welcoming, of non-monogamy in their long-term relationships than are heterosexual couples, and that open relationships are more common in same-sex relationships.[71]

Adultery laws are enforced not only through the criminal law but also as part of the law of divorce. Extramarital sex has already come up in cases where same-sex couples are divorcing and one spouse raises to the judge the other spouse's infidelity as a ground to undercut a claim for post-marriage financial support ("He fooled around during the marriage, therefore I shouldn't have to support him financially after the marriage is over"), or as a ground to award joint custody or visitation ("Her sexual immorality during the marriage makes her a less fit parent").

This kind of sexual moralism within the framework of marriage extends beyond adultery to other kinds of sexual conduct that might be legal but could be considered immoral. One attorney told me that he had a client who sought to deny his spouse equal access to their child after their divorce. When they drew a religiously conservative judge for their case the client informed the judge that his spouse often watched gay porn movies at night and that this rendered him a bad parent (even though he always waited until after their son had gone to sleep to turn on the "dirty movies"). The argument worked, as the non-dirty-movie-watching father gained custody of the boy and the other father was punished with limited visitation rights.

So even if we may not see a marked uptick in the enforcement of adultery or fornication laws against same-sex couples in the same way that we witnessed the criminal laws related to marriage used to discipline newly freed people in the nineteenth century, angry divorcing spouses may gain a strategic advantage when their marriages are unwinding by making charges against their spouses of adultery or other forms of sexual (mis)conduct. These appeals have already found a sympathetic ear among family court judges who are either unfamiliar with same-sex relationships or hostile to the notion that they are of the same moral fiber as different-sex relationships.

On the other hand, it is equally possible that same-sex couples' gaining the right to marry is part of a trend toward the liberalization of marriage more generally. In this sense, the conservatives who fear that traditional marriage is under threat may be right, though it may not be same-sex couples who are causing this change, but rather larger social trends that favor the relaxation of rigid, narrow notions of marriage.

In this sense, permitting same-sex couples to marry may be more of a symptom than a cause of this evolution. Time will tell, but same-sex couples who marry and later have sex outside their marriages would be well advised to keep an eye out for local sheriffs or judges who are not so sympathetic to their newly won right to marry or to the broader modernization of marriage.

Other concerns are less speculative. In the early summer of 2011, on the day the New York state legislature voted to allow same-sex couples to marry, an op-ed that I wrote appeared in the *New York Times* in which I voiced the view that the gay community's celebration of the right to marry ought to include some awareness of how we might be rushed to the altar by those who worship marriage—including people in the gay community.[72] I got a lot of e-mails in response to that piece, but one was particularly interesting. A female doctor in Connecticut who had entered into a civil union with her female partner in Vermont wrote me:

> Thank you, for writing the Opinion piece and describing something that most celebrating the New York legislature's recent vote don't fully understand. Marriage is a wholly different animal. I have been struggling with where to turn. . . . I was never married yet I've had to divorce. . . . I purposely did NOT get a civil union in Connecticut when they recognized civil unions, and didn't even know that my Vermont civil union turned into a marriage when Connecticut then recognized those civil unions as marriages. The VT CU was largely to support the general movement. I knew it expressly did not mean anything in Connecticut.

This lesbian doctor was appalled that her civil union got swept into a marriage when Connecticut amended its law in 2008 allowing same-sex couples to marry. She was right that the Connecticut legislature specifically intended that the law would convert all civil unions into marriages—whether or not the affected couples intended to or even knew that they would be automatically married. She was wrong, however, that her Vermont civil union would become a marriage in the state of Connecticut because the automatic marriage provision of the Connecticut law applied only to civil unions entered into in Connecticut—thus her Vermont civil union wasn't affected when same-sex couples could marry in her home state of Connecticut.

But truth be told, our Connecticut doctor's problems are bigger than she suspects. She somehow misunderstood the meaning of her Vermont civil union, believing that it committed her to much less than would a marriage. In fact, civil unions in Vermont fall into the category of what gay rights advocates call "everything but marriage," meaning that the law was intended to provide all the rights, benefits, and responsibilities of marriage, just under a different legal name. As a result, when she got civil unioned to her partner she was married in Vermont for all intents and purposes. To get out of her civil union she'd have to go through a legal divorce preceding, just like any married person. Here's the rub: Vermont makes it much easier to get into a civil union than to get out. Out-of-staters can drive up to Vermont and get civil unioned, then drive home that night. Getting civil disunioned or divorced can't be done as easily because Vermont, like many states, has a residency requirement for divorce. This means that a person must have been living in Vermont for at least six months at the time of filing for divorce, and for at least a year before the divorce can be granted. To end a civil union, out-of-staters must either move to Vermont temporarily or convince a court in their home state to recognize their union—at least long enough to dissolve it. In fact, town clerks in Vermont are required to provide civil union applicants with information to advise them "that Vermont residency may be required for dissolution of a civil union in Vermont."[73]

Connecticut courts have been clear that they do not have the power to dissolve civil unions entered into in Vermont.[74] The doctor who wrote me would have better luck in either Massachusetts or New York, where courts have been increasingly willing to dissolve civil unions entered into in Vermont, but she'd be no better off since she would still have to move to either of those states for a year in order to meet their residency requirements for divorce.[75] (The reason Nevada gained such a well-known reputation for "quickie" divorces was because it has a short, twenty-day residency requirement to dissolve a marriage entered into in another state.)

The Connecticut doctor has a problem that is not uncommon for many same-sex couples that have been civil unioned or married in the states that allow it: while it was easy to get hitched, it's almost impossible to get unhitched. They can fly to New York for the weekend to get married, but they'll have to move back to New York for a year before they can get themselves divorced. As a practical matter, the "lock" part of wedlock is no joke for them.[76]

Same-sex couples face another context where being swept into marriage without their knowledge resembles the plight of freed people in the nineteenth century. In 2000, the American Law Institute (a body of legal experts who draft new codes that serve as models for state legislatures to consider in order to clarify, modernize, and otherwise improve the law) adopted new principles relating to the formation and dissolution of domestic partnerships, whether involving same- or different-sex couples. They took the view that if your relationship looks a lot like a marriage, but you haven't actually gotten married, the law should treat you as if you have. They set their sights on "two persons of the same or opposite sex, not married to one another, who for a significant period of time share a primary residence and a life together as a couple."[77]

The ALI Principles of the Law of Family Dissolution recommend that courts adopt a default rule recognizing a domestic partnership if two persons have lived together in a joint household for a certain period of time, say two or three years. When such a couple breaks up, the ALI recommends that the rules of divorce should apply to how their relationship is dissolved and their property divided. To escape the presumption in favor of a domestic partnership, the couple must have made an enforceable contract explicitly opting out. Thus the law opts them into a marriage-like regime whether or not they reached a mutual and explicit agreement that they desired or intended to do so; instead it requires that they explicitly opt out to avoid the matrimonialization of their relationship. The form of the relationship, not the parties' intent, is fundamental here.[78]

These principles, largely applauded by the lesbian, gay, and progressive legal communities,[79] though with some notable exceptions,[80] risk a wholesale transformation of thousands of relationships into a marital form unbeknownst to the couples themselves. The assumption underlying this support is that couples that form relationships that share many similarities to a marriage either wish to have their relationships treated like a marriage or should want them to. If they become law the ALI principles will completely transform what it means to "just" live together, and will surely serve as a disincentive to doing so. What is more, such laws will frustrate, if not render impossible, the formation of economic, emotional, and sexual attachments and intimacies that are not like marriage and have no aim to be. The requirement that couples are automatically opted into the marriage-like regime unless they explicitly opt out runs contrary to common sense in many respects; it would be hard for many couples to sit down and agree that they've reached a point where they'd each like to have their relationship considered like a marriage, but surely it would be even more difficult to have that conversation with the aim of not committing to marriage's obligations. This was exactly what my correspondent from Connecticut was most worried about.

A more interesting proposal, though not one likely to be adopted any time soon, would be to require married couples to renew their vows periodically, and if they fail to do so their marriages will lapse or expire. This rule would force a conversation about expectations and disappointments, and would allow both parties to renegotiate and clarify the deal, rather than saying "I do" once and forever.

Besides these settings in which the law may marry people without their knowing or consenting to it, we've seen more explicit ways in which important institutional actors have gotten into the "marriage promotion business," strong-arming same-sex couples to marry, echoing the experiences of freed people when they were told that they had to marry in order to get basic humanitarian aid. For those who have for years received employment-related benefits coverage for domestic partners, they are now being told that if they don't marry, their partners will be dropped from the benefits plans. For example, since 1997 both same-sex and different-sex couples have been able to register their relationships as domestic partnerships with the City of New York. The law was designed "to recognize the diversity of family configurations, including lesbian, gay, and other non-traditional couples." To qualify, the couple has to have "a close and committed personal relationship, live together, and have been living together on a continuous basis."[81] The consequences of registering one's relationship as a domestic partnership are not the same as being married—what is involved is a mere "registry" that serves to publicly signal a committed relationship and does not specify anything about what the couple has agreed to in terms of monogamy, longevity, financial interdependence, etc. Perhaps most importantly, domestic partnership laws were not passed as a kind of consolation prize for same-sex couples who could not marry, but rather were designed to enable the recognition of a larger class of relationships than those encompassing people who could or wanted to marry. The use of the term "non-traditional couple" in the law was not meant to be a euphemism for same-sex couples, but rather meant what it said: couples who by intent or circumstance had created relationships that were not marital in form.

New York City provided health and other benefits to the registered domestic partners of city employees (both same-sex and different-sex partners), and other private employers used domestic partnership registration as a way to make benefits available to the non-spousal partners of their employees. But not all employers have required actual registration with the city in order to add a domestic partner to the company's benefit plan. At Columbia University, employees in same-sex partnerships could add a partner to the benefits plan by filling out a form saying they lived in the same household. Yet employees in different-sex partnerships had to marry their partners to get them on the health plan. A male graduate student I know, informed he'd have to marry his longtime girlfriend in order for her to get benefits, was told by a person in the Columbia benefits office: "Too bad your girlfriend isn't a man—it would be so much easier!" They ended up getting married, though they were politically and personally uninterested in doing so.

I was concerned that when same-sex couples gained the right to marry in New York State, Columbia University would require us to marry our domestic partners in order to keep them on the university-sponsored benefits plan. Just as the ink was drying on the wedding invitations same-sex couples had printed up when New York State legalized marriage for same-sex couples, major U.S. corporations were adjusting their personnel policies to recognize these new rights. As the *New York Times* reported the issue: "Corning, I.B.M. and Raytheon all provide domestic partner benefits to employees with same-sex partners in states where they cannot marry. But now that they can legally wed in New York, five other states and the District of Columbia, they will be required to do so if they want their partner to be covered for a routine checkup or a root canal."[82] The right to marry was collapsing into a compulsion to marry.

What's wrong with that? some might ask. All these policies do is put same-sex couples on an equal footing with heterosexual couples—they have always had to marry to get their partners/spouses on their employer-sponsored health plans. Surely employers may have an interest in minimizing their benefits-related expenses by using some criterion with which they decide who is eligible for the group plan, but that criterion shouldn't violate anti-discrimination laws. After all, a third or more of one's compensation comes in the form of benefits, and in the era when same-sex couples couldn't marry, limiting dependent coverage only to those who were married amounted to a kind of sexual orientation–based discrimination. To address this inequity, some employers provided domestic partner coverage as an enlightened way of addressing that gap in compensation for those barred by law from marrying. (Although discrimination against same-sex couples can't be entirely avoided because under federal law employees who put their domestic partners on their health plan must pay taxes on that coverage as "income" whereas hetero-sexuals who put their legal spouses on their plans do not.)

But when same-sex couples gained the right to marry, some em-ployers, including Columbia, announced a change in policy, giving all employees whose same-sex domestic partners were covered under the benefits plan one year to marry their partners or they'd be dropped from the plan.[83] Faculty and staff advocated strongly against this change after it was announced, pointing out that New York City still allowed the registration of both same- and different-sex partnerships, even though same-sex couples could now marry, and that Columbia University had no business promoting marriage, or worse, coercing its employees to marry—especially when it had used a suitable administrative process for recognizing domestic partnerships for years. What is more, we argued, the new benefits eligibility policy now discriminated against employees on the basis of marital status—those who married were compensated considerably higher than those who didn't. The policy change, in ef-fect, converted sexual orientation–based discrimination into marital status–based discrimination. We urged Columbia not only to reinstate domestic partner benefits for the same-sex partners of employees but to expand the policy to include different-sex partners, so as to mirror New York City's domestic partnership law. Reinstating same-sex benefits alone, we urged the provost, would merely result in reviving a policy that discriminated against heterosexual employees since they had to marry to get their partners on the plan, while employees in same-sex partner-ships had the option of marrying or registering as domestic partners.[84]

In the end Columbia revised its policy, giving us half a loaf. It re-instated domestic partnership benefits for same-sex couples only, set-ting up a system that discriminates against employees in different-sex domestic partnerships, who must still marry to gain coverage for their partners.

To avoid the Scylla and Charybdis of marital status– and sexual orientation–based discrimination in their benefits plans, some com-panies have adopted an "each one pick one" policy of allocating employment-related benefits. Rather than limiting policies to legal spouses, allow each employee to choose another person to put on the group plan; it could be your brother the musician who does not have insurance, your sister who lost her coverage when she was divorced, your mother who has expenses that exceed her Medicare coverage, or your spouse who is not otherwise insured.

It seems so natural and normal that dependent benefits coverage be rationed through the use of marriage or its proxy, domestic partnership. But if we step back for a moment, it really makes no sense, other than as a means of limiting employer expenses or as a subsidy for the nuclear family. Originally, the notion of employment-based health care and dependent coverage was designed to subsidize the family wage; the husband would work while the wife stayed home with the kids and received health insurance derivatively from *his* employment. Of course this left the wife and their children in a very vulnerable place, dependent not only on the husband's wage for their support but also on his employment for coverage of their health care needs. Many divorced women today find themselves without health insurance coverage or having to buy individual coverage on the private market at very high prices for inferior policies. The Obama administration's Patient Protection and Affordable Care Act was designed to address some of this need, particularly for divorced women, but it does not relieve married women's dependency on their husbands' employment-related health benefits since the Affordable Care Act presupposes an ongoing robust employment-related health insurance scheme. Some argue that only a single-payer system would resolve all of these problems, taking the primary source of health insurance away from employment and making it a right for everyone, regardless of whether they have a job that includes health benefits or are married to someone who has one.

⮑

In a range of ways—some predictable, others less so—marriage has been a thorny lever by which both formerly enslaved people and lesbian and gay people might be elevated up from their subordinate status. Marriage, then as now, has been a complicated vehicle through which to address the injustice of racism and homophobia. Too often the freedom to marry risks collapsing into a compulsion to marry, squeezing out marriage as a freely given choice and substituting in its place a form of government oversight, regulation, discipline, and punishment that is hard to reconcile with a vigorous notion of freedom. So too, gaining marriage equality may entail the overshadowing of other forms of intimate, family, or sexual relationships as viable, socially acceptable alternatives to marriage.

4

Am I My Brother's Keeper?

Policing Our Own with Marriage

In late May 1863 General Ulysses S. Grant launched the Siege of Vicksburg, circling the city and then shelling it for forty unrelenting days. Cut off from reinforcements and food supplies, Confederate soldiers and the Vicksburg civilian population suffered enormously during "the Siege," as they still call it today in Vicksburg. By the end of June over half of the soldiers defending the town were unable to fight due to scurvy, malaria, dysentery, or diarrhea. Some residents resorted to eating shoe leather when food ran out, and most of the inhabitants of Vicksburg took to digging and then living in caves to avoid the artillery shells lobbed into the city by Union gunboats anchored in the Mississippi River. Lieutenant General John Pemberton's surrender of Vicksburg to General Ulysses S. Grant on July 4, 1863, marked a pivotal Northern victory in the war, securing control of the Mississippi River in Union hands and splitting the Confederacy in half. To this day the Fourth of July is celebrated with great ambivalence in Vicksburg, and as I found when I visited the city to research this book, many whites live with the memory of "the Siege by the Federals" as if it had taken place a few years ago.

All the civil courts in Vicksburg's Warren County were shut down during the Civil War. Although the war officially concluded in April 1865 with General Lee's surrender to Grant at Appomattox, the courts in Warren County did not get up and running again until that December. A month later, on January 5, 1866, a freed woman named Matilda Damage did something quite bold and unheard of in that area. She tracked down Judge Mat Laughlin, a Warren County justice of the peace, and swore out a complaint against Ellen, another freed woman of color, claiming that the previous June, Ellen had assaulted Matilda in her home, biting her so maliciously that her right hand had to be amputated. Ellen was indicted and tried for this assault, yet ultimately was found not guilty.[1] This case marks the first time that a freed black person—never mind a freed *woman*—had initiated a criminal court proceeding against another member of her community. In every other case in Warren County prior to this time where a person of color was involved in some way in a legal proceeding it was as an item of property, as a defendant, or as a witness, but they most certainly did not initiate the proceeding.

Just six months later another freed woman in Vicksburg took an even bolder step. Josephine Watkins swore out a criminal complaint against her husband, Albert, and his new wife, Anna. Handwritten testimony reveals that Albert and Josephine had been automatically married by law, having cohabited prior to and after the effective date of the Mississippi automatic marriage statute. Like so many freed people during this period, Albert was unaware that he had been legally married to Josephine and that he had to divorce her before he could marry Anna. So, ignorant of the law, on June 8, 1866, Albert married Anna Williams while he was still legally wed to Josephine. Josephine immediately reported Albert and Anna to the authorities, and Warren County sheriff Marmaduke Shannon arrested both of them on charges of bigamy. They were brought before a grand jury and indicted; arraigned on June 26, they both pled not guilty before Judge William Yerger. Yerger was a well known member of the Mississippi legal community who, as a member of the Whig Party, had opposed the state's succession from the Union in 1861. He was one of the first white judges in postwar Mississippi to allow black people to testify in legal proceedings against both whites and blacks. Sherriff Shannon was likely less sympathetic to the freed people of Vicksburg. His house was shelled during the siege in July 1863, and his son was killed fighting for the Confederacy.[2]

Anna and Albert were tried before a jury and found not guilty for reasons that are not entirely clear from the records that remain. Maybe Judge Yerger or the jury felt less inclined to hold the freedmen to the strict letter of the law than did Josephine or Sheriff Shannon. Yet what is remarkable about this case is that rather than turning to black religious or community leaders to resolve her dispute with her husband, Josephine handed him over to the local white sheriff.

The *Damage* biting case was the first criminal case in Warren County ever to be initiated by a person of color, and the *Watkins* case was the first marriage-related prosecution in Warren County since well before the war started. These two cases signal an important shift in the ways in which freed people in the Vicksburg area were beginning to see themselves as legal subjects. Not only were they subject to law, in the sense of being required to heed the law's demands for marital fidelity and adherence to the strict rules of contract labor, but they also now regarded themselves as subjects who could make use of the law by turning to legal authorities to sort out the complicated disputes that arose in their lives, especially their intimate, domestic lives.

Josephine Watkins may have been the first, but she was certainly not the only freed woman to take the bold step of calling the police when her husband left her for another woman. By 1868, this tactic seemed to be a familiar one in the Vicksburg black community. That May, Isaac Shaffer and Maria Wright were indicted for "unlawful cohabitation" by District Attorney J. E. White. The complaining witness on the indictment was Mary Shaffer, most likely Isaac's spurned wife. The following November, however, the prosecutor dropped the case. Isaac had probably returned to Mary by then.[3] A few months later, Oliver Garret and Sallie Simpson were turned in to the local authorities by Oliver's wife, Martha. Oliver was indicted for adultery and Sallie for fornication and both were held on $50 bond. The 1870 census lists Oliver as a forty-eight-year-old mulatto barber born in South Carolina. Sallie was a twenty-six-year-old mulatto woman who kept house. For reasons that the records don't reveal, the case was later dropped by the district attorney.[4]

The criminal court archives in Vicksburg reveal a number of similar cases of freed people being prosecuted for marriage-related crimes. Oscar Sanders and Liz Smothers were indicted for unlawful cohabitation after Oscar's wife, Susan Sanders, turned them in. They were held over on $200 bond each, but six months later the district attorney dropped the case.[5] Then there was Phillip Brazil and Eliza Ann Clark. They were indicted on charges of bigamy in October 1871. Samuel Clark had been married to Eliza Ann Clark by their owner in 1861, and they had then been automatically married by operation of law on the effective date of the Mississippi freedmen's marriage statute. They had lived together in Vicksburg until March 1877 when Eliza Ann left Samuel and married Phillip Brazil. Samuel was not pleased, so he went to the local sheriff and swore out a criminal complaint against his wife and Phillip Brazil. The records do not indicate whether or not Phillip and Eliza Ann were convicted of bigamy.[6]

Interestingly enough, in all of these cases, freed women (and one man) used the criminal law to go after their spouses when they took up with other people, but every one of the cases was dropped by the prosecutor and no one was convicted of any crime. One has to wonder whether the freed women and men of Vicksburg were using the criminal law and criminal justice system strategically to get their husbands and wives to return to them. How could they be sure that when they turned in their spouses that they weren't going to end up going to prison? Surely they knew what a horrendous place the Mississippi prisons were for black men. The violence of the convict leasing and criminal surety systems that I described in chapter 3 were well known to black people at this time. Maybe they knew exactly what they were doing and were using the criminal laws as a way to exact revenge against family members and others who had hurt, shamed, or otherwise offended them.

Of course, it is very difficult to know the true motivations of the women who filed these criminal cases against their husbands. But I have a theory. Without question, these women needed their husband's wages in order to support their families, and they would have lost those wages for a long time, if not forever, had they been convicted of bigamy, adultery, or unlawful cohabitation. While we can't know this for sure, it's possible that a good number of the women in Vicksburg who resorted to criminal law to get their husbands back in the house may have done so in order to avoid having their children apprenticed out to their former owners. Mississippi passed a law in 1865 requiring sheriffs to notify the local probate judge if they knew of a freed man or woman who was considered too poor to support their child or children. The probate judge was then *required* to apprentice the child or children to a "competent or suitable person," with a preference for the former owner of the child. The statute required no notice to the child's parents, nor did it provide for any hearing on the merits of the claim that the parents did not have the means to support their children.[7] The laws empowering judges to remove children from their parents, often after they had just been reunited at the end of slavery, "came close to legalized kidnapping in many instances, depriving parents of children if a white judge deemed it 'better for the habits and comfort' of a child to be bound out to a white guardian."[8] According to historian Eric Foner, "to blacks, such apprenticeships represented nothing less than a continuation of slavery."[9]

Freedmen's Bureau agents were deluged with complaints from freed men and women about their children being taken from them without their consent and with no notice. "The act of takin children from their parents and binding them out, as they call it, is an every day occurrence," wrote Bureau agent J. T. Fisher in an 1866 monthly report to headquarters on "Outrages committed by whites against the blacks in State of Mississippi."[10] In January 1866, Virginia Cain, a freed woman, entered into a labor contract with Jesse Owen for her own and her two sons' labor. Virginia and the boys, Joe and Allen, ages sixteen and eighteen respectively, were to earn $24 per month plus room, board, and clothing for their work. The ability to contract for a wage was among the most fundamental freedoms formerly enslaved people enjoyed as a result of their emancipation, and was surely experienced as such by the likes of Ms. Owen and her sons. Yet a couple of weeks after Virginia signed the contract, Hardy Cain, the white man who had formerly owned Virginia and her boys, entered her home and forcibly took the boys into his own service under the Mississippi apprentice statute. Since Virginia was not at home, her sons were taken to the local courthouse without her knowledge or consent. Just before they were brought before a judge by her former owner, the clerk of the court called her name three times from the courthouse steps in order to give her "notice" of the proceedings to take away her boys. When she did not appear, the hearing began and Hardy Cain testified that Virginia could not support them and that her whereabouts were unknown (she was probably at work). The probate judge then apprenticed the boys to Mr. Cain. As soon as she found out about this, Virginia approached the Freedmen's Bureau for help in getting her sons back given that she clearly had the means to support them and risked arrest herself for breaching her contract with Mr. Owen.[11]

Nelson Gill, a Freedmen's Bureau agent in Holly Springs, Mississippi, urgently wrote his superiors in March 1866 about a woman who had come to him for help after she had traveled all the way from Arkansas to get her two sons, ages fourteen and sixteen, back from a man who had apprenticed them without her consent. She was desperate to get her boys back, having left her family, including a small baby, in Arkansas. She told Agent Gill that she had approached the man, asking for the boys, but he refused and threatened to arrest her if she didn't leave. Exasperated, Gill reported that he received complaints of this sort almost every day.[12]

Surely news of cases like this spread quickly through the communities of freed people, leading them to keep their children always within sight, and to live in a constant state of terror that their old masters or "the law" would come take their children. It is impossible to overstate how horrifying this possibility was for a community whose excruciating memories of owners seizing and selling away family members on a moment's notice were still fresh in their minds. The monthly Mississippi Freedmen's Bureau reports are full of frustration and outrage with the way in which the apprenticeship laws were being "oppressively enforced" against newly freed families.[13]

The everyday nightmare that the children of freed people could be removed from their parents' homes and apprenticed to white people— usually their former owners—may have provided ample motivation for freed women to turn to the law when their husbands left them for other women. Maybe they had already exhausted avenues within the black community in Vicksburg to shame or coerce their husbands to come back home. We can't know for sure. But the resort to this risky strategy of going to the local white sheriff and swearing out criminal complaints against their husbands may have been the only avenue they had left to keep their husbands and, most importantly, their wages in the home. Where there were two wage-earning adults in the home it would be less likely that the children could be removed on account of the family's inability to support them adequately. It is certainly a plausible explanation for why freed women voluntarily involved themselves and their families in the criminal justice system almost immediately after the close of the Civil War.

Whatever their motivation, recently emancipated black people in the Vicksburg area were aware of how the criminal law worked and that it could impose a kind of discipline and punishment that at times echoed the ill treatment they received while enslaved. In the months following Grant's capture of Vicksburg in 1863, military provost marshals and Freedmen's Bureau agents acted as judicial officers to adjudicate and settle legal disputes involving freed people. When Captain A. W. Preston reported to his superior, Lieutenant Stuart Eldridge, on the state of the civil courts in Vicksburg, he noted that in the preceding month the court in Warren County had eleven cases come before it. Ten of the eleven defendants had been charged with vagrancy, six men, four women—all colored. One other defendant, Cornelia Washington, was convicted of larceny (theft). Washington and William Wright, who had been convicted of vagrancy, were sentenced to suspension by their thumbs for two hours a day for ten days. The rest of the vagrants were fined $1 plus court costs and were hired out to white plantation owners as a way to pay their fines.[14]

These cases and sentences were representative of the kinds of prosecutions involving freed people in the immediate postwar period. Vagrancy and "hunting with a gun on Sunday" were the most common crimes, but it was not unheard of for freed women to be charged with keeping houses of prostitution. Vagrancy laws, adopted as part of the immediate postwar Black Codes, notoriously discriminated against the newly freed people,[15] sweeping within their jurisdiction those who had not signed a year-long labor contract, walked away from the contract they had signed, not paid their taxes, misspent what they earned, were in town when they weren't supposed to be, or were there without a pass (in Mississippi black people needed a written pass from their employer granting them permission to leave their residences on the plantations and travel into town—a holdover from times of slavery). In Vicksburg, city officials were requiring freed people to pay $5 for a pass or labor license. If they were found without a pass they were arrested as vagrants and fined. As such, vagrancy laws were the catch basin for regulating the deeds, work, location, and movements of freed people after the war. They were an extremely effective way of keeping black people *in their place*, and were designed "to keep the Negro exactly what he was: a propertyless rural laborer under strict controls, without political rights, and with inferior legal rights."[16]

The entanglement of law enforcement in freed people's marital lives in the postwar period was not unique to Vicksburg, Mississippi. Something rather odd was going on in the black community in Oak Hill, North Carolina, as well. Located in Granville County in the north-central part of the state in what they called the Bright Tobacco Belt, Oak Hill had a disproportionately large black community compared with the rest of North Carolina, and a significant number of the black people—both men and women—owned land.[17]

The fact of a large black community is not what was strange. Rather it was what they were up to that is worthy of attention. Take Willis and Charry Chandler for example. They lived together in Oak Hill as a married couple. According to census data, Willis was a thirty-three-year-old black man who worked on a farm—meaning that he did not own any land but that he might have worked the tobacco crop as a contract laborer on a white-owned farm. Charry was listed as a member of Willis's household, was the same age as Willis, and the census taker reported that she "ke[pt] house"—something he noted about almost every black woman in Granville County. Keeping house typically meant that freed women were cleaning, mending, preserving vegetables, and otherwise tending to the needs of the family in ways that would never have been allowed during enslavement when their labor would have been almost entirely committed to their owner's needs. Now freed, these women may have contributed to the household income doing washing, cooking, and sewing for local whites—work that the census agents would not have recognized as "employment." It is possible that Charry preferred home-work as a refuge from sexual exploitation by white men that was an all too common horror for black women who worked outside the home.[18] In 1870 Willis and Charry lived with their four children, Oliver, or Olley (ten), Rachaul (seven), Mary (five), and their little brother Lenay (three). A third son, Henry, was born in late 1875, and a fourth, Doc, came two years later. At the time of the 1880 census, Willis still lived in Oak Hill with his six children, listing himself as a widower. Charry does not appear anywhere in the 1880 Oak Hill census; presumably she passed away sometime between 1875 and 1880.[19]

In many respects the Chandler family's work and home life were quite typical for freed people in this part of North Carolina. Yet the records from the county criminal court show that in July 1875 Willis and Charry were indicted for "fornication and adultery," a charge that was brought against anyone who "being lewd and vicious persons, and not united together in marriage did unlawfully and adulterously bed and cohabit together, and then and there did unlawfully commit fornication and adultery, in contempt of the hold rite of matrimony." Charry was identified on the indictment as Charry Downey.[20] Given her last name—Downey—she probably had been a slave on the Downey plantation, a plantation so large that it was the first in Granville County to have a railroad spur running out to it to deliver supplies and pick up tobacco for shipment.

Willis and Charry ultimately paid $8 to the court as a penalty for their illegal living arrangement, yet they continued to live together and had another two children. There is no record of their ever getting a marriage license. North Carolina's "automatic marriage" statute required freed people who had lived together "as" husband and wife to "go before the clerk of the court of pleas and quarter sessions of the county in which they reside, at his office, or before some justice of the peace, and acknowledge the fact of such cohabitation, and the time of its commencement, and the clerk shall enter the same in a book kept for that purpose."[21]

The indictment of Willis and Charry Chandler, standing alone, isn't hugely remarkable. What happened next is. The fall of 1875 was a busy time for fornication and adultery prosecutions in Granville County. Shortly after Willis and Charry were picked up by the authorities for "F&A," so were seven other couples: Berry and Bett Downey, Stephen and Margaret Downey, Frank Pointer and Ereline Wilkenson, Rich Overby and Julie Downey, Charles Winston and Mary Hester, Jim Royster and Meely Overby, and Seth Royster and Mesan Royster. Not only were all of these couples black, but they were neighbors in the Oak Hill community. According to the census records Berry and Bett Downey lived two doors down from the Willis and Charry Chandler. Who were the complaining witnesses on the indictments of these couples? *Willis and Charry Chandler.* Did they turn state's evidence? Was there some kind of feud being waged in the Oak Hill community of Granville County? Was the local sheriff on a morality campaign and strong-armed the Chandlers into squealing on their neighbors? The records do not answer these questions, but it seems that once Willis and Charry got picked up by the police, they ended up in everybody else's business.[22]

Only some of these couples were indicted. Seth Royster and Mesan Royster, Charles Winston and Mary Hester, and Jim Royster and Meely Overby were not. According to the 1880 census, these three couples were still living together as if married five years after their arrests, though there is no record of any of them getting a marriage license. On the other hand, Berry and Bett Downey pled guilty to "F&A" yet kept living together without being married. The others were all indicted, and some paid fines of $8 just like Willis and Charry. They all continued to live in the community at least through 1880, and none of them was formally married. The fact that these criminal prosecutions resulted neither in motivating these couples to marry or in breaking up their illegal co-habitations makes me wonder how the criminal justice component of marriage laws was being used in this community. To this day fornication remains a crime in North Carolina, though it is rarely enforced.[23]

Fornication wasn't the only way that black people experienced the law getting into their business. As I was sifting through the county court records at the state archives in Raleigh, I noticed that in the late 1860s the criminal courts in Granville County began to experience a substantial uptick in "bastardy" cases. North Carolina had a legal pro-ceeding whereby "any justice of the peace, upon his own knowledge, or information made to him, that any single woman within his county is big with child, or delivered of a child or children, may cause her to be brought before him to be examined upon oath respecting the father."[24] Any woman brought into court in a bastardy case could be fined $5 if she refused to declare the father of her child or children, and would be committed to prison until she divulged his name or posted a bond as security. The goal of these provisions was to keep the wife and children from becoming a public charge. The assumption behind the statute was that unwed mothers would be unable to support their "bastard" chil-dren, who would eventually become the responsibility of the local gov-ernment. Through these proceedings the statute sought to shift those costs to the putative father.

Once the woman provided the court with the name of the absent fa-ther he would be brought into custody and a hearing would be held on whether he was, in fact, the father. In the pre-DNA era these cases were typically very hard to prove, but the statute made her testimony presumptive evidence of paternity—meaning that he was presumed to be the father unless he could convince the court otherwise. This was the one anomalous context in which freed women's testimony was given the weight of law. The stakes in these cases were pretty high: in addition to a father's duty to support his children financially, willful abandonment of a child amounted to a misdemeanor in North Carolina.

In the February 1868 term of the Granville County criminal court, nineteen bastardy prosecutions were filed—a large share of the total of twenty-three cases that came before the court that month. By the spring of 1874 the court system was so overrun by bastardy petitions that it opened up a special bastardy part that would hear only such cases. An overwhelming number of these cases were filed by black women. The records do not reveal why the cases were filed or whether they were begun at the instigation of a justice of the peace who knew of unwed mothers in his jurisdiction. It is possible that the women "turned themselves in" to the local authorities.

Once the cases were filed a warrant would issue for the arrest of the putative father, who would be brought into court to deny or admit paternity. Yet curiously, almost none of the cases filed resulted in a determination of paternity—indeed, few men were even successfully served with arrest warrants as almost all were returned marked *Not found in the county*. Still the bastardy cases mounted. Assuming a good number of them were initiated by the women themselves, just as were the "F&A" cases, what was motivating them to pursue a seemingly fruitless legal formality that led to a dead end, yet created a formal legal record of their status as unwed mothers?

Of course we can't know for sure, as the court documents tell us far too little. But I have a couple of guesses about why these unwed mothers went to court and filed formal papers announcing the fathers of their children. One possibility is the connection the bastardy law bore to the North Carolina apprenticeship law. Under a law passed in 1837 and still in force in the 1860s, the state's civil courts had the authority to bind out, as apprentices, "all infants whose fathers have deserted their families and been absent for one year, leaving them without sufficient support; [and] all infants whose parents do not habitually employ their time in some honest, industrious occupation." The law allowed male apprentices to be bound until the age of twenty-one and female apprentices to age eighteen. The person to whom the apprentice was bound, termed "master" in the law, was required to provide "diet, clothes, lodgings and accommodation fit and necessary; education in reading, writing and arithmetic; six dollars in cash, a new suit of clothes and a new Bible at the end of [the] apprenticeship." The law did not require that the parent of the apprentice be notified of or consulted about the proceeding to remove the child from home.[25]

The obligations imposed on the "masters" by the North Carolina apprenticeship law were observed mostly in the breach. "The law is regarded generally with a feeling of dread both on account of the wrongs it caused, and those it was capable of inflicting," wrote the reporter for the North Carolina Department of Labor. "It has been the instrument of much wrong and oppression to indigent and helpless children."[26] Quite often poor black children were apprenticed to indigent white employers who failed to pay apprentices at the end of their service, and the law provided no remedy for these defaults of statutory obligations.[27] Freedmen's Bureau agents working in North Carolina immediately after the close of the war frequently heard complaints from the new freedmen about the way that the apprenticeship system was destroying their families.[28] In 1866, members of a delegation of freedmen claimed that "our children, the dearest ties which bind us to domestic life, and which makes the time of home endearing, are ruthlessly taken from us, and bound out without our consent."[29]

The North Carolina apprenticeship law, thus, elevated the parental rights of fathers over mothers, treating children who were being raised only by their mothers as the equivalent of orphans. The absence of the father in the home rendered the children fair game for removal by "masters" through a simple court proceeding. In 1867, the North Carolina Supreme Court stepped in in a case where the children of a freedwoman had been apprenticed without notice to her or her consent. Writing for the court, Justice Reade noted,

> I remember that when I was at the bar, the County Court of Granville had ordered sundry orphans to be brought to court to be bound out. Among them were three or four who were neat and clean, and their mother was with them. She cried much, but said not a word. Upon enquiring it was found that she was an honest, industrious woman and widow, who had labored hard for her children, and that just when they could begin to help her the rapacity of some bad man sought to take them away.[30]

The court ruled that any court order binding out a child under the apprenticeship law without proper notice to the parent or parents was void, in effect treating it as a kidnapping. Yet the court left intact the part of the apprenticeship law that required parents to prove that they were honest and industrious, thus forcing them to legally overcome the general sentiment among whites that freed people were dishonest and shiftless.

It may be that the rise in bastardy petitions in North Carolina was a symptom of the frequency with which black children were being removed from their mothers' care and custody, just as we saw in Mississippi. While the freed women of Vicksburg turned to the law of adultery, bigamy, and fornication to get their husbands and their wages back in the home, the freed women of North Carolina used bastardy proceedings to force the same result.

Another possible explanation for the frequent filing of bastardy petitions was that the mothers were initiating these cases not for a local legal audience, but for one up north. In the postwar period, numerous benevolent societies were formed in the North to send aid to deserving and needy freed women and children.[31] This form of private welfare played an important role in addressing the crushing poverty experienced by so many black women, especially those with children and no husbands. Many of those women were widowed after their husbands died fighting in the Union army. Others lost their husbands to workplace accidents, white violence, or the brutality of the criminal justice system's prisoner leasing programs. Still others had never married. The women who had children without marrying would have needed the aid these Northern benevolent associations made available. Most likely, however, they would have had to show they were respectable women, and bearing children "out of wedlock" may have disqualified them for these benefits. Many Northern societies sent their funds to a local minister in the South whose judgment they could trust about the respectability of needy women in the community. Possibly a norm developed in Granville County that needy unwed mothers could establish a modicum of respectability by filing bastardy petitions in court. The mere legal formality of filing the petitions—even if they didn't result in an order of paternity—could elevate them from loose women to abandoned mothers. I don't know this, I'm just guessing. But it is possible.

The black women of Granville County may have also been drawn to the bastardy procedure for another reason: "therapeutic jurisprudence." Drawing from a mix of law and psychoanalysis, some scholars have argued that there are therapeutic payoffs, or costs, to legal proceedings that have value separate and apart from any monetary award that a person might win as a result of filing a lawsuit, including being able to tell your story, being taken seriously by an official with important social status such as a judge, and having the power through a legal proceeding to force another person to come to court and answer a complaint. Freed people must have felt a kind of exhilaration when they found they could launch a legal proceeding on their own behalf and for their own benefit simply by signing a legal document.

It's not hard to imagine unmarried mothers' turn to "bastardy petitions" as a way of healing the deprivation of kinship that all enslaved people suffered. This injury was an intergenerational inheritance for the enslaved people in the Americas. Saidiya Hartman describes what happened to the notion of family, of place, and of kin when a person was sold into slavery and shipped across the Atlantic: "Slavery made your mother into a myth, banished your father's name, and exiled your siblings to the far corners of the earth."[32] Frederick Douglass, writing about the effects of slavery on those born into enslavement, described the slave as an orphan.[33] While enslaved people had many blood relatives, slavery made them strangers. Bonds of blood could not keep family together and were not enough to generate a notion of kin. The only thing a mother could pass to her children was her status as a slave, since U.S. law incorporated a rule from British law that had its roots in Roman law, *partus sequitur ventrem*, "that which is brought forth follows the womb," whereby the slave status of a child followed that of his or her mother. Enslaved fathers had no patrimony to endow their children, thus they were not fathers at all. Perhaps the bastardy petitions were an inexact way for newly freed mothers to suture those lost fathers back into the family or to conjure a form of paternity and kinship that enslaved families had been denied for so long.

⤺

The freed people of the South Carolina Sea Islands took a somewhat different tack when it came to turning to the law with marital problems. Edward Pierce, appointed by the treasury secretary to oversee the freed people at Port Royal in 1861, asked Henry Judd, a forty-year-old manufacturer from New York, to serve as the Sea Island Colony's judicial officer, settling complaints among the freedmen. When asked by the American Freedmen's Inquiry Commission about the nature of his cases, Judd replied that "nine tenths grew out of domestic difficulties; one man having so many wives. A man picks up a woman he thinks he can live with her, he goes through some form of marriage. In a short time they fall out and this woman applies for redress."[34]

Records of the provost court in Beaufort, South Carolina, tell these stories. Nanny Bacon lived with Titus Bacon in Beaufort for a number of years, raising a large family together and farming four acres of land that they had purchased with their own money. In the spring of 1868 Titus took up with another woman and barred Nanny from the land they had bought together. Nanny went to the provost marshal in Beaufort to file a complaint against Titus, asking not that he be arrested and returned to her, but instead for a divorce and an equitable settlement of their interest in the land. Titus did not contest Nanny's version of the facts, agreeing that they should be divorced. Testimony was taken from white people living near the Bacons and the provost marshal granted the divorce.[35]

Rose Warren filed a complaint against her husband, Joe, with the provost court in April 1868. They had four children together and owned ten acres of land on St. Helena Island they had purchased at government-run tax sales. They had a horse and a couple hogs, and farmed the land for cotton. According to witnesses who testified to the court, Rose did most of work on the farm, and they fought frequently—often violently. After a particularly violent fight in which Joe had Rose on the ground and punched her in the eye, Rose left him and sought a divorce and financial settlement from the provost court. After hearing from five witnesses, Provost Judge A. S. Hitchcock granted the divorce, and gave Rose and her children four acres of arable land for her individual cultivation. Judge Hitchcock ordered Joe to leave Rose alone and gave him sole use of the horse. By any account, this was not a terribly favorable settlement for Rose—four acres was enough land to raise provision crops for her and her children, but not enough to raise a profitable cotton crop. Moreover, without the horse it would be very difficult for her to work the land—it was said at the time that tilling the land without a horse or a mule was like working with one hand tied behind your back. The judgment was unclear as to whether Rose would have access to the remaining six acres of land, whether she had to negotiate with Joe about sharing it for cultivation, or if it was left to Joe's exclusive use.

Since military officials and the Freedmen's Bureau favored a system where ownership of all property and the signing of labor contracts was done through the male heads of households, divorcing wives had to turn to law to gain legal title to the land held in their husbands' names. To some degree, the Freedmen's Bureau created the problem that made divorcing wives dependent upon the Bureau's intervention when the household broke up, since married women did not have a legally recognizable ownership interest in the fruits of their labor or the land they purchased with their husbands. This problem was not unique to freed women, of course, as the institution of coverture, by which women's legal identity was subsumed under, or *covered* by, her husband's, was the norm for white women in most states at this time. Formerly enslaved women were emancipated into the second-class status that white women enjoyed when it came both to owning property and having their own legal and economic identity.

As these cases from Beaufort show, the freed women of the South Carolina Sea Islands used law in a more straightforward way than the women in North Carolina or Mississippi. Or better yet, they used law the way it was intended. They filed legal actions to divorce their husbands and got financial settlements as part of those legal separations. Sometimes they got what they were after, sometimes they didn't. But these cases did not have the air of a desperate ploy to save their children or redeem the good name of the women involved, as we saw in Granville, North Carolina. Unlike the women in Vicksburg, the women of Port Royal did not seem to use the law strategically to get their husbands back, rather they turned to law to get cash and/or title to property they had earned or bought with their husbands. Perhaps this regional difference can be attributed to the fact that the child apprenticeship system was not as much a factor in the Sea Islands as it was in Mississippi and North Carolina, or that relatively speaking, freed people in the Sea Islands had more land and other resources than did their brethren in Vicksburg and north-central North Carolina. Or they felt less motivated to separate the "good blacks" from the "bad blacks" through resort to marriage. It is hard to say for sure, but the regional differences are worth noting.

Did these women see themselves as making a "choice" that their new emancipated status now made possible, or did they feel boxed in without alternatives when they turned their husbands into the sheriff, reported them to Freedmen's Bureau officers, filed for divorce, or initiated a bastardy petition? Maybe they felt that each time they turned to the law and it responded, setting in motion a range of procedures and governmental action, they were putting farther and farther behind them enslavement, powerlessness, and the invisibility of non-personhood. Perhaps all these things were in play.

～

What lessons are to be found for today's LGBT movement in the way that criminal laws related to marriage were used *within* the black community at the end of the Civil War? Some freed women turned in their husbands when they entered adulterous relationships in Warren County, Mississippi; might we expect that today when a jealous or desperate partner sees an advantage in dragging their relationship problems before a homophobic state official? Willis and Charry Chandler turned state's evidence against their neighbors in Granville County, North Carolina. So why wouldn't we expect that gay men and lesbians will "use" legal advantages made possible with marriage laws?

The thought of it isn't far-fetched at all. On the night of September 17, 1998, the police broke into the Dallas apartment of John Lawrence (who was white) where he was found in bed with Tyrone Garner (who was black). The police had been summoned by another of Garner's lovers who was jealous and had reported to the police that "a black man was going crazy" in Lawrence's apartment "and he was armed with a gun" (a racial epithet rather than "black man" was, in fact, probably used). The case ended up in the Supreme Court five years later culminating in the famous *Lawrence v. Texas* decision, in which the Court found that criminal sodomy laws were unconstitutional.[36]

Lisa Miller tried to deny her partner and coparent Janet Jenkins from any right to custody or visitation with their daughter, Isabella, by kidnapping Isabella and moving to Virginia, a state with laws hostile to lesbian families and parenting. Miller isn't alone in using this tactic, as a growing number of spouses in same-sex relationships see a strategic advantage when the relationship breaks up in filing for divorce and/or custody of their children in states that won't recognize their marriage and/or refuse to acknowledge the legal status of gay or lesbian parents. I hear of this kind of cynical maneuver every month as lawyers serving the lesbian and gay community try to manage the complex evolution in the legal status of same-sex couples at the time when some states embraced them and others still shunned them.

Of course gay or lesbian people are unlikely to be any different from heterosexual people when it comes to using the law to hurt one another or to gain advantage. All people can be jealous, petty, vengeful, and greedy toward lovers/partners/spouses, regardless of sexual orientation.

Beyond the shared experience of newly freed black people and same-sex couples in having their spouses exploit residual racism or homophobia to gain an interpersonal advantage, what other lessons lie in the stories this chapter tells in Vicksburg, Mississippi; Granville County, North Carolina; and the Sea Islands in South Carolina?

One relates to the vulnerability of children in low-income families. Marriage is not, and cannot be, a tool to address the personal and family vulnerability caused by poverty. In all three aforementioned communities, being married did little to alleviate the financial stress with which poor black women contended. In some cases it made them even more vulnerable to poverty-based exploitation, such as having their children apprenticed because of their inability to adequately provide for them. At best, marriage laws provided them with a tool to work *within* the crushing reality of the oppression of Southern Black Codes.

Apprenticeship laws enacted throughout the South in the immediate postbellum period resulted in the removal of thousands of black children from the homes of their newly freed parents on the grounds that their families were too poor to support them or were otherwise unfit. Bound out to white planters, often the family's former owners, these children were abused and overworked. Recently freed mothers and fathers tried everything they could to keep their families intact, and defend against the loss of their children on account of the family's poverty.

Fortunately, by the turn of the century most of the apprenticeship laws had been repealed or found unconstitutional by the courts. But the vulnerability of black families is hardly something we can relegate to the past. Today's child welfare system continues to treat black families more harshly than whites, and enables the removal of children from poor and black families in ways that bear a strong resemblance to and bear the legacy of the apprenticeship laws of the nineteenth century.

Consider this: black children are grossly overrepresented in today's foster care system. While black children make up roughly 14% of the national child population, 31% of the children in the foster care system are black.[37] Even this number understates the problem. In thirty-two states, the percentage of black children entering foster care is at least one and a half times greater than the percentage of these children in the state's population, and in seven of these thirty-two states, the percentage is at least three times greater (California, Iowa, Minnesota, Nevada, Pennsylvania, Utah, and Wisconsin). In New York City black children are ten times as likely to be in protective custody than are white children. There is no state in which the percentage of white children entering foster care exceeds the percentage of white children in the state's population.

Overall, black mothers are reported more often for abuse and neglect, and are more likely to have these charges substantiated. Black children are less likely to receive needed mental health services once in foster care, they have fewer visits with parents and siblings, and black families receive fewer preventive, reunification, and other services. Black families have fewer contacts with caseworkers, and black parents' rights are more likely to be terminated.[38] At every stage of the child welfare system, race seems to matter. Studies show that emergency room doctors are more likely to suspect and report abuse when black children come in with broken bones.[39] In essence, the U.S. Department of Health and Human Services found that "minority children, and in particular African American children, are more likely to be in foster care placement than receive in-home services, even when they have the same problems and characteristics as white children."[40]

When New York City's foster care system was challenged in federal court, Judge Jack Weinstein explicitly compared the way African American children were being treated to a form of "enthrallation" or "slavery." He wrote: "The exact language of the Thirteenth Amendment could be construed to cover children forcibly and unnecessarily removed without due process and then consigned to the control of foster caretakers. They are continually forcibly removed from mothers who themselves have been abused by their male partners without a court adjudication and placed in a forced state custody in either state or privately run institutions for long periods of time. There they are disciplined by people not their parents. This is a form of enthrallation that bears on their due process rights under the Fourteenth Amendment."[41] Sounds a lot like the now-repudiated nineteenth-century apprenticeship system.

Why do so many black children end up in foster care? Race is part of the answer, but so is class. As scholar Dorothy Roberts has observed, the ostensible reason for the placement of a child in the foster care system is abuse or neglect, yet "the public child welfare system often equates poverty with neglect. Most child maltreatment addressed by child protective services involves neglect related to poverty." Indeed, "poverty—not the type or severity of maltreatment—is the single most important predictor of placement in foster care and the amount of time spent there."[42] Roberts argues persuasively that rather than address the needs of poor children by improving the economic situation of poor families, U.S. policy "solves" the problem by pathologizing and blaming poor parents, removing the children from the family, and placing them in foster care with an aim of having them adopted by families with greater means to support them.

Changes to the child welfare law in the 1990s made this problem even worse when the Adoption and Safe Families Act of 1997 reversed federal policy that had previously required that state child welfare programs make reasonable efforts to keep a child from entering foster care and once in the system return the child to its family of origin. The new law imposes a swifter and rigid time frame for state agencies to initiate petitions to terminate parental rights and offers financial incentives for states to increase the number of adoptions of children in foster care.

Thus adoption is now supposed to solve both the problems of child poverty and the ills of the foster care system, thereby resulting in the permanent removal of poor, disproportionately black children from their families of origin.

The issue of children being removed from their families of origin through the foster care and adoption systems, an issue of great urgency for the African American community, has a "gay angle," even a "gay marriage" angle. When Reagan appointee Judge Richard Posner wrote a unanimous decision for the Seventh Circuit Court of Appeals in the fall of 2014 finding that the Indiana and Wisconsin laws banning same-sex couples from marrying were unconstitutional he pointed frequently to the fact that same-sex couples, just like "opposite-sex" [sic] couples, adopt children and raise them in families, families that would be strengthened by the structure and security of marriage. (Judge Posner seemed not to know that same-sex couples "have" children through methods other than adoption. Even the sources he cited in the opinion note that "[m]ore than eight in ten of the children being raised by same-sex couples in Wisconsin are biologically related to one member of the couple (81%)" and "[n]early two thirds (62%) of children being raised by same-sex couples in Indiana are biological children.")[43] Judge Posner argued that adoption was a worthy and socially desirable solution to the vexing social problem of unwanted children. "Unintentional offspring are the children most likely to be put up for adoption, and if not adopted, to end up in a foster home. Accidental pregnancies are the major source of unwanted children, and unwanted children are a major problem for society, which is doubtless the reason homosexuals are permitted to adopt in most states—including Indiana and Wisconsin."[44]

The judge went on to note that gay or lesbian couples ("homosexual couples" in his parlance) are five times as likely in Indiana and two and a half times as likely in Wisconsin to raise an adopted child than are heterosexual couples. Thus, he concluded, "[m]arried homosexuals are more likely to want to adopt than unmarried ones if only because of the many state and federal benefits to which married people are entitled.

And so same-sex marriage improves the prospects of unintended children by increasing the number and resources of prospective adopters. Notably, same-sex couples are *more* likely to adopt foster children than opposite-sex couples are."[45]

The argument boils down to this: Kids in foster care or who are otherwise "unwanted" by their birth parents are a public problem, perhaps even a public nuisance, in need of a solution. Same-sex couples are that solution. Thus it is in the state's interest to allow them to marry as it will make that solution even more attractive to same-sex couples and will minimize the burden of the care of unwanted children on the public.

The studies Judge Posner cited to document the important role that same-sex couples play in solving the "children of unwanted pregnancies" problem each have sections on "race/ethnicity," but those sections concern the race of the adoptive parents, not the race of the children. Other studies, however, have shown that same-sex couples are almost twice as likely as different-sex couples to adopt a child of a different race from their own (54% vs. 30%).[46] (Data relating to the race of children adopted by same-sex couples was available to the researcher who produced one study on which Judge Posner relied, but it was not analyzed in the study.) Given that most people who adopt, including gay and lesbian people, are white and African American children are enormously overrepresented in the population of children in foster care or who are up for adoption, the data shows that same-sex couples are contributing disproportionately to a situation where black children are being removed from black families to be raised by white people. Judge Posner's reasoning frames this social fact as a kind of public service, in which children, disproportionately children of color, are "rescued" from their unfortunate circumstances by adoptive parents, predominantly white, who are able to do a better job of raising those children than their birth parents, particularly if the adoptive parents are married.

This critique in no way aims to suggest that same-sex couples are ill suited to parent, whether as birth or adoptive parents, but rather to note the implications of a litigation and advocacy strategy that has featured gay couples' interests as parents. Judge Posner unfortunately rested his decision in the Indiana and Wisconsin marriage equality case on adoption, something none of the gay groups urged him to do. Yet there have been foreseeable implications in the transformation of the legal subject in the gay rights cases from a sexual subject who resists being criminalized to a parenting couple who seeks the right to marry. Those implications include a kind of passive collaboration in the racial violence of African American children's overrepresentation in the foster care and adoption systems. So too, advances in the fight for marriage equality for same-sex couples have been built, in some cases, on the vulnerability of poor and black families.

Judge Posner's inclination to rest the marriage equality argument on the social virtue of adoption also implicates reproductive rights. Lying just below the surface of his opinion is the problem of "unwanted pregnancies." Many of these pregnancies are surely the result of limited access to contraception or abortion rather than irresponsibility or degeneracy. The "problem" gay marriage rights for same-sex couples can felicitously solve surely results from the twin evils of a denial of reproductive health care to women *and* the racism of the child welfare system. Same-sex couples swooping in to solve the problem of these unfortunate pregnancies most surely enlists the marriage equality movement in the normalization of other forms of injustice.

Some of the advocacy in favor of marriage equality would have been well served by anticipating these racial and reproductive rights implications and minimizing them in advance by avoiding arguments that either explicitly or implicitly reinforce the notion of same-sex couples' respectability, responsibility, and dignity. For better or for worse, in some circumstances winning marriage equality has been a zero-sum game that has entailed shifting the stigma same-sex couples have endured to other, already stigmatized people and groups. As the stories in this book illustrate, African Americans, particularly poor African American women and their families, have always been an easy target for that stigma.

5

The Afterlife of Racism and Homophobia

When I set out to write this book, over a decade ago, I began with the hypothesis that newly freed peoples' experience of the right to marry had a "be careful what you wish for" lesson for today's marriage equality movement. I expected that just as marriage revealed itself to be a supple and effective means by which racism could reproduce itself through the state licensure of intimate relationships, it would be equally up to the task of reproducing homophobic bias in the contemporary context. Despite significant victories in the courts and legislatures extending the right to marry to same-sex couples, homophobia, I conjectured, would have an afterlife that outlasted the exhilaration of the first fabulous gay weddings.

In some respects my hypothesis was correct. And in others I was wrong, as events on the ground outpaced my working hypothesis.

How was I right? There has indeed been a backlash against the overwhelming success of the marriage equality movement. While there have been great successes expanding marriage rights for same-sex couples in a number of jurisdictions, the voters in other states moved precipitously and preemptively to clarify different local norms by passing laws that limited marriage to one man and one woman. Explicitly undertaken in response to the success of the marriage equality effort, these clarifications or revisions of state marriage laws were undertaken either through the passage of amendments to the laws defining marriage or through state constitutional amendments. California's Proposition 8, which put a referendum to voters to reverse a victory for marriage equality won before the California Supreme Court, is perhaps the most prominent example of this sort of measure.[1] But this kind of legal backlash against marriage rights for same-sex couples took place in thirty-one states. Twelve such measures barring marriage rights for same-sex couples were enacted in the November 2004 elections alone. A majority of these measures contain language to explicitly deny recognition not only to marriages between same-sex couples but also to civil unions, domestic partners, or any other legal status.[2] Their aim was twofold: to clarify the essential heterosexual nature of the institution of marriage, and to make sure that marriage didn't have to compete with any other legal status that was "marriage-like" or "marriage lite."

Advocates who supported these measures used them as an opportunity to express a wide range of hostility toward gay people generally, toward their fitness as parents, and toward the notion of legal marriage for same-sex couples. In the spring of 2013 the president of the Southern Baptist Convention along with a televangelist colleague speculated that threats to the U.S. from North Korean leader Kim Jong-un might be attributable to the rise in marriage rights for same-sex couples in the United States: "Could our slide into immorality be what is unleashing this mad man over here in Asia to punish us?"[3] A pastor in New York City went on TV and claimed that if same-sex couples were allowed to marry they would "take a nine-year-old boy to an Arabic nation" and marry him, then come back to the U.S. and force the state to recognize the marriage.[4] In response to President Obama's support of marriage rights for same-sex couples, Republican Mississippi state representative Andy Gipson posted a status update on Facebook citing a passage from Leviticus that calls for gay men to be "put to death," and then followed up with a response to a constituent's post:

[I]n addition to the basic principal that it is morally wrong, here are three social reasons it's horrific social policy: 1) Unnatural behavior which results in disease, not the least of which is its high association with the development and spread of HIV/AIDS; 2) Confusing behavior which is harmful to children who have a deep need to understand the proper role of men and women in society and the important differences between men and women, and fathers and mothers; and 3) Undermines the longstanding definition of marriage as between one man and one woman, a definition which has been key to all aspects of social order and prosperity. Anytime that definition is weakened our culture is also weakened. And yes, that is also true for other conduct which weakens marriage's importance in society.[5]

Then, in early 2015, a Huntington Beach lawyer filed paperwork with the California attorney general's office to have an initiative, the "Sodomite Suppression Act," placed on the ballot that would recriminalize sodomy: "any person who willingly touches another person of the same gender for purposes of sexual gratification be put to death by bullets to the head or by any other convenient method."[6]

Latent and explicit hatred toward same-sex couples that have exercised a new legal right to marry has surfaced in another context created by the disarray that resulted from allowing each state to decide whether to allow same-sex couples to marry, before a single, national rule on the issue was set down. In states that limited marriage to one man and one woman a question arose as to whether the courts in those states would recognize the marriages of same-sex couples entered into in states that allowed them to marry. If, for instance, a lesbian couple living in South Carolina, a state that limited marriage to one man and one woman,[7] traveled to New York to marry legally and then returned to South Carolina to continue with their lives, what should the South Carolina courts do when the couple later files for divorce? Recognize the marriage as valid under another state's law and proceed with the divorce (as they would for any other couple validly married in another state), or refuse to recognize the validity of the marriage and dismiss the divorce action as a legal impossibility (you can't get divorced if you were never legally married)? Tobias Wolff has argued that when courts refused to recognize the validity of same-sex couples' marriages entered into lawfully in states that allowed such marriages, the courts were essentially sending a message to those couples: you are unwelcome here. The hostility against same-sex couples in courts in some regions, he claims, is greater than it was against interracial couples. Even in states with the most draconian anti-miscegenation laws, courts would sometimes recognize the validity of interracial marriages for at least some purposes, like inheritance. The categorical nature of the refusal to recognize same-sex marriages for any purposes is unprecedented, he insists. Rather than engendering respect for other states' laws, these cases set off a kind of "social alarm" that justified harsh condemnation of the underlying immorality upon which these relationships rested.[8]

Particularly in jurisdictions that haven't signed up for this new civil rights revolution, gay men and lesbians may find themselves suffering a kind of "price tag" for gay rights victories in other states. Gay people in Mississippi, Alabama, Georgia, Louisiana, Idaho, and Montana reported an increase in hostility in their communities that negatively tracked the success of the marriage equality movement nationwide. In their churches, workplaces, and at family dinners they often bore painful witness to religious conservatives' need to hold the line on marriage equality while the rest of the nation went to hell. This climate forced many gay and lesbian people, particularly people of color, even deeper into the closet. Advocates from Mississippi have told me that their low-income gay and lesbian clients are having more and more difficulty accessing social services delivered through churches (many state and local aid programs that provide food, housing, and other assistance contract with churches to provide these services). Rather than outing themselves to their fellow parishioners and enduring likely harassment or ostracism, many same-sex couples will lie about their relationships by telling people that they are cousins, not lovers. Or in small communities where this kind of lie would be impossible since everyone knows everyone else, they are forced to make a tragic choice between foregoing social services out of fear for the hostility they are likely to endure or closeting themselves so deeply that a normal relationship is impossible.

The story of how Tom Wojtowick and Paul Huff were kicked out of their Catholic church chillingly illustrates the kind of backlash some couples are experiencing when they get married. After living together as a couple for over thirty years, Wojtowick and Huff, aged sixty-six and seventy-three respectively, decided to get married and traveled from their small town in Montana to Seattle, Washington, for their nuptials. When they returned home they expected to take up their lives as they had been before—living together, known in the community as gay, and active in their church, the Kiwanis Club, and other civic organizations. They had set an example to their community of how gay people are not all that different from everyone else. Yet a little over a year after their marriage, a new priest assumed the pulpit at their church and summoned them for a conference. He told them that they could no longer sing in the church choir or participate in any other church rituals or functions, including communion. He demanded that they get divorced, stop living together, and sign a statement affirming that marriage was a sacrament of one man and one woman.

This incident divided the parishioners at their church, roughly half opposing the priest's excommunication of the gay couple and half supporting it. Meanwhile the Episcopalians in town offered to take them in. What's remarkable about this incident is the fact that that church and half of its membership had no problem with Wojtowick and Huff, an openly gay couple, being part of the parish. It was their *marriage* that set them off. As Frank Bruni put it on the opinion page of the *New York Times*, "'I do' means you're done."[9]

To be sure, the law can't fix all of the backlash against same-sex couples who marry and "enjoy private intimacy and . . . share a household in which they can hold themselves out to their community as participants in a committed relationship."[10] Nevertheless, this condemnation of hostility toward gay people asserted in legal precedents has been met with a NIMBY-like response in more conservative parts of the country: you can have your marriage rights in San Francisco, New York, and other sinful cities, but not in our backyard and not in my church! In this sense, some communities approach the claims to marital legitimacy that same-sex couples present as a kind of public nuisance. And some churches, while able to love the sinner, find the sin intolerable when same-sex couples marry.

This intolerance toward the very idea of same-sex couples marrying solidified quite quickly into a state-by-state strategy in the 2014–15 legislative session to enact new laws that would allow individuals and businesses to ignore same-sex couples' marriages, or to outright discriminate against them, all in the name of religious liberty. These Religious Freedom Restoration Acts (RFRAs) granted public officials the right to refuse to issue a marriage license if doing so would conflict with their religious beliefs, and permitted individuals and businesses an exemption from compliance with an otherwise generally applicable law if compliance with that law would offend their religious beliefs. The timing of these proposals—in the legislative session just before the Supreme Court was to hear oral argument in the marriage equality cases—was no accident, as they were seen as a way of getting a jump on the Court, prophylactically "restoring" rights that were about to be threatened and setting in place a means by which opponents of marriage equality could house that opposition in a "restored" right to religious liberty.

This clear backlash against the growing inevitability of the Supreme Court recognizing a constitutional right to marriage for same-sex couples mirrored in uncanny ways the use of religious liberty as a tool to perpetuate forms of racial injustice at important junctures in U.S. history. In 1869 the Georgia Supreme Court turned to religious teaching when it upheld the criminal conviction of Charlotte Scott, a black woman, who had married a white man, Leopold Daniels, and thereby violated Georgia's 1788 law criminalizing interracial marriage, known legally as an anti-miscegenation law. The chief judge of the Georgia Supreme Court, Joseph E. Brown, wrote:

> This, in my opinion, is one of the wisest provisions in the Constitution. . . . Before the laws, the Code of Georgia makes all citizens equal, without regard to race or color. But it does not create, nor does any law of the State attempt to enforce, moral or social equality between the dif-

ferent races or citizens of the State. Such equality does not in fact exist, and never can. The God of nature made it otherwise, and no human law can produce it, and no human tribunal can enforce it. There are gradations and classes throughout the universe. From the tallest arch angel in Heaven, down to the meanest reptile on earth, moral and social inequalities exist, and must continue to exist through all eternity.[11]

The Indiana and Alabama supreme courts similarly used god's plan as the justification for upholding their states' anti-miscegenation laws in 1871 and 1877 respectively.[12] In the 1960s, the trial court in *Loving v. Virginia* relied on similar reasoning when it upheld the conviction of Mildred and Richard Loving, an interracial couple who had married in violation of Virginia's criminal prohibition against miscegenation: "'Almighty God created the races white, black, yellow, malay and red, and he placed them on separate continents. And but for the interference with his arrangement there would be no cause for such marriages. The fact that he separated the races shows that he did not intend for the races to mix.'"[13]

Assertions of religious liberty were used as a defense against compliance with newly enacted laws prohibiting racial discrimination in the mid-nineteenth century as well. In 1956 Senator Strom Thurmond drafted the "Southern Manifesto" defending the morality of racial segregation immediately after the Supreme Court's decision in *Brown v. Board of Education*. A central ploy was to set up private religious schools that were racially segregated. This worked for a while, until the Treasury Department withdrew the schools' non-profit status on account of their failure to comply with federal non-discrimination laws. In 1983 the Supreme Court upheld the Treasury regulations in *Bob Jones University v. United States*, wherein religious schools argued that the Bible instructed that "[c]ultural or biological mixing of the races [was] regarded as a violation of God's command." Thus, the Treasury rule could not constitutionally apply to schools engaging in racial segregation, the schools argued, because it conflicted with their sincerely held religious beliefs.

The Court rejected the schools' claims, holding that the government's interest in eradicating racial discrimination in education outweighed any burdens on their religious beliefs.[14]

The Civil Rights Act of 1964 met ample resistance in the name of religion as well. The owner of a barbecue chain who was sued for refusing to serve blacks defended himself by claiming that serving blacks violated his religious beliefs. A court rejected the restaurant owner's defense, holding that the owner

> has a constitutional right to espouse the religious beliefs of his own choosing, however, he does not have the absolute right to exercise and practice such beliefs in utter disregard of the clear constitutional rights of other citizens. This court refuses to lend credence or support to his position that he has a constitutional right to refuse to serve members of the Negro race in his business establishments upon the ground that to do so would violate his sacred religious beliefs.[15]

These decisions reflect an evolving national consensus that religion can't be used as a justification for discrimination on the basis of race. The recent wave of state RFRAs enacted in response to the surge of rights prohibiting discrimination against LGBT people and same-sex couples seeks to exploit the absence of a similar consensus around the primacy of laws prohibiting sexual orientation–based discrimination.

∽

Ironically, in a number of cases, married gay men and lesbians have taken advantage of enduring homophobic sentiment by seeking to exploit disdain for gay people when their marriages end. Just as people with spouses of a different sex have sought to have their divorces adjudicated in a state that would give them the most leverage in dividing up joint assets or would favor them as a parent, some gay people engaged in similar "forum shopping," seeking to have their marriages dissolved in states that were hostile to the very idea of same-sex couples marrying. A court order annulling a marriage on the grounds of its illegality might be a highly favorable disposition for the more affluent person in the couple—it's like the marriage never happened and they can just walk away, owing their spouse/partner nothing. Or—as in the case of Lisa Miller and Janet Jenkins—where a married couple is raising a child, the biological parent could seek to have custody and visitation issues adjudicated in a jurisdiction that is hostile to the idea of lesbian or gay coparenting.[16]

All of these examples testify to the shared experience of a newly won right to marry for recently emancipated black people in the nineteenth century and same-sex couples today: the enduring potency of bigotry, a bigotry that justified a long-standing exclusion from civil marriage, survives the repeal of that exclusion and fuels a backlash against these new rights holders. In this sense, one of the lessons to be drawn for today's marriage equality movement from African Americans' early celebration of the ability to legally marry is that homophobia, like racism, will have an afterlife. Same-sex couples would be well counseled to prepare for the ways in which a marriage license inaugurates new forms of state discipline and regulation that can be easily deployed in the service of a durable and crushing homophobic itinerary. Just as the institution of marriage has been sufficiently supple to host both emancipatory and racist ends for African Americans, same-sex couples are likely to find marriage to be a worthy standard bearer for both new forms of citizenship and familiar forms of disgrace and exclusion.

⟿

Surely some dots are amenable to connecting when we compare the afterlives of racism and homophobia and how these resilient social blights have been sustained by and through the institution of marriage. Yet the discontinuities between the experiences of African Americans and same-sex couples in marriage are striking and are worthy of careful consideration as well.

The examples I gave earlier in this chapter of a backlash against married same-sex couples might be best understood as the exceptions that prove the rule. They are significantly less representative of the conse-quences of the rollout of marriage equality today than I had expected. Quite contrary to my predictions of a systemic homophobic recoil in response to the successes of the struggle for marriage equality (predic-tions that have earned me a reputation in the gay community as a kind of "turd in the punchbowl," to borrow a less than flattering moniker I learned from my mother), the trend has been in favor of embracing the right to marry for same-sex couples, even in sectors where it seemed unlikely just a few years ago. Same-sex marriage rights have found sup-port from prominent conservative political actors and celebrities such as David Blankenhorn, the star witness against marriage equality in the trial challenging Proposition 8; former Bush-era solicitor general Ted Olson; Ken Mehlman, former head of the Republican National Com-mittee; Meg Whitman, who supported Proposition 8 when she ran for California governor; representatives Ileana Ros-Lehtinen of Florida and Richard Hanna of New York; Stephen J. Hadley, a Bush national secu-rity adviser; Carlos Gutierrez, a commerce secretary to Mr. Bush; James B. Comey, a top Bush Justice Department official; David A. Stockman, President Ronald Reagan's first budget director; and actor Clint East-wood.[17] Their change of heart on this issue says something about their hearts, I suppose, but also about how the appeal for support has been framed. Many of these conservative leaders have seen a convergence of their deep *traditionalist* commitments with the arguments in favor of marriage equality. As they observed in a brief submitted to the Supreme Court in the Prop 8 case: "Many of the signatories to this brief previ-ously did not support civil marriage for same-sex couples . . . [but] amici have concluded that marriage is strengthened, not undermined, and its benefits and importance to society as well as the support and stability it gives to children and families promoted, not undercut, by providing access to civil marriage for same-sex couples."[18] Like President Obama, their views on marriage rights for same-sex couples have evolved.[19]

Why, then, have gay men and lesbians been able to find a kind of redemption in marriage that has eluded African Americans? Why have marriage rights been such a successful tool for gay people to achieve greater standing as full and equal citizens while marriage has remained a potent tool to shame, punish, and discipline African Americans? Why, in other words, have gay people been so successful at using marriage to redeem their good name, while marriage continues to be a site of failure and dysfunction for many African Americans?

I pose the questions in this manner not to ratify the premises that underlie them (for instance that marriage is redemptive for gay people and dysfunctional for African Americans) but to acknowledge the kind of social reputation that these two groups enjoy or suffer in relation to marriage. So too, I pose the questions this way not to ignore that these two social groups overlap with one another (there are plenty of African Americans who are lesbians or gay men) but rather to acknowledge the social reputation that the gay rights movement and its subsidiary, the marriage equality movement, enjoy as white, and the African American community enjoys as heterosexual. By design or not, the gay community has been able to leverage its social capital in whiteness to their advantage in the marriage equality movement, yet African Americans have received little benefit in any endowment they might enjoy from the stereotype that all or most black people are heterosexual.

The juxtaposition this book aims to take on, and particularly the discontinuities it illuminates, tells us something very important about the relative mark of inferiority soldered to blackness as compared with that of homosexuality.

Advocates advancing the cause of marriage equality for same-sex couples have drawn from this powerful metaphor, arguing that the injury they suffer inflicts a similar badge of inferiority on same-sex couples who cannot marry or who are discriminated against for having done so. Invoking a clear analogy to the history of racial inequality in the United States, Ted Olson and David Boies argued in their brief to the Supreme Court in the Prop 8 case:

Although opening to [same-sex couples] participation in the unique and immensely valuable institution of marriage will not diminish the value or status of marriage for heterosexuals, withholding it causes infinite and permanent stigma, pain, and isolation. It denies gay men and lesbians their identity and their dignity; it labels their families as second-rate. That outcome cannot be squared with the principle of equality and the unalienable right to liberty and the pursuit of happiness that is the bedrock promise of America from the Declaration of Independence to the Fourteenth Amendment, and the dream of all Americans. This badge of inferiority, separateness, and inequality must be extinguished. When it is, America will be closer to fulfilling the aspirations of all its citizens.[20]

Similarly, a group of law professors urged the Illinois legislature to reject a religious exemption in the Illinois marriage equality bill and condemned such a license to discriminate in the name of religion on the ground that it "stamps a badge of inferiority on married same-sex couples that permits their exclusion wherever they go."[21]

The invocation of the notion of a "badge of inferiority" as a way to denounce state policies that offend overarching principles of equality or liberty, whether on the grounds of racism or homophobia, suggests careful thought about the work that must be done to either resist that stamp or remove its mark once imprinted. What notions of the self in relation to larger societal stereotyping, violence, exclusion, and abjection are deployed in efforts to cleanse bodies marked with the moral stain of inferiority? Is there anything peculiar about a strategy that turns to law to remove a mark that is the remainder of law itself?

The badge of inferiority borne by people of color is, to be sure, central to the logic that makes blackness intelligible and black bodies legible in a larger racist society. Testifying to the spectacular and violent way in which the signature of race becomes written on the body, Langston Hughes wrote in 1949, "They've hung a black man . . . For the world to see."[22] The shooting of Michael Brown in Ferguson, Missouri, in the summer of 2014 is only one recent iteration of these acts of signing and signification. Frantz Fanon similarly suggested the spectacular way in which race is written on the body: "'*Maman*, look, a Negro; I'm scared!'"[23] This signature is not one written by black people, but its mark is truly "theirs" in the sense of belonging to them, as being a property of their blackness. Yet Fanon, among so many others, provides the analysis necessary to understand how race is more a moral category than one biological in nature, more an indictment than a fact: "I am overdetermined from the outside," Fanon observed.[24]

When advocates for marriage equality today conjure a "badge of inferiority" in their arguments to courts, are they mobilizing a notion of injustice that works in ways similar to the writing of race on black bodies? Judge Vaughn Walker, ruling in the case challenging Proposition 8's ban on same-sex marriage, credited expert testimony (from an economist, oddly enough) that the marriage ban "conveys a message of inferiority"[25] and an Iowa trial court found that:

> Plaintiffs suffer great dignitary harm because the State's denial to Plaintiffs of access to an institution, so woven into the fabric of daily life and so determinative of legal rights and status, amounts to a badge of inferiority imposed on them and Minor plaintiffs. Plaintiffs are continually reminded of their own and their family's second-class status in daily interactions in their neighborhoods, workplaces, schools, and other arenas in which their relationships and families are poorly or unequally treated, or are not recognized at all.[26]

Presumably, winning these cases, particularly after naming the injury of suffering as a "badge of inferiority," results in the removal of that badge and the signature of disgust and perversion suffered by homosexuals in its name. Motivating these victories is the notion that gay couples don't deserve such a degrading signature, or worse, that they have been wrongly mistaken for those who do.

This is what distinguishes the work done by the marriage equality cases for gay people that has not, and cannot, be accomplished for people bearing the signature of racial inferiority. In the marriage cases, lesbians and gay men have accomplished a kind of rebranding of what it means to be homosexual. They have been awarded a kind of "dignity of self-definition" that law and culture have never recognized in African Americans. In this sense, the dignity at stake in the marriage cases is not that conferred by the blessings of marriage but rather in a kind of self-possession that has allowed them to tell a counter narrative of "who gay people are." If the marriage equality cases have been about anything, they've been about the demand that gay people have been misrecognized by law and society, and that the time has come to tell a more respectable, decent story that, if believed, justifies a city official's signature on a marriage license. Marriage, it turns out, has been not only an end in itself for the gay community, but the container for a rebranding project as well.

The success of this political project is truly stunning, particularly when viewed in contrast to the challenges faced over time by the cause for racial equality. For two social movements organized around particular identity-based claims to justice and quality, both seeking to escape the subordinating consequences of a conception of difference anchored in a biological difference from the norm, gay people have enjoyed astonishing success revealing the irrelevance of biology and the injustice done in its name.

Hughes' invocation of lynching when he wrote, "They've hung a black man . . . For the world to see," might be contrasted with "They've held a wedding . . . For the world to see." The difference between these two events and the subjects they spectacularly produce is to be found in the power, or dignity, of redefinition to be found in the gay wedding. It both reflects and then reproduces a new form of respectability so yearned for in many sectors of the gay community. It enunciates a new norm and a new normal. In an earlier era a same-sex commitment ceremony or "marriage" elicited disgust, incredulity, or even violence. It operated as a kind of pastiche that mimicked the original but where the joke, if there was one, was on the couple doing the imitation insofar as the gap between the imitation and the original bore witness to the blasphemous nature of this inferior version of the sacred. Now, the marriages of same-sex couples are neither pastiche nor parody of the original, as they *are* the real deal.

In this sense, gay people have been able to reshape the response elicited by these spectacular performances, from disgust to empathy or even identification—something African Americans have never been allowed. Instead, for the most part marriage for African Americans has been a vehicle for reinforcing their inferiority and for eliciting familiar responses that assign a badge of inferiority. Made explicit in the Freedmen's Bureau records, in the rulings of postbellum Southern judges, and in the Moynihan Report, marriage has been and largely remains a kind of test that the African American community is seen as failing.

What the marriage equality movement has shown, and the historical comparisons I draw in this book aim to illustrate on a granular level, is how lesbian and gay people have been better able to use a form of legal pleading to redefine what it means to be gay than have African Americans to redefine what it means to be black. Blackness, we learn, is both a durable badge *and* a badge of inferiority. What it marks is the residue of racism that no legal victory has been able to dissolve. At best, legal victories for African Americans award restitutions for injury, reinscribing an inferior status at the same time as they compensate for it. By comparison, the gay marriage cases have pulled off something altogether different, by converting marriage into a badge of superiority. Of course, this badge is awarded or "enjoyed" only by those members of the gay community who are willing or able to present their relationships within a logic of respectability. The work that badge does in redeeming the social reputation of "good gays" depends on a contrast with "bad gays" who don't want to marry or discipline their sexual selves into a tidy couple form.

How has this been possible? How has the gay community been so successful in deploying marriage to remake its public reputation so convincingly?

First of all, the team for marriage equality has been enormously successful in shaping their struggle as essentially conservative in nature. They don't seek to destroy marriage or to radicalize it, they have insisted, but rather aim to fold same-sex couples into the institution on its own terms. The claim for marriage rights for same-sex couples offers a striking lesson in how a social justice movement has effectively and relatively swiftly transformed the perception of its agenda from radical and beyond the pale to essentially traditional in nature.

When the conservatives sign up for marriage equality, they do so because it dawns on them that their interests in traditional family values, in the nuclear family, in privatizing dependency, and in bourgeois respectability are stronger than their homophobia. As marriage equality advocates make the plausible case that they share with conservatives the same basic values about marriage, conservatives come around to see same-sex couples who want to marry as "just like us," or enough like us, to recognize a shared identity.[27] "My brother is gay and I know what he goes through and went through when he was younger. I don't see the problem with gay marriage. They are just like us but they like the [same] sex. That's no problem," writes a straight ally of the gay community in an online debate on marriage rights for same-sex couples.[28] Country-western singer Dolly Parton took the comparison one step further when she quipped, "I think gay couples should be allowed to marry. They should suffer just like us heterosexuals."[29]

But if the "just like us" argument is what made a significant difference in turning the marriage equality argument into such a raging success, then why hasn't a similar argument worked for African Americans? They are just as able to deploy a narrative of traditional family values as the gay community—perhaps even more so. In fact, the peculiar American commitment to a notion of racial equality grounded in the idea of "color-blindness" is, in significant respects, another version of the "just like us" claim made by gays and lesbians. It posits that skin color should be irrelevant in determining a person's worth and that we all share a basic humanity and dignity that should not be inflected or diminished by considerations of race or color.

Yet the argument from color-blindness has never been effective in diminishing indelible notions of difference and inferiority for African Americans. It certainly hasn't worked to remove a badge of inferiority for people of color the way the appeal to a shared traditional notion of marriage and "just like us" arguments have functioned in the marriage equality cases.

The stories in this book, holding up side by side two experiences of newly won rights to marry, help us see how racial difference is a difference more indelible than that of sexual orientation. African Americans' relationship to marriage, particularly compared with that of same-sex couples, shows us how fixed the signature of racial inferiority is for black people in American culture. No appeal to decency, tradition, or respectability can overcome the logic of difference that structures racial identity in this country. The history of marriage helps us see how that difference is sutured to black bodies in ways that made being freed something less than being free, and marriage a tool of discipline and failure rather than security and full citizenship for African Americans.

Even more, it's worth noting that the successes of the marriage equality movement may have been won precisely because of the negative reputation African Americans suffer when it comes to marriage. The racial endowment as white from which the marriage equality movement has benefited (even if not grounded in reality, since many of the members of the LGBT community who sought marriage rights were people of color) surely helped conservative courts, legislators, and others come to see an affinity of interest with this cause.

When the lawyers and clients in the gay marriage cases stand on the steps of the Supreme Court after arguing their case for marriage equality, all, or nearly all, of them are white. When the *New York Times* published a piece in the fall of 2014 by Adam Liptak, the paper's chief Supreme Court reporter, speculating about which of the several competing same-sex marriage cases were likely to be taken up by the Court, the

Times ran a photo to capture this horserace in the gay community. It featured three photographs, one of Ted Olson and the two male plaintiffs in "his" case, Paul Katami and Jeff Zarrillo; one of Jeffrey L. Fisher, the lawyer in the Oklahoma marriage case; and one of Roberta Kaplan, the lawyer in the Utah case who also argued the case for Edie Windsor in the Supreme Court in 2013. All of these people are white.[30] The heads of the biggest gay rights organizations—Lambda Legal, the Human Rights Campaign, the ACLU Lesbian Gay Bisexual & Transgender Project, the National Gay and Lesbian Task Force, the National Center for Lesbian Rights—are all white,[31] as are the attorneys most visibly identified with this issue. Organizations in the LGBT community that have elevated people of color into leadership roles tend to be more grassroots oriented, and have not prioritized marriage equality to the same degree, or at all, as compared with the "Big Gay" shops.

For this reason, it's not surprising that "gay marriage" is publically perceived to be a white issue. As Kenyon Farrow writes, "in order to be mainstream in America, one has to be seen as white."[32] "Being seen as white" is a task the marriage equality movement could pull off, while African Americans, by definition, just can't.

Rightly or wrongly, homosexuality in general and the marriage equality movement specifically enjoy a kind of racial privilege that has underwritten the plausibility of this positive transformation in the meaning of gay identity. Here, as elsewhere, the project of identifying with another group, of seeing a shared sameness, is accomplished not only on the level of acknowledging a shared identity, but of recognizing a shared sense of what you are not. As such, identities are constituted through, not outside, difference. When judges, policy makers, or the media are persuaded that same-sex couples are sufficiently similar to different-sex couples when it comes to marriage, that recognition of shared identity is premised upon the specter of a constitutive outsider that gay couples are *not* like. And what they are not like is African Americans (even though, of course, many lesbians and gay men *are* African American).

This is what we see at work when the marriage equality movement enjoyed unimagined success at the same time that the Family Leader's "Marriage Vow" gained support for the idea that black people were better able to maintain stable, two-parent households when they were enslaved than they are today.[33] A conservative agenda that has demonized unmarried African American mothers as "welfare queens" and disparaged African American fathers as "deadbeats" is not undermined, and indeed might be furthered, by supporting marriage rights for same-sex couples. At the same time, the claims of same-sex couples to marriage rights is enhanced to the degree that they can differentiate themselves from dysfunctional, "broken" families. Of course, none of the advocates for marriage equality have argued this dissimilarity by explicitly referring to African American families. But they don't need to, as that work is being done more than competently by groups such as the Family Leader and their ilk. But, in many ways, that work is already part of the historical framing and ongoing moral imagination of marriage in the United States. A conception of marriage as the pinnacle of mature personhood and mutual responsibility is so saturated with racial and gender stereotypes that some things do not even have to be said to convey the feeling of truth and obviousness.

One of the challenges for the supporters of the marriage equality movement is to appreciate the costs to others of same-sex couples gaining rights in this context. This entails careful consideration of the negative externalities of certain arguments being made in the gay marriage cases, and attention to minimizing those externalized costs. Appeals to dignity, respectability, and the virtues of marriage ought to figure prominently in the inventory of arguments that are likely to offload stigma from gay couples to their constitutive outside, African American families most prominently.

6

What Marriage Equality Teaches Us about Gender and Sex

A close look at the history of marriage among African Americans and the newly won rights of same-sex couples illuminate how gaining marriage rights can come at the price of stigmatizing other groups and ways of life on marriage's outside. So too, the half-lives of both racism and homophobia render marriage a more complicated rite of passage than its advocates have fully appreciated. This chapter takes up two more concerns with a political project that figures marriage as a primary institutional site within which to elaborate a fuller and freer notion of a gay self. One involves the durability of gender-based power on marriage's inside. The other involves the negative consequences for sex and sexuality on marriage's outside.

For formerly enslaved people in the nineteenth century, the right to marry was something they both demanded and endured. A marriage license signified a new civil status as a person not property, but it also worked as a tool to arrest and imprison newly freed black people who became entangled in the complex rules of marriage. The power that underwrote that tool was both racial and gendered in nature. Racial in the sense that enforcing the laws of marriage became a racial project as soon as newly freed people were permitted to marry. And gendered insofar as the institution of marriage was, and still is, structured around gender roles and inequalities. Notwithstanding its other benefits, marriage created new domains of private dependency and vulnerability that rendered women the property of their husbands.

Chapter 1 recounts the stories of enslaved women in Kentucky and their first experiences of marriage in 1864, showing how they suffered the blessings of matrimony with the lash. For the wives of the first Negro soldiers serving in the Union Army, marriage triggered new forms of gendered vulnerability that amplified the racial violence to which they were accustomed. Stories in other chapters show how newly emancipated people were taught by law and civil authorities that marriage entailed the assumption of rigid roles as husband/head of household and wife/domestic dependent. These new status-based positions entailed a range of new responsibilities and vulnerabilities that were both welcomed and suffered by newly freed people. In this sense, as Catherine Hall describes, "the richness of the concept of 'family' was that it offered a way of combining inequalities of power with belonging within a family. Just as men and women, parents and children, were equal, unequal and different, so white people and black could also be contained within this embracing framework."[1] For newly freed black people, marriage functioned as a primer for other structural discriminations to come—discriminations that were not inconsonant with citizenship, freedom, or equality in nineteenth- and twentieth-century America.

As an ideal, most African Americans say they think marriage is a good idea. But as a reality, marriage continues to be a more complicated proposition. As the historical tales in previous chapters illustrate, for newly emancipated African Americans marriage provided both an opportunity to celebrate new, yearned-for freedoms *and* an easy way for the criminal law to insinuate itself into freed people's lives.

This complicated legacy of marriage in the African American community persists today. For many African American women, marriage looms as a just-out-of-reach promise. African Americans are the least likely racial/ethnic group to marry and the most likely to divorce.[2] Stanford Law professor Rick Banks's book, *Is Marriage for White People?*, provocatively asks why so few African American women choose not to marry or to marry "down" rather than marry a man of equal class and educational background from "outside the race."[3]

One might also provocatively ask whether marriage is better suited for straight people. By posing this question I don't mean to align myself with those, such as the conservative National Organization for Marriage, who feel that only straight people should be allowed to marry, but rather to ask whether the legal rules and social norms that make up civil marriage have heterosexual couples in mind. Put another way, is there something essentially heterosexual about the institution of marriage? Are marriage's rules and norms well suited to govern the lives and interests of same-sex couples?

Given that hundreds of thousands of same-sex couples have legally married,[4] now is the time to ask this important, if not painful, question: What have we gotten ourselves into? What will it mean to be governed by a set of rules that allocate rights and responsibilities and distribute and redistribute property in ways that were developed with heterosexual relationships in mind? Marriage law—and, most importantly, feminist reforms to marriage law in the last fifty years—take matrimony to be a legal relationship that is fundamentally structured by gender inequality. The rules of support within marriage and the rules of distribution upon divorce are designed to take that underlying structural gender inequality into account. In fact, the taken-for-grantedness of this evolution in the law of marriage and divorce we chalk up as a victory for feminist lawyering and advocacy.

First, as a legal matter, gaining marriage rights really boils down to surrendering the breakup of your relationship to governance by rules set by the state, rather than the ad hoc improvisations that same-sex couples used before they were able to marry. What should we expect from this new form of governance? How will the heterosexual history of marriage map onto same-sex relationships when they are subject to the rules of divorce?

A woman I met in late 2012 helped me understand just how complicated both marriage and divorce can be for same-sex couples. I was invited to give a talk at St. Bartholomew's Episcopal Church on 5th Avenue in New York City. The church was founded in 1835 and has a rather affluent and diverse membership. Their lesbian and gay fellowship invited me to talk to them about the marriage cases that were before the Supreme Court that year. I don't get asked to talk at church very often, so I welcomed the opportunity to reach a new and different audience.

About seventy-five people showed up, including one woman, whom I'll call Beth, who lives in New Jersey and comes in to mass at St. Bart's every Sunday. She raised her hand at the end of my talk and shared the following story:

Nine years ago, when she was legally separated from but still married to a man, Beth was set up on a blind date with a woman—let's call her Ruth. They dated steadily for several years, broke up for two years during which time they lived in different cities and dated other people, and then got back together again. Beth bought, renovated, and flipped houses for a living and had become quite successful doing so. Ruth was a licensed electrician working through the electrician's union. Their relationship was both hot and volatile, and they wanted to try to figure out how to make it work. They had some deep issues that caused recurring conflict between them—largely having to do with their class differences and, of course, money—that they could not resolve and kept returning to in their fights. Beth, the more affluent of the two, had two teenage children from her marriage and had primary custody of the kids. In 2007, when Beth and Ruth reunited after having broken up for a couple years they went to a counselor to set out some ground rules about their separate and joint financial lives. With the counselor's help they agreed not to commingle their assets but to live together and contribute to their daily living expenses in proportion to their abilities: Beth would contribute 80% and Ruth 20%. They both agreed in front of the counselor to the terms of the financial arrangement and promised to abide by it, hoping that this would minimize future conflict in the relationship.

Not surprisingly, it didn't. Rather than splitting up again they did something pretty wacky: "We decided to go to Massachusetts and get married," Beth later told me over the phone, chuckling to herself at the wisdom of this idea. "We just thought that getting married would allow us to work things out without the threat of breaking up. We both thought it would make us feel safer to work through the hard stuff if we had the legal structure of marriage around our relationship. I don't know what I was thinking; it's like people deciding that having a baby will help keep them together."

Fifteen months later they had a terrible fight and Ruth moved out. Beth then filed for divorce. Ruth's lawyer responded by demanding that Ruth get half of all of Beth's assets, as well as ongoing financial support. These were her rights as a divorcing spouse under New Jersey law. Beth was shocked since they had made a very different agreement with each other when they were in counseling. The case went to trial before a seasoned female family court judge. The judge, a Catholic, had dealt with many messy divorces. This was, however, her first same-sex divorce.

At the trial Beth's lawyer argued that the standard rules of equitable distribution (splitting the marital assets fifty-fifty) should not apply because of the premarital financial agreement they had reached when they saw the counselor before they moved back in together. Since they had never put this agreement in writing, Beth's lawyer called the counselor to testify and she described the details to the judge.

When the judge ruled she noted that under New Jersey law a prenuptial financial agreement must be in writing,[5] therefore their premarital agreement was considered irrelevant and unenforceable, and the rules of marital distribution in New Jersey law would apply instead. The question then became what assets would be subject to equitable distribution. This required that the judge determine when the marital clock started ticking. The easy and obvious choice would be when they married in Massachusetts, but instead the judge "backdated" their marriage to when Beth and Ruth started dating rather than to when they legally married. She wrote in her judgment that prior to marriage, "they had a nine year relationship when they functioned as a couple." She treated Beth's total assets as marital property and granted Ruth a half share in all of it—including assets Beth had acquired long before she and Ruth were legally married.

Given that same-sex people were not able to marry at the point that Beth and Ruth got together, the judge reasoned that it was only fair that she backdate the marriage to early in their relationship on the assumption that they would have married if they could have. In this sense, the shadow of the law of marriage[6] is cast backward as a kind of restitution for a status injury suffered by same-sex couples. As Beth explained it to me later in an email, "The judge and all the lawyers involved have assumed that from the day we met, we were 'a joint enterprise,' essentially a monogamous, committed life partnership. And that [Ruth] is entitled to half of my net worth based on a 9 year acquaintance, even though for 3 years of it I was still married to [my former husband], and for almost 2 of those years she was living in Massachusetts and Maine and dating and finally in another relationship."

Beth and I have talked quite a bit since the meeting at St. Bart's, and I have gotten a pretty good sense of what she's going through. She is outraged that the judge retroactively married them and that the laws of equitable distribution applied to their divorce even though they had explicitly agreed otherwise. "I want my experience to be a cautionary tale for others—gay people should be wary of marriage," she told me. "You have no idea what you're getting yourself into."

This case highlights the way in which marriage, and particularly divorce, risk gendering two same-sex spouses in ways that are recognizable from the vantage point of heterosexual marriage. Beth's perspective reflects what I've come to call the "lesbian husband" position. She feels she earned her own money fair and square, not due to any gender-based advantage that a male husband married to a female wife might have. Ruth should not have any legal entitlement to her money; in fact, Ruth agreed not to make such a claim before they got married. In so many ways Beth's position is not unfamiliar in divorce cases—it's the husband position, seeking to minimize financial exposure in a divorce from a wife who has lower wage-labor market power and trying to limit that exposure through a prenuptial agreement.

On the other hand, Ruth looks a lot like a "lesbian wife"—going in and out of the wage-labor market, earning less money, and contributing less financially to the family's joint support. The judge even understood her to be a "housewife" for part of their marriage, performing unpaid domestic labor as is customary for wives/mothers. On this view, Beth should not be able to just walk away from Ruth, leaving her destitute while Beth retains her substantial assets.

On this telling, Beth and Ruth's case looks a lot like a traditional heterosexual divorce—the husband, the one with more assets, trying to part with as few of those assets as possible; the wife, the one with fewer resources, trying to gain as many of those assets as she can; and both parties arguing a notion of fairness that is shot through with gender stereotypes.

But is this the right way to understand what went on in this relationship and what would be a fair way to dissolve it? Does it make sense to render these parties legible through a heteronormative lens, translating them into the more familiar stock characters that populate family court? Does this act of translation do violence to Beth and/or Ruth, or for that matter to lesbian relationships more generally?

Shifting our focus to the front end of marriage, specifically to prenuptial agreements, illuminates other complexities in the way same-sex couples' marriages enter a socio-legal landscape already mapped by gender.

A friend of mine practices family law in California's Bay Area and has been doing so for years—long before same-sex marriage or civil unions. He tells me that he's seeing a trend emerging in a number of the gay male divorces he has handled. Where the two men in the couple have different earning power or assets, the less affluent spouse is declining to demand his half share at the time of divorce because it genders him *as a wife* to do so. He would rather leave the marriage with his masculinity intact than be turned into an ex-wife receiving alimony. For gay men in this situation, the fear of marriage law gendering them motivates them to forgo economic advantage. This dynamic contrasts with my first example where the gendering of the weaker party provides her with an economic advantage that she is more than happy to seize.

Another lawyer who practices in Virginia tells a similar story. Courts, he notes, reinforce the view that men are individual economic units. "I worked with a male couple where the younger one was the stay-at-home spouse raising the children and the older one was working and making lots of money. When the older one found a younger playmate he walked away and filed for divorce. In the straight context, the court would order spousal and child support. Yet with gay male spouses there is less of an expectation that the stay-at-home male spouse needs to be supported because, after all, he's a man."

As these examples illustrate, the law of marriage and divorce risk imposing—if not imprinting—status-based gendered identities on the parties in ways that clearly change how they might have seen themselves had marriage law not been on the scene. The desirability of these identities may cut in opposite directions depending upon whether masculinity or femininity is at issue—Ruth sees a benefit in being treated as a wife insofar as the dependency it entails will enable access to Beth's assets, while the male "wives" often want nothing to do with an association with wifeliness and the unmanly dependency with which it is associated.

The new world we live in, one in which lesbian and gay couples are increasingly marrying, holds out two different ways of thinking about the subversive feminist potential of this important change in the law.

We could see the revolutionary project as disassociating gender from sex. That is, we could entertain the notion that women can be husbands and men can be wives. That's pretty "gender-y," as Eve Sedgwick once said.[7]

The lesbian-husbands and gay-wives analysis illuminates gender differences and advantages that are quite familiar in marriage and in society more generally. Yet this account ratifies marriage as essentially a status-based relationship populated by pre-scripted characters locked into roles that predetermine their relative rights and responsibilities, powers, and vulnerabilities. Of course, these status-based rules were developed to address the all too common problem of wives giving up their careers to raise the kids while supporting their husbands' professional lives, thus leaving wives economically vulnerable at the time of divorce. There is a vast literature documenting the impoverishing effect of divorce on heterosexual women/mothers, particularly as compared with the favorable economic consequences of divorce for heterosexual men/ fathers.[8] However, the reform of divorce laws to allow for the distribution of assets at the end of a marriage in a way that is sensitive to wives' economic vulnerability post-marriage ironically reinforces the heterosexist structure of marriage more generally since the problems of inequality *within* marriage are to be "taken care of" when marriages end. The feminist reforms to divorce law, in essence, take status inequalities within marriage as a given and, as a result, target reforms at the consequences of those entrenched inequities rather than at their source.

If we were to focus concern about the status inequalities in marriage not only on their consequences but also on their source, we might conclude that wives have a deep investment in destabilizing the notion that marriage entails traditional role-based behavior from each spouse. If feminism stands for anything it is that being a wife or a husband need not necessarily predetermine any particular relationship to caretaking or breadwinning, dependence, or self-sufficiency.

So let's return to the judge in New Jersey who conscripted Beth and Ruth into the roles of husband and wife at the time of their divorce. In that particular case, this was "good" for Ruth. But was it "good" for marriage, or even "good" for the project of folding same-sex couples into marriage more generally? What Beth and Ruth's divorce may teach us is that—at least in the near term—the only way that power inequalities in marriage can become legible to family court judges is through the epistemic violence of casting the parties into familiar gendered roles that were long ago scripted by traditional heterosexist notions of marriage.

Another approach to the problem would be to see this as an opportunity to disorganize marriage and gender altogether. By this I mean, what if the increasingly common phenomenon of same-sex spouses had the effect of blowing up the very notion of roles in marriage completely?

To do this, rather than starting with the traditions and norms of heterosexual marriage, picking them up and dropping them onto lesbian and gay relationships, what if we started with the traditions and norms of gay and lesbian relationships and see what happens when we try to honor those forms of attachment, responsibility, and dependence through the rules of marriage?

We don't have to look very far to come up with examples, since lawyers are asked every day by lesbian and gay couples to write into prenuptial agreements the idiosyncratic, creative, and varied commitments gay men and lesbians have made to one another. The aim of these agreements is to opt out of the default rules of marriage and to make marriage adapt to the polymorphous notions of responsibility these couples have pledged to one another. Pretty much every lawyer who does family law in the lesbian and gay community can attest to having the following couple in their office:

Steve, a balding, less than fit sixty-year-old investment banker has been with Rob, a hot thirty-five-year-old former bartender and occasional model, for eight years. The couple splits their time between a penthouse in Manhattan and a house in the Hamptons. Title to both properties is held solely in Steve's name, and Steve contributes 100% to the financial support of both houses and their lifestyle. As is common among many gay men in similar relationships, there is an implicit understanding that Steve will support Rob as long as the relationship lasts, and when it's over, it's over. Neither Rob nor Steve expects that Steve will owe Rob anything financially if/when they split. They decide to marry and go to a lawyer, asking that a prenuptial agreement be drawn up stating that in the event of divorce Rob will get nothing. The lawyer asks them: But why are you getting married if you want to opt out of all of the rights and duties that marriage entails? They answer: Because this is such an important civil right we just won—everyone's getting married and we want to throw a fabulous wedding!

Should guys like Steve and Rob be able to keep their *laissez-faire* deal with each other once they marry? Does getting married necessarily entail a shift in what they owe one another, including a responsibility for the more affluent one to support the less affluent one after the marriage ends? If Rob freely chose to live for eight years with this understanding of what Steve owed him before they got married, why can't he freely choose to waive any rights to support after they marry?

As the Virginia lawyer I know explains it, men are much more willing to sign prenups in which they essentially waive all the rights of economic support or distribution in the event of divorce. Overall, he has observed, men are much more comfortable with economic inequality than are women.

Many of the same-sex couples who are the first to marry in states that change their laws have been together for many years, sometimes decades. They have worked hard to structure their relationships, responsibilities, and financial lives in ways that work for them outside of formal legal and cultural regulation. Why shouldn't they be able to continue those arrangements once they marry? In this sense, shouldn't marriage be more of a contractual relationship between the two parties than one that comes with set rules that the state is loath to waive or bend? This position has been argued by family law scholars such as Cynthia Lee Starnes, who aims to treat marriage more like a business partnership than a special, intimate relationship. Starnes urges us to adopt "an enriched partnership model that analogizes alimony to a buyout."[9]

This model, to some, would allow couples like Steve and Rob to opt out of the requirements of equitable distribution and duties of support entirely would threaten to undue decades of feminist reform of the law of marriage. Husbands have argued for ages that the money they earn is "theirs" and that their wives who stay home and "do nothing" are not entitled to it upon divorce. Modern reforms of the law of divorce have come to recognize the gendered nature of this position, pointing out that the unpaid work done by wives and mothers "at home" contributes to the overall wealth and well-being of the family, and that the breadwinner could not be out in the wage-labor market winning bread if it were not for the work that the homemaker was doing to enable and support his work at the office. In this sense, the modern law of divorce recognizes the married couple as an economic unit and the resources that come into the household during the marriage are to be treated as joint assets, split equitably upon the marriage's dissolution. Prior to these reforms, divorce was notoriously an impoverishing event for wives and an enriching one for husbands.

But Steve and Rob could respond that it is unfair to limit their freedom to shape their relationship as they wish, and to burden them with concerns about gender inequality that do not characterize their relationship. Sure, maybe "straight" rules of support and equitable distribution should apply to a heterosexual couple whose relationship is shaped by gender inequality, but those rules shouldn't apply to gay men. Rob got a great deal while it lasted with Steve supporting him in a lifestyle he never would have been able to afford on his own, and Steve got the benefit of a relationship with a sexy younger man. They each got something valuable to them for as long as it lasted and it would be unfair to force upon them ongoing commitments that neither of them wanted. In some respects, Rob and Steve's relationship and their "contractual freedom" approach to the financial commitments marriage entails may mirror marriage trends more generally, insofar as the parties in both different- and same-sex couples increasingly enter marriage more as economic equals than under the traditional scenario where there is a substantial difference in their wage-earning potential.[10]

So what should courts do when faced with enforcing Steve and Rob's prenup? In essence, the question boils down to this: should Rob be treated as a man or as a wife? What's at stake here is a tension between liberty on the one hand and equality on the other. Respecting Steve and Rob's liberty interests threatens to undermine the integrity of the equality-based reforms that have been built into the law of divorce as a way to protect women/wives from structural gender bias. If Rob were treated as a man would this resolve the question of his agency and liberty to enter into a contract in which he waives rights he would have had if he had been a wife? Surely there are inequalities between and among men that are worthy of public policy concern, whether based in race, class, or other vectors of social and economic vulnerability. Indeed, might there be gender inequalities in gay male relationships that should be of concern to those committed to gender justice? Surely feminine men suffer a range of social and economic disadvantages with which masculine men are not burdened. Should a court faced with enforcing Steve and Rob's prenup undertake an inquiry of this robust range of inequalities that might render their agreement unworthy of enforcement in ways that echo the justifications for the default rules of equitable distribution for heterosexuals?

On the other hand, if the court treats Rob as a wife, does this require that his assent to their agreement be seen through a prism that paternalistically genders him as having made a bad bargain that oppressed him? This structural approach, adjudicating the matter as a question of Rob's collaboration in his own subordination, risks essentializing this specific relationship, and marriage more generally, as impervious to autonomous action and the renegotiation of the lives that can be elaborated in the name of "spouse." This conclusion is bad for marriage, risky for women and wives, and likely offensive to Rob.

Steve and Rob are not unusual. Lawyers serving the lesbian and gay community now have a booming practice of same-sex couples asking for prenups that allow them to marry while opting out of some of the most basic rules of marriage. These are only a few other common examples.

Consider the same kind of relationship as the one just described except the couple agrees that if they divorce after ten years of marriage, Steve must pay Rob ongoing support unless either of them die or Rob gets into another relationship. The challenge for them and for the lawyer is to put in writing what they mean by "relationship." Here's what one lawyer came up with:

The monthly payments made by Steve pursuant to this Article shall continue to be made on the first day of each subsequent month until the earliest to occur of the following "Termination Events":

(1) Steve's death;
(2) Rob's death;

(3) Rob's remarriage or entry into a civil union or domestic partnership with someone other than Steve;

(4) Rob's cohabitation ("cohabitation" defined as a party's living or residing on a reasonably continuous basis of 90 days or more with an adult other than Steve) with an adult with whom he is having or has had a romantic, sexual, or non-platonic relationship, regardless of whether said adult maintains an independent residence away from the Party's residence, and also regardless of whether or not either contributes to or shares the other's living expenses.

This agreement differs from what one might see in a "regular" prenup or divorce settlement only with respect to (4), the provision that cuts off Steve's duty of support in the event that Rob cohabits with someone else with whom he is in a relationship even if Rob is not supported financially by that other person. Basically, Steve will agree to support Rob after their breakup only if Rob stays single and lives alone.

Consider other complex arrangements: Liza and Francine have been together for twenty-two years and have always had an open relationship, meaning that they have agreed not to be monogamous. They decide to marry and ask their lawyer to draft a prenup that contains a clause stating that they agree to continue this understanding of non-monogamy into the marriage and that neither of them may use a claim of infidelity or adultery against the other for any purpose in the case of a divorce.

After being together for five years Fred and Melvin decide to have a child through the use of a surrogate. Fred is much more interested in being a parent than is Melvin. Melvin loves his work and loves to travel, and is clear with Fred that he'd rather have an "uncle-like" role in the child's life. Melvin adds that this also means that he doesn't want to split the costs of supporting the child; rather he's willing to pay only a quarter of the costs so that he still has the ability to afford trips abroad. This deal is just fine with Fred, as he'd actually prefer to be the primary parent. When their child is seven years old Fred and Melvin decide to get married, but they want a prenup containing the agreement about their different commitments to being parents while they remain married and that in the event that they divorce Fred would maintain primary custody of the child and Melvin would have limited visitation and duty of support.

What should courts do when faced with the problem of enforcing these prenups? Family court judges seem distinctly ill equipped to take on the task of a nuanced investigation of the relative powers and inequalities that characterize relationships, whether gay or straight. Nor can we expect them to be particularly suited to take on the impossible balancing of liberty and equality these cases raise.

One other set of issues poses even more difficult questions when it comes to the way same-sex couples are approaching the legalization of their relationships. It seems that for many men, marriage becomes an opportunity not only to legally formalize their commitments to one another but also to monetize those vows in ways that might not have been considered possible in the absence of marriage. So, for instance, a soon-to-be married gay man asked his lawyer to negotiate an adultery penalty clause in a prenup that would require his soon-to-be spouse to pay him $100,000 if he has sex with another man after they are married. (I asked the lawyer if this penalty was to be assessed per adulterous sexual act or as a one-time fine. She wasn't sure.) In another case a lawyer was asked to draft a prenup that include a $500,000 payout if the client's spouse exposes him to HIV. It's not clear that courts will enforce these efforts to contractually monetize the hurts and heartbreaks common in marriages. But they do signal an interesting way in which some gay people regard the legal structure of marriage as an opportunity to render each of the commitments of a relationship into legal agreements with a dollar value in the case of breach. For some couples that have been together a long time, marriage is treated more like a transaction than a sacrament.

So here's where I come out: given that most divorces that family courts will preside over will continue to be between men and women, and that gender inequality remains a sticky form of injustice that characterizes many of those relationships, I am loath to allow same-sex divorces to open the door to weaken the gender-justice enhancing mechanisms in the current rules of divorce.

For this reason I am inclined to push the question back to the moment when the Steves and Robs consider whether to marry. It strikes me that what they are seeking is to have it all—all of the social, legal, and financial benefits of marriage without being bound by marriage rules that they don't like or think shouldn't apply to them. In this sense, we ought to make room for them to conclude that on balance marriage isn't for them and is better left to straight people and their concerns.

Some may be troubled by this approach—marriage should be made to work for all, whether straight or gay, and to the extent that it can't bend to meet the needs and interests of the Steves and Robs of the world it should be forced to do so as a matter of equality. But that argument is wrong, as it conflates the problem at issue into a problem of sexual orientation discrimination, which it surely isn't. Rather, what produces the problem is a question of scarcity—of asking one institution to work for too wide a range of relational commitments. Were we to offer a broader range of options by which couples could obtain different forms of recognition, responsibility, commitment, and security less pressure would be put on marriage, and some of what marriage laws have evolved to take account of (such as gender inequality in heterosexual relationships) would not be undermined by trying to accommodate relationships that bear very little resemblance to traditional straight marriages.

In this sense I'm inclined to agree with those who argue that marriage is a traditional, conservative institution. By this I mean marriage is made up of traditions, some of which are worth preserving as a matter of gender justice. Those same-sex couples prepared to assume the implications of those traditions are best suited to organize their relationship within the structure of civil marriage. Those who aren't should consider alternative structures within which to organize their relationships, rather than demanding or expecting that marriage can or should accommodate "side deals" that risk undermining or weakening the justice-enhancing traditions that women's rights advocates have worked hard to build into marriage. This suggests an extremely uncomfortable conversation within the gay community—one that suggests that the "collective win" the community has gained in attaining access to marriage may also entail "collective responsibilities" toward others governed by marriage. There tends to be a strong individualistic vein that runs through some sectors of the gay community: "this is *my right* and I'm free to do with it what I want." The hard conversation I am suggesting is one where new rights holders understand themselves to bear some accountability to a larger set of concerns about inequality.

This is the juncture at which the gay community has arrived. Now that we have reached a tipping point in the repeal of the prohibition against same-sex couples marrying, it's time to ask whether marriage is for us. Or rather, for all of us. This question was too difficult to ask as long as the federal government and the majority of the American people favored the exclusion of same-sex couples from civil marriage. During the long period of exclusion many people in the gay community developed an attachment to the idea of the benefit to which they were being denied access. (Some might call it a kind of reaction formation.) Even among the members of the lesbian and gay community who entertain strong critiques of the marriage institution, some find themselves faced with an uncomfortable choice now that they can marry: they feel it would be legally and financially irresponsible to refuse the security and financial advantages that marriage offers. So they marry, holding their noses and feeling they have, in some odd way, sold out. This tragic choice arises because marriage has a monopoly on relationship recognition. But it need not, and our politics shouldn't surrender to this status quo.

A friend of mine who does LGBT family law in New York recently said, "Unless you have a very gendered relationship, you need a prenup." If she's right, then most of us ought to get lawyers before we get married. Or maybe we ought to think hard about what it means for same-sex relationships to be "very gendered." What my lawyer friend probably means is that the default rules of marriage work best for same-sex relationships that are gendered in heteronormative terms: where one person is more like a husband and a higher wage earner and the other is more like a wife who invests his or her time in unpaid domestic work.

But lesbian and gay relationships can be very gendered in all manner of other ways that do not necessarily have any relationship to hetero-normative gender inequality. Gender can be a vernacular for desire in many relationships where, for instance, the sexual orientation of one person in a lesbian couple is toward women gendered in a particular way, either feminine/femme or masculine/butch. Wealth or wage labor market power may or may not be coextensive with one's gender in these relationships. The butch may enjoy a labor market endowment by virtue of her masculinity, but could just as easily suffer workplace discrimination on account of her failure to conform to gender norms appropriate for her sex. What is more, in many "very gendered" lesbian relationships the way one performs one's gender may bear no relationship whatsoever to the way power is distributed within the relationship or how tasks in the domestic sphere are allocated. It isn't always safe to assume that the femme is doing all the cooking and cleaning before the butch comes home from work looking for her pipe, slippers, and a scotch. Although some couples may find that scenario totally hot, to be sure.

We can tell a similarly complex story about gay men, their gendered identities, gendered desires, and the ways in which "very gendered" relationships may or may not translate into power outside the home and inside the couple that mirrors gendered power in traditional heterosexual relationships.

What we're starting to see, and what we can expect to see more of when the law of marriage and divorce are brought to bear on the dissolution of gay and lesbian marriages, is a tendency to recognize gender in same-sex marriages as something familiar, as something "just like" what goes on in heterosexual marriages. This is where we should be attentive to a worrisome kind of misrecognition, where family court judges interpret the dynamics of same-sex relationships from the vantage point of the hetero-gendered dynamics they are accustomed to, just as we saw with Beth and Ruth. (In the context of lesbian intimate partner violence there is much evidence that this kind of misrecognition takes place all the time, where butches are stereotyped by law enforcement officials to be the batterers and femmes to be the victims/survivors of that violence. In fact, intimate partner violence in same-sex relationships does not necessarily mirror the gendered forms of violence in different-sex relationships.)[11]

One lesson we can draw from the early experience of same-sex couples with the right to marry is that marriage may not be for all of us. While we might all support the repeal of an exclusion from marriage as a matter of basic constitutional fairness, we need not all jump into marriage to demonstrate our new rights-bearing identity. If this book has any overarching message it is that we ought to slow down, take a breath, and evaluate whether marriage is "for us."

Yet for some members of the lesbian and gay community the financial and legal advantages of marriage are too compelling. For this group—the "nose-holding" pragmatists who marry to protect their legal and economic interests but do so "under protest"; who bear the weight of a new kind of dual consciousness and get married, but do so ambivalently; and who suffer a guilty queer conscience, with their queer tails between their legs—I have a platform of action. Most of my friends and colleagues find themselves in this situation. They promise to keep up their critiques of marriage and defense of non-marital forms of family even though they're getting married. They all have good economic or legal reasons to get married, and they insist that they have not surrendered their critique of marriage—it's just that their lawyers or financial advisors convinced them that it is foolish not to avail themselves of the advantages of marriage now that they are available. Or maybe their employers told them they had to marry or else their partners would be kicked off the health plan.

Without minimizing the importance of these reasons to marry, I find that too often the promises these folks make to keep up their critiques of marriage are just empty words that soothe a guilty conscience. To them I issue a challenge: that *you*, even more than those of us who aren't marrying, need to make real your promise of progressive engagement with marriage from its inside. It will not only assuage your guilt, it will make those who aren't marrying less resentful, and most importantly you will make a real difference.

I have eight important things you can, you should, and you must do to make your ongoing commitment to a critique of marriage real. All of them will help nurture queer counterpublics in the era of same-sex marriage. This eight-point progressive call to action for married queers is attached at the end of the book as an appendix.

↬

Just as same-sex couples must contend with the gender-based history and values of civil marriage, gaining marriage rights may also threaten the gay community's own history and values. Chapter 5 surveys how homophobia's afterlife is animating a backlash against same-sex couples that marry. But that afterlife can do other work that may split the gay community from itself and from its history. One of the costs of winning a right to marry lies in the negative externalities those victories are producing.

This reassignment of stigma is, in important ways, the by-product of the great success of the marriage equality movement's capacity to rebrand itself and what it means to be homosexual. Marriage has proven a useful trope by which to pull the *sex* out of homo*sex*uality, thereby leaving a remainder of same-sex attachment, love, and care that is distinctly unsexual in nature. In the wake of this social transformation, a badge of inferiority has been shifted from decent same-sex couples—many of whom are portrayed in the media and in legal papers as wanting dignity for their relationships and their children that only marriage can confer—to indecent others whose intimate attachments don't or won't march politely down the aisle.

The dignity and respectability enjoyed by same-sex couples through the right to marry does not merely dissolve the shame and humiliation that underwrote their exclusion from civil marriage. Rather, that abjection typically finds another worthy home, usually close by. Tragically, the new luster of matrimony is rendered all the more radiant in contrast to newly revealed forms of perversion or scandal. I don't mean to imply that this was an intended narrative of redemption deliberately sought out by the advocates of marriage equality, but rather that it was a foreseeable and tragic consequence of certain arguments they emphasized in the road to gaining marriage rights.

Consider two events that dominated the news in the summer of 2011: Democratic New York congressman Anthony Weiner resigned from office after it became public that he had been tweeting to female Twitter followers photos of himself in various stages of undress and arousal. At the same time New York became the largest U.S. state to grant same-sex couples the right to marry. Two iconic images captured this moment: a thumbnail of Weiner's bulging briefs and wedding cakes topped with same-sex couples.

While these events may seem unrelated, they are meaningfully connected. That summer marked an important turning point in the geography and politics of sex: public sex, previously a domain often dominated by the specter of a hypersexualized gay man, became the province of the irresponsible, foolish, and self-destructive heterosexual man, in the body and bits of Anthony Weiner. Meanwhile, homosexuals were busy domesticating their sexuality in the private domain of the family. Just as undignified, hetero sex-on-the-loose seeped out into the open, homo-sex disappeared from view into the respectable pickets of legalized private kinship. In important ways, the panic that unfolded with the revelation of Representative Weiner's publicly sexual tweets was fueled by homophobia's resilience, a resilience that made itself felt in the wake of the success of same-sex couples' demand for marriage equality rights.

How so? Well, the emplotment of gay life that drove Supreme Court Justice Anthony Kennedy's story of the Lawrence/Garner "relationship" in *Lawrence v. Texas*, one animated by characters who are intimate, committed kin, not participants in a casual hookup, whose connection is romantic not sexual, is taken up in the marriage equality cases. The homosexuals portrayed in the marriage cases are the soccer mom, the good provider, the loving father, the de facto daughter-in-law, and the fellow who attends stamp-collecting conventions. The respectable homosexual keeps quiet about the sex part of homo*sex*ual. In this sense, the space cleared out when the homophobia that justified criminal sodomy laws is repudiated is a space for the desexualized, non-threatening gay subjects who long for the stability and fidelity of "enduring personal bonds."[12]

In the marriage cases, the decent, loving, faithful gay character is met by adamant arguments from the other side insisting marriage is essentially a procreative, child-rearing enterprise, and since only a man and a woman can procreate, marriage should be made up of husbands and wives. In response to this heterosexualization of marriage, the same-sex couples insist: we too have children, just not the way you do.[13] It makes sense for the plaintiffs in these cases to insist that there are ways to make babies that aren't essentially heterosexual, but the consequence of this argument is that homo-sex loses any political, legal, social, or erotic meaning. Or worse, it becomes conscripted into racialized state projects, such as when Judge Richard Posner announced that marrying gay couples is in the state's interest because they (presumptively white gay couples) will be more likely to adopt children from the foster care system (presumptively children of color) and thus relieve the public of an economic burden.[14]

For same-sex couples, marriage, just like fun at the University of Chicago, is where homo-sex goes to die. Who, if not lesbian and gay people, see themselves as having an interest in carrying a brief for sex? Sex for its own sake, and as part of a politics of freedom. The gay rights agenda used to be a crucial site for imagining a kind of sexual citizenship that wasn't defined by and through the redemptive pastoralization of marriage. It is time sex pushed back and resisted a hygienic sexual politics that aims to cleanse homosexuality of its more erotic inclinations. Since same-sex marriage advocates have surrendered to, if not embraced, the heteronormativity of the private family, public spaces may be the last refuge for sexual liberty. In this sense, Anthony Weiner may be more of an ally in the cause to defend sexual liberty than are marriage equality advocates. The elaboration of sexual publics (and by this I don't mean weddings) is essential as a counterweight that can challenge the hegemony of the matrimonialized gay subject/gay couple.

The stories we tell about gay and lesbian people in the marriage litigation, and that are told back to us in the legal opinions in these cases, are stories of self-discipline, commitment, monogamy, and respectability. The most salient desires of those who seek to marry are for kinship, love, fidelity, and security. Sex is nowhere on the scene, except in one capacity that I'll discuss in a moment. This story—which I will acknowledge makes sense given the benefits the parties are seeking—both reproduces and reinforces the narrative Justice Kennedy began telling about us in *Lawrence*: the Constitution stands to protect us so long as we can plausibly discipline our desires into the form of kinship. Sex for its own sake remains without constitutional protection.

Sex that is not potentially reproductive in nature, but is rather engaged in for pleasure, comfort, or elaborating the self in complex ways, for instance, has lost ground in the cause to secure marriage rights for same-sex couples. The marriage cases, thus, do the final work in the project of homosocializing gay and lesbian legal subjects, a job first begun in *Lawrence*. Thus, in the twenty-five years since the Supreme Court decided *Bowers v. Hardwick* (the case that found no constitutional problem with criminalizing homosexuality), lesbians and gay men have gone from having their legal identity defined entirely on the basis of the sex to a legal and social identity now organized around love, joint tax returns, and parenting.

In this world view, kinship, love, intimacy, and care for the ones we love are what married people have, thereby reinforcing the notion that lives outside of marriage take place in a zone characterized by insecurity, dysfunction, self-interest, and perhaps most importantly: the wrong kinds of sex. For similar reasons, reproductive rights, both the right to abortion and to contraception, enjoy a kind of second-class constitutional status, alive, but just barely, on life support waiting for a conservative Supreme Court to pull the plug.

Now, as in the nineteenth century when African Americans made a similar claim to a right to civil marriage as a necessary component of freedom, the right to marry for same-sex couples has launched what David Scott has termed a form of responsibilized freedom.[15] The civil rights paradigm does not take the form of a demand that we be left alone to determine our own sense of the good or be given the freedom to order our intimate private lives as we wish. Rather, today's marriage equality movement makes the demand that we have earned state licensure of our families because we have satisfied the state's criteria of eligibility for legitimate family status. This is a curious notion of freedom indeed. What it does is inaugurate a new regulatory relationship with the state, exchanging the ignominy of criminal regulation for the dignity of civil regulation.

If the stories in this book teach us anything, it is that the laws of marriage have the potential to lock us into roles, responsibilities, and limitations from which it is very hard to break free. Surely it made sense for advocates in the nineteenth century and today to argue that exclusion from the institution of marriage amounted to a profound form of state-sponsored discrimination for newly freed people. So too does it make sense to argue that state-sponsored discrimination against same-sex couples today is fundamentally wrong. But once the exclusion is lifted and marriage rights become available we are obliged to carefully evaluate what it means to elaborate a freer and more equal self by surrender to legal governance of our intimate lives by the state.

As the most blatant forms of bias against gay people are defeated, homophobia will find refuge in other precincts of public and private life—precincts where it has always lurked, but may not have gained attention as it was overshadowed by recent victories in addressing bias in the military and marriage. Just as racism in the era after *Brown v. Board of Education* has proven to be increasingly subtle and difficult to address, so too will be challenges in addressing homophobia's afterlife. As with race, those who are disfavored by mainstream norms and opportunities will find themselves responsible for their own misfortune. We can imagine how this will go: "What was he thinking having sex with some-one not his husband?" "If they had gotten married the court would have recognized both of them as legal parents." "It's too bad they fired him, but after all it's reasonable for an employer to insist that he wear 'men's' clothing to work—he can dress like that after hours." "That homeless gay kid was turning tricks; did he really think he wouldn't get arrested?"

There was a time, albeit not long ago, when the gay community saw these issues—supporting modes of alternative parenting, forming com-mitted relationships outside the watch of the government, and loosen-ing the grip of rigid gender norms—as core to the ways we were taking on homophobia. In many ways, addressing these issues requires harder work than gaining marriage rights.[16] This is the difficult, slogging work we need to return to, just as the African American community continues to combat the underfunding of majority black schools, systemic gun vi-olence in their neighborhoods, racial profiling, police violence, debtors' prisons, and crushing poverty—to name only a few of the ways in which racism does its daily, dirty work marginalizing and undermining the life chances of black men and women.

Such perils can come from bigoted legal actors using marriage laws as a tool to punish new rights holders. But today we're learning that the perils of marriage may inhere in the institution of marriage itself. Ex-amining the ways in which marriage does not work for many same-sex couples promises to illuminate its limits as a structure for different-sex couples as well. Like it or not, the social, legal, and economic structure of marriage can exert overwhelming power that threatens to turn us into husbands and wives, as those roles are traditionally understood. If those are roles you're happy with, then marriage is for you. But if you intend to resist their pull, then alternative relationship forms ought to be a viable alternative. In ways as yet underexamined by the lesbian and gay com-munity, to be wed is to be locked into a set of traditions and roles that we had no part in creating and that were not formed with us in mind. The aim of this book is to begin the careful work of understanding why and how this is so.

APPENDIX: A PROGRESSIVE CALL TO ACTION FOR MARRIED QUEERS

So often when progressive queer people make the decision to marry, they suffer a deep sense of ambivalence about having "sold out" or "bought in" to a traditional, mainstream institution that they have long critiqued. Typically, they promise to keep up their critiques of marriage and defense of non-marital forms of family after they marry. In order to make good on those promises, here are eight fundamentally important things you can do:

1. Resist the repeal of domestic partner benefits programs (for both same- and different-sex couples) at the same time that you advocate for marriage rights.

2. Refuse to give your support to marriage equality laws that surrender other rights in the name of religion. Many statutes granting marriage rights to same-sex couples include gaping religious exemption clauses that create a new kind of license to discriminate against same-sex couples. Some advocates lobbying for marriage equality have seen this bargain as worth making. New York's 2011 Marriage Equality Act and Utah's 2015 Antidiscrimination and Religious Freedom law prohibiting sexual orientation–based discrimination in employment and housing contained truck-size religious exemptions.[1] Resist the urge to make this bargain. The more we accede to the legitimacy of religion-based exemptions to civil rights laws, the more acceptable and common they will be—not only as a tactic to undermine the right of same-sex couples to marry, but as a means to attack reproductive rights and racial equality laws as well.[2]

3. Think hard about the degree to which you are expecting to have it all when you marry on terms that work best for you, but that doing so may undermine important advances in gender equality for others. When you ask your lawyer to draft a prenuptial agreement that exempts your relationship from all of the default rules of marriage, consider first why those rules exist and how the enforcement of your marriage contract may have negative spillover effects for others—particularly women—who may not enjoy equal bargaining power when entering a marriage.

4. Cease making arguments in support of marriage rights for same-sex couples that (i) turn on the dignity that marriage confers to qualifying couples, (ii) turn on the benefits to children of having two parents who are married, and (iii) advertently or inadvertently make it easier to disparage non-marital and non-reproductive sexual activity. While it may be tempting to pitch these arguments to judges and policy makers to gain ground for the cause of marriage equality, these positions accrue credibility for the cause largely by reinforcing the stigma suffered by other people whose identities and behaviors don't look marital in form.

5. Pledge to think about how strategies to fight homophobia might be linked to other causes, such as anti-racist organizing or defending reproductive rights. That harder thinking ought to include a sensitivity to the ways in which the same-sex marriage movement has been the beneficiary of a racial endowment, and how some arguments made in furtherance of marriage equality may have amplified the ways in which marriage has not been a liberating experience for many people of color. Similarly, that hard thinking must include a sensitivity to the intersection of interests between the gay rights movement and the reproductive rights movement.

6. Resist making arguments in support of marriage rights that rest on a negative judgment toward paying taxes. While it is unfair for same-sex couples to be taxed differently and more highly than different-sex couples (particularly when it comes to estate taxes),

a progressive agenda should embrace the payment of taxes, estate taxes in particular. Too often the arguments made in favor of marriage equality echo a kind of Tea Party cynicism toward paying taxes. Commit to a progressive queer critique of the state *and* of the private accumulation of property and wealth by abandoning and repudiating any anti-tax ethos haunting some corners of the same-sex marriage movement.

7. Calculate the tax benefits you receive from being married, including estate taxes, and rather than pocketing it, give the money away to a worthy cause.

8. Think about what it means to gain an economic advantage through marriage, passing money tax-free to "preferred relatives" such as spouses rather than to the broader kin networks so prevalent in the lesbian and gay community. Find other, creative ways to support the needs of our extended kin/family *even if* the state does not recognize them as "family" and there is no tax benefit for doing so.

NOTES

ACKNOWLEDGMENTS

1 Megan J. McClintock, "Civil War Pensions and the Reconstruction of Union Families," *Journal of American History* 83 (1996), p. 456.

INTRODUCTION

1 George Washington's will is available at http://gwpapers.virginia.edu/documents/george-washingtons-last-will-and-testament/.

2 I prefer the term "black" to "African American" when writing about this period because black people in the United States did not become citizens until 1868 with the passage of the Fourteenth Amendment to the Constitution.

3 I use the male pronoun here because only freed or free black men were allowed to conduct business dealings, enter into contracts, or acquire debt. Black women, even if not enslaved, were subject to the same laws of coverture as were white women. That is, as women they did not enjoy a legal personality independent of their fathers or husbands.

4 On the laws and customs that regulated the lives of free black people in the antebellum period, see Ira Berlin, *Slaves without Masters: The Free Negro in the Antebellum South* (New York: New Press, 1974); Mark Tushnet, *The American Law of Slavery, 1810–1860: Considerations of Humanity and Interest* (Princeton, NJ: Princeton University Press, 1981); Marina Wikramanayake, *A World in Shadow: The Free Black in Antebellum South Carolina* (Columbia: University of South Carolina Press, 1973).

5 Andrew Koppelman, in works such as "The Miscegenation Analogy: Sodomy Law as Sex Discrimination," *Yale Law Journal* 98 (1988), has made this argument earliest and most often.

6 Judith Butler, *Frames of War: When Is Life Grievable?* (London: Verso, 2009), p. 6.

7 For further reading on this question, see Reva Siegel, "Discrimination in the Eyes of the Law: How "Color Blindness" Discourse Disrupts and Rationalizes Social Stratification," *California Law Review* 88 (2000); Eva Paterson, Kimberly Thomas Rapp, and Sara Jackson, "The Id, the Ego, and Equal Protection in the 21st Century: Building upon Charles Lawrence's Vision to Mount a Contemporary Challenge to the Intent Doctrine," *Connecticut Law Review* 40 (2008).

8 Edward W. Said, *Representations of the Intellectual: The 1993 Reith Lectures* (New York: Vintage Books, 1996), p. 44.

9 Michael Bronski, Ann Pellegrini, and Michael Amico, *"You Can Tell Just by Looking": And 20 Other Myths about LGBT Life and People* (Boston: Beacon Press, 2013), p. 97.

10 Said, *Representations of the Intellectual*, p. 44.

11 Statement of Col. William A. Pile, testimony taken in Kentucky, Tennessee, and Missouri, Nov. and Dec. 1863, Record Group 94 (hereinafter RG), M 619, roll 201, frame 139, National Archives, Washington, D.C. (hereinafter NA) (this statement hereinafter Pile Testimony).

12 Mark Oppenheimer, "Married, with Infidelities," *New York Times Magazine*, June 30, 2011, p. 22.

CHAPTER 1. FREEDOM BY MARRIAGE

1 Edwin M. Stanton to Abraham Lincoln, Mar. 3, 1865, in *The War of the Rebellion: A Compilation of the Official Records of the Union and Confederate Armies, series 3, vol. 4* (Washington, DC: Govt. Print. Off., 1900), p. 1219 (hereinafter *The War of the Rebellion*).

2 Victor B. Howard, *Black Liberation in Kentucky: Emancipation and Freedom, 1862–1884* (Lexington: University of Kentucky Press, 1983), pp. 6–8; Lincoln to Fremont, Sept. 2, 1861, available at http://www.thelincolnlog.org/view/1861/9; Lincoln to O. H. Browning, Sept. 22, 1861, available at http://www.thelincolnlog.org/view/1861/9.

3 Abraham Lincoln, "Remarks to a Deputation of Western Gentlemen, August 4, 1862," *New York Tribune*, Aug. 5, 1862.

4 Ira Berlin, "Emancipation and Its Meaning," in David W. Blight and Brooks D. Simpson, eds., *Union and Emancipation: Essays on Politics and Race in the Civil War Era* (Kent, OH: Kent State University Press, 1997), pp. 110–11; John David Smith, "Let Us All Be Grateful That We Have Colored Troops That Will Fight," in John David Smith, ed., *Black Soldiers in Blue: African American Troops in the Civil War Era* (Chapel Hill: University of North Carolina Press, 2002), pp. 17–18. Lincoln's evolution on the question of arming black soldiers was well summarized in a conversation he had with three Kentuckians (Governor Thomas E. Bramlette, Albert Hodges, and Archibald Dixon) in April 1864 in which he explained how he became convinced that the sure benefits of gaining hundreds of thousands of able new troops outweighed the unlikely cost of losing Kentucky. Lincoln to A. G. Hodges, Esq. Executive Mansion, Frankfort, Kentucky, Washington, Apr. 4, 1864, in Roy P. Basler, Marion Dolores Pratt, and Lloyd A. Dunlap, eds., *The Collected Works of Abraham Lincoln* (New Brunswick, NJ: Rutgers University Press, 1953), pp. 7, 281–83.

5 William C. Davis, *The Orphan Brigade: The Kentucky Confederates Who Couldn't Go Home,* (Garden City, NY: Doubleday and Co., 1980).

6 Thomas to Stanton, Feb. 1, 1864, Letters Sent RG 393, NA; Michael T. Meir, "Lorenzo Thomas and the Recruitment of Blacks in the Mississippi Valley, 1863–1865," in John David Smith, ed., *Black Soldiers in Blue: African American Troops in the Civil War Era* (Chapel Hill: University of North Carolina Press, 2002), pp. 263–64.

7 General Orders No. 34, Headquarters, District of Kentucky, Louisville, Kentucky, Apr. 18, 1864, available at http://www.afrigeneas.com/forumdarchive/index.cgi/ md/read/id/6791/sbj/general-orders-no-34/.

8 "Market Price of Slaves," *New York Times*, Aug. 22, 1863.

9 Richard D. Sears, "A Long Way from Freedom: Camp Nelson Refugees," in Kent T. Dollar, Larry H. Whiteaker, and W. Calvin Dickinson, eds., *Sister States Enemy States: The Civil War in Kentucky and Tennessee* (Lexington: University of Kentucky Press, 2009), p. 225; Victor B. Howard, *Black Liberation in Kentucky: Emancipation and Freedom, 1862–1884* (Lexington: University of Kentucky Press, 1983), p. 67.

10 Thomas D. Mays, *The Saltville Massacre* (Abilene, TX: McWhiney Foundation Press, 1995).

11 Affidavit of Patsy Leach, Camp Nelson, Kentucky, Mar. 25, 1865, Bureau of Refugees, Freedmen, and Abandoned Lands (hereinafter BRFAL), RG 105; M 999, roll 7, NA.

12 Affidavit of Martha Cooley, Camp Nelson, Kentucky, Mar. 24, 1865, ibid.

13 Affidavit of Clarissa Burdett, Camp Nelson, Kentucky, Mar. 27, 1865, ibid.

14 General Orders No. 24, L. Thomas, July 6, 1864, in *The War of the Rebellion*, p. 474.

15 Affidavit of John Vetter, Camp Nelson, Kentucky, Dec. 16, 1864, BRFAL, RG 105, M 999, roll 7, NA. Abisha Scofield, another missionary working at Camp Nelson, testified to similar facts and atrocities as a result of the expulsion of the women and children from Camp Nelson. Affidavit of Abisha Scofield, Camp Nelson, Kentucky, Dec. 16, 1864, ibid.

16 Affidavit of Joseph Miller, Camp Nelson, Kentucky, Nov. 26, 1864, ibid.

17 Affidavit of Albert A. Livermore, Camp Nelson, Kentucky, June 26, 1865, ibid. See generally Richard D. Sears, *Camp Nelson, Kentucky: A Civil War History* (Lexington: University of Kentucky Press, 2002), pp. 220–21.

18 "Can nothing be done for the poor women and children sent from this Camp by order of Genl Fry? They are literally starving to death." Hall to Restieaux, Dec. 16, 1864, Box 720, RG 92, NA; Sears, *Camp Nelson, Kentucky*, pp. 134–35.

19 Humanitas, "From Kentucky: Cruel Treatment of the Wives and Children of U.S. Colored Soldiers, Camp Nelson, Kentucky, Nov. 28, 1864," *New York Daily Tribune*, Dec. 2, 1864.

20 Murray Davis, "Abstract of Report of Special Inspection of Camp Nelson, Kentucky, May 13, 1865," BRFAL, RG 105, M 999, roll 7, pp. 173–75, NA; John Gregg Fee, *Autobiography of John G. Fee* (Berea, KY, and Chicago: National Christian Association, 1891), pp. 175–78.

21 Victor B. Howard, *Black Liberation in Kentucky: Emancipation and Freedom, 1862–1884* (Lexington: University of Kentucky Press, 1983), pp. 117–18.

22 Abisha Scofield, Letter to William Goodell, Camp Nelson, Kentucky, Nov. 30, 1864, MS American Missionary Association Archives, 1839–1882; 44058, Amistad Research Center at Tulane University.

23 Statements of Senator Wade, Cong. Globe, 28th Cong. 2d Sess. 161 (1865).

24 *A Resolution to Encourage Enlistments and to Promote the Efficiency of the Military Forces*, 38 Res. No. 29, 3 Stat. 571 (1865). Curiously, Congress did not borrow the language it had used a year earlier in the war widow's pension statute that enabled black women to file pension claims as widows of deceased colored soldiers, even though they were not legally married. The principal difference between the two definitions of marriage used to distribute both pensions and freedom to black women was that the pension statute required that they have lived together as husband and wife for at least two years prior to the soldier's enlistment. The Pension Statute of July 4, 1864, entitled the widows and children of colored soldiers killed in the war to a pension "without other proof of marriage than that the parties had habitually recognized each other as man and wife, and lived together as such for a definite period next preceding the soldier's enlistment, not less than two years, to be shown by the affidavits of credible witnesses." Act of July 4, 1864, ch. 247, § 14, 13 Stat. 387 (1864) (supplementing Act of July 14, 1862, which granted pensions to white widows of fallen Union soldiers).

25 General Orders No. 33, Mar. 11, 1865, in *The War of the Rebellion*, p. 1228; *The Union*, Aug. 11, 1865.

26 In 1860 there were 225,483 enslaved people in Kentucky. Marion A. Lucas, *A History of Blacks in Kentucky: From Slavery to Segregation, 1760–1891* (Frankfort: Kentucky Historical Society, 1992), p. xvi.

27 Jas. S. Brisbin to Governor Bramlette, Apr. 22, 1865, published in *New York Tribune*, May 1, 1865.

28 Ibid.

29 D. W. Lindsey, Adjutant General of Kentucky, to Brigadier General C.B. Fisk, July 26, 1865, with enclosed blank certificate, BRFAL, RG 105, M 999, roll 7, NA.

30 R. J. Hinton, Captain and District Inspector, to Captain T. W. Clarke, Sept. 21, 1865, ibid.

31 Affidavit of Mary Wilson, Camp Nelson, Kentucky, June 17, 1865, ibid.

32 Edwin M. Stanton to Abraham Lincoln, Mar. 3, 1865, *The War of the Rebellion*, p. 1219 (my emphasis).

33 For a fuller explanation of the origins and nature of the law of coverture, see Richard Chused, "Married Women's Property Law: 1800–1850," *Georgetown Law Journal* 71 (1983).

34 John Gregg Fee, letter to the editor, *Louisville Press*, Mar. 20, 1865.

35 Hannah Arendt, *The Origins of Totalitarianism* (San Diego: Harcourt, Brace, Jovanovich, 1973), p. 301.

36 Lieutenant R. W. Thing to Major J. H. Cochran, Dec. 22, 1865, BRFAL, RG 105, M 999, roll 7, NA.

37 Gayatri Chakravorty Spivak, *Outside in the Teaching Machine* (New York: Routledge, 1993), p. 46.

38 *Dred Scott v. Sandford*, 60 U.S. 393 (1857).

39 The text of the Manhattan Declaration is available at manhattandeclaration.org.

40 From page 2 of the declaration (see http://manhattandeclaration.org/#2).

41 Also known as Hunter Wallace, the founder of the racist blog *Occidental Dissent*, www.occidentaldissent.com, according to the Anti-Defamation League, blog.adl.org/extremism/matthew-heimbach-publically-returns-to-racist-street-activism.

42 See Southern Poverty Law Center Intelligence Files, "Council of Conservative Citizens," http://www.splcenter.org/get-informed/intelligence-files/groups/council-of-conservative-citizens.

43 Ibid.

44 Scott Johnson, "Groups Protest SPLC, Same-Sex Marriage," *Montgomery Advertiser*, May 9, 2014, available at http://www.montgomeryadvertiser.com/story/news/local/2014/05/09/groups-protest-splc-sex-marriage/8905525/.

45 For Griffin's text, see the *White Reference* blog at http://whitereference.blogspot.com/2014/05/council-of-conservative-citizens-and.html.

46 David Badash, "Fischer: 'We Need an Underground Railroad' to Abduct Children from Gays," *New Civil Rights Movement* (blog), Aug. 8, 2012, http://thenewcivilrightsmovement.com/fischer-we-need-an-underground-railroad-to-abduct-children-from-gays/discrimination/2012/08/08/45849.

47 Transcript of Record at 83–84, *Perry v. Schwarzenegger*, 704 F. Supp.2d 921 (N.D. Cal. 2010), available at http://www.afer.org/wp-content/uploads/2010/01/Perry-Vol-1-1-11-10.pdf.

48 Megan R. Wilson, "Lobbyists Quietly Advise GOP on Gay Marriage shift," *The Hill*, July 30, 2014, http://thehill.com/business-a-lobbying/business-a-lobbying/213747-lobbyists-quietly-advise-gop-on-gay-marriage-shift; "Attorneys General Switching Sides on Gay Marriage," Associated Press, Feb. 14, 2014, available at http://www.usatoday.com/story/news/politics/2014/02/14/attorneys-general-gay-marriage/5492785/.

49 *Skinner v. Okla. ex rel. Williamson*, 316 U.S. 535, 541 (1942); *Maynard v. Hill*, 125 U.S. 190, 205, 211 (1888).

CHAPTER 2. FLUID FAMILIES

1 Petition to the Governor, the Council, and the House of Representatives of Massachusetts (May 25, 1774), reprinted in Herbert Apetheker, *American Negro Slave Revolts* (New York: Columbia University Press, 1943), pp. 8–9, quoted in Peggy Cooper Davis, *Neglected Stories: The Constitution and Family Values* (New York: Hill & Wang, 1997), p. 109.

2 Memorandum in Support of Plaintiffs' Motion for Summary Judgment, *Goodridge v. Dep't of Public Health*, No. 01–1647-A, Massachusetts Superior Court, Aug. 20, 2001.

3 This is essentially the view of historians such as Kenneth Stampp, *The Peculiar Institution: Slavery in the Ante-Bellum South* (New York: Vintage, 1956); E. Franklin Frazier, *The Negro Family in the United States* (Chicago: University of Chicago Press, 1939); and Stanley Elkins, *Slavery: A Problem in American Institutional and Intellectual Life* (Chicago: University of Chicago Press, 1959), and, oddly enough, some of the advocates for same-sex marriage rights today.

4 "There is one topic to which I will allude, which will serve to establish the heathenism of this population. I allude to the universal licentiousness which prevails. It may be said emphatically that chastity is no virtue among them—that it's violation neither injures female character in their own estimation, or that of their master or mistress." Rev. La Roy Sunderland, ed., "Testimony of the Western Luminary," in *Anti-Slavery Manual, Containing a Collection of Facts and Arguments on American Slavery* (New York: Piercy & Reed, 1837); David A. McElroy, "Freedom: Loving Liberty or Licentious Anarchy?" *Freedom's Phoenix* (blog), Mar. 5, 2011, http://www.freedomsphoenix.com/Opinion/085109–2011–03–05-freedom-loving-liberty-or-licentious-anarchy.htm.

5 *Skinner v. Oklahoma*, 316 U.S. 535, 541 (1942).

6 *Zablocki v. Redhail*, 434 U.S. 374, 384 (1978).

7 See, e.g., Paula Giddings, *When and Where I Enter: The Impact of Black Women on Race and Sex in America* (New York: William Morrow, 1984), pp. 85–90; Deborah Grey White, *Ar'n't I a Woman?: Female Slaves in the Plantation South* (New York: W.W. Norton, 1985), pp. 27–61, 164–65.

8 Pile Testimony.

9 American Freedmen's Inquiry Commission, S. Exec. Doc. No. 38–53, Preliminary Report Touching the Condition and Management of Emancipated Refugees (1863), p. 5 (hereinafter Preliminary Report).

10 *Debow's Review* 623 (1836), quoted in J. W. Blassingame, *The Slave Community: Plantation Life in the Antebellum South* (New York: Oxford University Press, 1972), p. 153.

11 Mary V. Thompson, *The Lives of Enslaved Workers on George Washington's Outlying Farms: A Talk for the Neighborhood Friends of Mount Vernon*, June 16, 1999, available at http://www.mountvernon.org/sites/mountvernon.org/files/Lives%20of%20Enslaved_JS%20edits.pdf.

12 Stampp, *The Peculiar Institution*, p. 346; Donna L. Franklin, *Ensuring Inequality: The Structural Transformation of the African-American Family* (New York: Oxford University Press, 1997), pp. 7–8.

13 Frazier, *The Negro Family*, p. 32. See also Elkins, *Slavery*. Kenneth Stampp argued that

[i]n Africa the Negroes had been accustomed to a strictly regulated family life and a rigidly enforced moral code. But in America the disintegration of their social organization removed the traditional sanctions which had encouraged them to respect their old customs. . . . Here, as at so many other points, the slaves had lost their native culture without being able to find a workable substitute and therefore lived in a kind of cultural chaos. (Stampp, *The Peculiar Institution*, p. 340)

14 Brenda Stevenson, "Black Family Structure in Colonial and Antebellum Virginia: Amending the Revisionist Perspective," in M. Belinda Tucker and Claudia Mitchell-Kernan, eds., *The Decline in Marriage among African Americans: Causes, Consequences, and Policy Implications* (New York: Russell Sage Foundation, 1995), pp. 27, 30.

15 Scholars of the time "largely attributed the long-term survival of enslaved African Americans to the viability of the slave family as their principal sociocultural institution" (ibid., p. 28).

16 Preliminary Report, p. 6.

17 Laura Edwards, *Gendered Strife and Confusion: The Political Culture of Reconstruction* (Champaign: University of Illinois, 1997); Brenda E. Stevenson, *Life in Black and White: Family and Community in the Slave South* (Oxford: Oxford University Press, 1997); Tera W. Hunter, *To 'Joy My Freedom: Southern Black Women's Lives and Labors after the Civil War* (Cambridge, MA: Harvard University Press, 1997).

18 Megan J. McClintock, "Civil War Pensions and the Reconstruction of Union Families," *Journal of American History* 83 (1996), pp. 456, 461 (providing an outstanding account of the Civil War pension system and what its records reveal about family formations in the nineteenth century).

19 See Act of July 14, 1862, ch. 166, 12 Stat. 566 (1862) (establishing Civil War pensions).

20 David Herbert Donald, *Lincoln* (New York: Simon & Schuster, 1995), p. 430.

21 Ibid., p. 431. Dudley Taylor, *The Sable Arm: Negro Troops in the Union Army, 1861–1865* (New York: Longhorn, 1956), is authoritative on this issue. See also Leo F. Litwack, *Been in the Storm So Long: The Aftermath of Slavery* (New York: Vintage, 1979), pp. 65–79 (describing black interest in and white resistance to the recruitment of black men for a "liberating army").

22 Litwack, *Been in the Storm So Long*, pp. 88–89. ("'No orders, threats, or commands,' a Confederate soldier reported, 'could restrain the men from vengeance on the negroes, and they were piled in great heaps about the wagons, in the tangled brushwood, and upon muddy and trampled roads.'")

23 McClintock, "Civil War Pensions," p. 473.

24 Statement of Sen. Lafayette Foster, Republican of Connecticut, Cong. Globe, 38th Cong., 1st Sess. 3233 (1864).

25 Act of July 4, 1864, ch. 247, § 14, 13 Stat. 387 (1864) (supplementing Act of July 14, 1862, which granted pensions to white widows of fallen Union soldiers).

26 Act of June 6, 1866, ch. 106, § 14, 14 Stat. 56 (1866) (supplementing several acts relating to pensions).

27 Act of June 6, 1873, ch. 234, § 11, 17 Stat. 566 (1873) (revising, consolidating, and amending laws relating to pensions).

28 Secondary Proof of Marriage, Pension File of Collin Johnson, Nov. 12, 1896, Bureau of Pensions, Civil War and Later Pension Files, 1861–1942, Application 643,658, Widow's Certificate Series (hereinafter BPCWLPF, WCS), RG 15, NA. The pension files are boxed as original paper documents. The files contain application numbers if a pension was applied for but never awarded and certificate numbers if a pension was awarded.

29 Summary of Proof, Affidavit of Ellen Waters, Mar. 14, 1871, and Agnes Waters and Lucinda Waters, July 16, 1866, Pension File of Aaron Waters, Certificate 157,761, BPCWLPF, WCS, RG 15, NA.

30 Affidavit of William Brent, Clerk of the Circuit Court of the District of Columbia, Oct. 2, 1843, Affidavit of Joseph Dozier and James H. Johnson, July 21, 1881, in Pension File of Elias Johnson, Certificate 56,536, ibid.

31 Affidavit of Rev. Nathan C. Conner, in Pension File of Elijah Johnson, Dec. 23, 1867, Certificate 114,336, ibid.

32 United States Sanitary Commission, *Sanitary Memoires of the War of the Rebellion, Vol. 1*, (1867), p. 322. Dr. Russell's treatment relationship with black soldiers was, at best, complicated, as he was known to study the bodies of black people in order to debunk stories of physical differences between black and mulatto bodies. See Margaret Humphreys, *Intensely Human: The Health of the Black Soldier in the American Civil War* (Baltimore: Johns Hopkins University Press, 2008).

33 Ira Russell, M.D., "Pneumonia as It Appeared among the Colored Troops at Benton Barracks, Mo., During the Winter of 1864," in United States Sanitary Commission, Contributions Relating to the Causation and Prevention of Disease, and to Camp Diseases (1867).

34 Affidavit of Theodore Stanley and Martha M. Stanley, July 14, 1869, in Pension File of George Williams, Certificate 157,858, BPCWLPF, WCS, RG 15, NA.

35 Affidavit of Susan Alexander, Dec. 26, 1874, Affidavit of Louisa Woods, Dec. 30, 1874, in Pension File of Allen Alexander, Certificate 97,533, ibid. ("[T]hey were married a great many years ago, she can not tell when.")

36 John Smith Kendall, *History of New Orleans, Volume 3* (New Orleans: Lewis Publishing Co., 1922) p. 1095.

37 Pension File of Julia Alfred, Certificate 146,842, BPCWLPF, WCS, RG 15, NA.

38 Ibid.

39 An image of Joseph Bostick's headstone at Arlington Cemetery is available at http://www.19usct.com/bostick-joseph.html.

40 Affidavit of Dilly Bostick, Dec. 19, 1887, in Pension File of Joseph Bostick, Certificate 171,629, BPCWLPF, WCS, RG 15, NA.

41 Affidavit of Christianna Poole, Dec. 8, 1890, in Pension File of Robert Poole, Certificate 286,824, ibid. See also Pension File of Charles Alfred, Certificate 177,642, ibid ("She and her said husband being slaves at the time [1857] and no marriage ceremony being recognized by the then existing laws of the State of Louisiana—their marriage was simply a voluntary union between themselves as man and wife.").

42 Herbert G. Gutman, *The Black Family in Slavery and Freedom, 1750–1925* (New York: Pantheon Books, 1979), pp. 270, 275.

43 See, e.g., Pension File of Charles Alfred, Certificate 146,842, BPCWLPF, WCS, RG 15, NA; Pension File of Daniel Allen, Application 167,134, ibid.; Pension File of Robert Poole, Certificate 286,824,.

44 Letter to the Commission of Pensions from F. Farrow, Auditor, Apr. 16, 1897, in Pension File of Collin Johnson, Application 643,658, ibid.

45 See Blassingame, *The Slave Community*, p. 165 (explaining that "the marriage ceremony in most cases consisted of the slaves' simply getting the master's permission and moving into a cabin together").

46 Tera W. Hunter, "Putting an Antebellum Myth to Rest," *New York Times*, Aug. 1, 2011, available at http://www.nytimes.com/2011/08/02/opinion/putting-an-antebellum-myth-about-slave-families-to-rest.html?_r=0.

47 Pension File of Daniel Allen, Application 167,134, BPCWLPF, WCS, RG 15, NA.

48 Affidavit of Mary E. Johnson, in Pension File of Frank Johnson, Mar. 24, 1907, Certificate 296,067, BPCWLPF, WCS, RG 15, NA.

49 Anthony E. Kaye, "The Personality of Power: The Ideology of Slaves in the Natchez District and the Delta of Mississippi, 1830–1865" (Ph.D. Dissertation, Columbia University, 1999), pp. 7–9; Anthony E. Kaye, *Joining Places: Slave Neighborhoods in the Old South* (Chapel Hill: University of North Carolina Press, 2007), pp. 56–60.

50 Testimony of Susan Alexander, Dec. 26, 1874, in Pension File of Allen Alexander, Certificate 97,533, BPCWLPF, WCS, RG 15, NA.

51 Kaye, *Joining Places*, pp. 56–70; Stevenson, "Black Family Structure," pp. 36, 233.

52 Edwards, *Gendered Strife and Confusion*, p. 109; Harriet Beecher Stowe, *The Key to Uncle Tom's Cabin* (Boston: John P. Jewett & Co., 1854), pp. 298–301, quoted in Gutman, *Black Family in Slavery and Freedom*, p. 64.

53 See Robert William Fogel, *Without Consent or Contract: The Rise and Fall of American Slavery* (New York: W.W. Norton, 1989). Many authors have documented the common practice by which slave men and women were forced by their masters to "marry" and reproduce. See, e.g., Litwack, *Been in the Storm So Long*, p. 234.

54 See Fogel, *Without Consent*, p. 153; Jacqueline Jones, *Labor of Love, Labor of Sorrow: Black Women, Work, and the Family from Slavery to the Present* (New

York: Basic Books, 1985), p. 20; Ann Patton Malone, *Sweet Charity: Slave Family and Household Structure in Nineteenth-Century Louisiana* (Chapel Hill: University of North Carolina Press, 1992), pp. 16–18, 180; Leslie A. Schwalm, *A Hard Fight for We: Women's Transition from Slavery to Freedom in South Carolina* (Urbana: University of Illinois Press, 1997), pp. 19–44; John Campbell, "Work, Pregnancy, and Infant Mortality among Southern Slaves," *Journal of Interdisciplinary History* 14 (1984), p. 793.

55 Christopher Morris, "The Articulation of Two Worlds: The Master-Slave Relationship Reconsidered," *Journal of American History* 85 (1998), pp. 982, 988–89.

56 See Barbara Bush, *Slave Women in Caribbean Society, 1650–1838* (Bloomington: Indiana University Press, 1990), pp. 120–50; Sidney W. Mintz, *Caribbean Transformations* (New York: Columbia University Press, 1984); Barbara Bush-Slimani, "Hard Labour: Women, Childbirth, and Resistance in British Caribbean Slave Societies," *History Workshop Journal* 36 (1993), p. 36.

57 "Marriage Vow—A Declaration of Dependence Upon Marriage and FAMiLY," available at http://www.thefamilyleader.com/wpcontent/uploads/2011/07/themarriagevow.final.7.7.111.pdf.

58 The "Marriage Vow" also included a promise that signers "solemnly vow to honor and cherish, to defend and uphold the institution of marriage as only between one man and one woman," and would remain faithful to their spouses, oppose any "redefinition" of marriage, such as that between same-sex couples and embrace a federal marriage amendment to the U.S. Constitution. Ibid.

59 See Gutman, *Black Family in Slavery and Freedom*, pp. xvii–xviii; *The Negro Family: The Case for National Action* (Washington, DC: Office of Policy Planning and Research, 1965) (aka the Moynihan Report; hereinafter *The Negro Family*), available at http://www.blackpast.org/?q=primary/moynihan-report-1965.

60 Gutman, *Black Family in Slavery and Freedom*, p. 3.

61 S. Philip Morgan, Antonio McDaniel, Andrew T. Miller, and Samuel H. Preston, "Racial Differences in Household Structure at the Turn of the Century," *American Journal of Sociology* 98 (1993), p. 798; Steven Ruggles, "The Origins of African American Family Structure," *American Sociological Review* 59 (1994), p. 136.

62 Joseph Epstein, a conservative essayist who has been described as a "curmudgeonly cultural critic" by *Kirkus Reviews*, wrote in a *Wall Street Journal* op-ed that the absence of fathers in the black family could explain "what's missing in Ferguson." Joseph Epstein, "What's Missing in Ferguson, Mo," *Wall Street Journal*, Aug. 12, 2014, available at http://online.wsj.com/articles/joseph-epstein-whats-missing-in-ferguson-mo-1407885042.

63 According to 2013 census data 35.6% of African American women are not married by age 45 as compared with 12.3% of white women. U.S. Census Bureau, "Marital Status Of People 15 Years and Over, by Age, Sex, Personal Earnings, Race, and Hispanic Origin: 2013," available at http://www.census.gov/hhes/families/data/

cps2013A.html. Richard Fry and D'Vera Cohn, "Women, Men and the New Economics of Marriage: Social & Demographic Trends Report" (Pew Research Center, 2010), p. 22; Natalie Nitsche and Hannah Brueckner, "Opting out of the Family? Social Change in Racial Inequality in Family Formation Patterns and Marriage Outcomes among Highly Educated Women" (Yale University Center for Research on Inequalities and the Life Course, 2009).

64 According to 2013 census data 29.8% of African American men are not married by age 45 as compared with 18.6% of white men. U.S. Census Bureau, "Marital Status of People 15 Years and Over, by Age, Sex, Personal Earnings, Race, and Hispanic Origin: 2013," available at http://www.census.gov/hhes/families/data/cps2013A.html.

65 Kids Count Data Center, "Children in Single-Parent Families by Race," available athttp://datacenter.kidscount.org/data/tables/107-children-in-single-parent-families-by#detailed/1/any/false/868,867,133,38,35/10,168,9,12,1,13,185/432,431. Other data show a lower number, 55%; Jonathan Vespa, Jamie M. Lewis, and Rose M. Kreider, "America's Families and Living Arrangements: 2012" (U.S. Census Bureau, Population Characteristics, 2013), available at http://www.census.gov/prod/2013pubs/p20-570.pdf. See also Patricia Dixon, "Marriage among African Americans: What Does the Research Reveal," *Journal of African American Studies* 13 (2009), p. 29; Robert A. Hummer and Erin R. Hamilton, "Race and Ethnicity in Fragile Families," *Future of Children* 20:2 (Fall 2010), p. 113; Ralph Banks, *Is Marriage for White People? How African American Marriage Decline Effects Everyone* (New York: Dutton, 2011); R. M. Kreider and D. B. Elliot, "America's Families and Living Arrangements: 2007" (Current Population Reports, 2009); D. Popenoe, "The State of Our Unions 2009: The Social Health of Marriage in America: Updates of Social Indicators" (2009), retrieved from http://marriage.rutgers.edu/Publications/SOOU/2008update.pdf; B. E. Hamilton, J. A. Martin, and S. J. Ventura, "Births: Preliminary Data for 2007, National Vital Statistics Report" (Centers for Disease Control and Prevention, 2009) retrieved from http://www.cdc.gov/nchs/data/nvsr/nvsr57/nvsr57_12.pdf.

66 *The Negro Family,* chap. 2.

67 Michelle Alexander, *The New Jim Crow: Mass Incarceration in the Age of Colorblindness* (New York: New Press, 2010).

68 Linda M. Burton and M. Belinda Tucker, "Romantic Unions in an Era of Uncertainty: A Post-Moynihan Perspective on African American Women and Marriage," *Annals of the American Academy of Political and Social Science* 621 (2008), pp. 132, 138.

69 Burton and Tucker, "Romantic Unions in an Era of Uncertainty," p. 136.

70 For the debunking of these myths, see Anne Marie Cammisa, *From Rhetoric to Reform: Welfare Policy in American Politics* (Boulder, CO: Westview Press, 1998); Jill Duerr Berrick, *Faces of Poverty: Portraits of Women and Children on Welfare* (New York: Oxford University Press, 1995).

71 Bureau of Labor Statistics, U.S. Department of Labor, "Usual Weekly Earnings of Wage and Salary Workers Fourth Quarter 2014" (2015), available at http://www.bls.gov/news.release/pdf/wkyeng.pdf.

72 Jo Jones and William D. Mosher, "Fathers' Involvement with Their Children: United States, 2006–2010, National Vital Statistics Report" (Centers for Disease Control and Prevention, 2013), available at: http://www.cdc.gov/nchs/data/nhsr/nhsr071.pdf.

73 Robert L. Rubinstein, Maine B. Alexander, Marcene Goodman, and Mark Luborsky, "Key Relationships of Never Married, Childless Older Women: A Cultural Analysis," *Journal of Gerontology: Social Sciences* 45 (1991), p. 270.

74 Jessica Dickler, "Moms: 'I Can't Afford to Work,'" *CNN Money*, Apr. 20, 2012, http://money.cnn.com/2012/04/18/pf/moms-work/index.htm.

75 Carol B. Stack, *All Our Kin: Strategies for Survival in a Black Community* (New York: Harper & Row, 1974).

76 Patricia Hill Collins, *Black Feminist Thought: Knowledge, Consciousness, and the Politics of Empowerment* (New York: Routledge, 2000).

77 Meredith Minkler and Esme Fuller-Thomson, "African American Grandparents Raising Grandchildren: A National Study Using the Census 2000 American Community Survey," *Journal of Gerontology Social Sciences* S82–S89 (2005).

78 See, e.g., Regina Davis-Sowers, "'It Just Kind of Like Falls in Your Hands': Factors That Influence Black Aunts' Decisions to Parent Their Nieces and Nephews," *Journal of Black Studies* 43 (2012); Gaynell Marie Simpson and Claudia Lawrence-Webb, "Responsibility without Community Resources: Informal Kinship Care among Low-Income, African American Grandmother Caregivers," *Journal of Black Studies* 39 (2009).

79 Banks, *Is Marriage for White People?*; Ronald Angel and Marta Tienda, "Determinants of Extended Household Structure: Cultural Pattern or Economic Need?," *American Journal of Sociology* 87 (1982), p. 1360 ; Dennis P. Hogan, Ling-Xin Hao, and William L. Parish, "Race, Kin Networks, and Assistance to Mother-Headed Families," *Social Forces* 68 (1990), p. 797.

80 Hamilton I. McCubbin, Elizabeth A. Thompson, Anne I. Thompson, and Julie E. Fromer, eds., *Resiliency in African-American Families* (Thousand Oaks, CA: Sage Publications, 1998); Ronald D. Taylor, "Risk and Resilience in Low-Income African American Families: Moderating Effects of Kinship Social Support," *Cultural Diversity and Ethnic Minority Psychology* 16 (2010), p. 344; Maria Scannapieco and Sondra Jackson, "Kinship Care: The African American Response to Family Preservation," *Social Work* 41 (1996), p. 190; Gladys J. Hildreth, Major L. Boglin, and Keith Mask, "Review of Literature on Resiliency in Black Families: Implications for the 21st Century" (University of Michigan, 2000), available at www.rcgd.isr.umich.edu/prba/perspectives/winter2000/ghildreth.pdf.

81 Stepping out of role, at an NAACP dinner commemorating the fiftieth anniversary of *Brown v. Board of Education* in 2004, Cosby chastised

the lower economic and lower middle economic people who are not holding their end in this deal. In the neighborhood that most of us grew up in, parenting is not going on. . . . I'm talking about these people who cry when their son is standing there in an orange suit. Where were you when he was two? Where were you when he was twelve? Where were you when he was eighteen, and how come you don't know he had a pistol? And where is his father, and why don't you know where he is? And why doesn't the father show up to talk to this boy?" (available at *AmericanRhetoric.com*, http://www.americanrhetoric.com/speeches/PDFFiles/Bill%20Cosby%20-%20NAACP.pdf)

82 Some of the identifying information has been changed to protect the privacy of the people involved, but key elements of the story are basically true.

83 Darren Rosenblum, "Pregnant Man?: A Conversation," *Yale Journal of Law and Feminism* 22 (2010), p. 256.

84 Ibid., pp. 257, 261.

85 Ibid., p. 207.

86 Joseph F. Sullivan, "Brief by Feminists Opposes Surrogate Parenthood," *New York Times*, July 31, 1987, available at http://www.nytimes.com/1987/07/31/nyregion/brief-by-feminists-opposes-surrogate-parenthood.html?pagewanted=1.

87 Robert Oscar Lopez, "Breeders: How Gay Men Destroyed the Left," *American Thinker* (blog) March 11, 2014, http://www.americanthinker.com/2014/03/breeders_how_gay_men_destroyed_the_left.html; Nancy Ehrenreich, *The Reproductive Rights Reader: Law, Medicine and the Construction of Motherhood* (New York: NYU Press, 2008), 309.

88 I have changed their names to protect their privacy.

89 *Debra H. v. Janice R.*, 14 N.Y.3d 576 (2010), available at http://www.nycourts.gov/reporter/3dseries/2010/2010_03755.htm.

90 *AA v. BB*, [2007] ONCA 2 (Can.), available at http://www.ontariocourts.ca/decisions/2007/january/2007ONCA0002.pdf.

91 As of the start of 2015 California, Massachusetts, Washington, Louisiana, Delaware, Maine, Pennsylvania, the District of Columbia, Oregon, and Alaska allow three or more people to be the legal parents of a child. See Gabrielle Emanuel, "Three (Parents) Can Be a Crowd, But for Some It's a Family," *NPR*, Mar. 30, 2014,http://www.npr.org/2014/03/30/296851662/three-parents-can-be-a-crowd-but-for-some-its-a-family. Courts in Pennsylvania and Maine have recognized that a child can have more than two people with all the rights and responsibilities of parentage. *Jacob v. Shultz-Jacob*, 2007 PA Super 118, 923 A.2d 473 (2007) (upholding an award of primary custody to the biological mother's same-sex partner, with partial custody to the biological mother and sperm donor, who had been involved as a parent since infancy, and holding that all three had an obligation to support the child); *C.E.W. v. D.E.W.*, 2004 ME 43, 845 A.2d 1146, 1149–51 (Me. 2004) (explaining that a child can have a non-biological parent with

all the rights and responsibilities of parentage in addition to two legally-recognized biological parents). Delaware and the District of Columbia allow a child to have more than two people with all the rights and responsibilities of parentage by statute. Del. Code Ann. tit. 13, §§8–201, 8–203, 8–204; D.C. Code §16–831.01, et seq. Courts in a number of states have allowed third-parent adoptions that have resulted in a child having three legal parents. Deborah H. Wald, "The Parentage Puzzle: The Interplay between Genetics, Procreative Intent, and Parental Conduct in Determining Legal Parentage," *American University Journal of Gender, Social Policy & the Law* 15 (2007), pp. 379, 406–7.

92 Steve Rothaus, "Miami-Dade Circuit Judge OK's Plan for Gay Man, Lesbian Couple to Be on Daughter's Birth Certificate," *Gay South Florida*, Feb. 6, 2013, available at http://miamiherald.typepad.com/gaysouthflorida/2013/02/miami-dade-circuit-judge-oks-plan-for-gay-man-lesbian-couple-to-be-legal-parents-of-young-daughter.html.

93 La. Civil Code Article 185; La. Revised Statutes 46:236.1(F); *Finnerty v. Boyett*, 469 So. 2d 287 (La. App. 2d Cir. 1985); *Smith v. Cole*, 553 So. 2d 847 (La. 1989).

94 *Jacob v. Shultz-Jacob*, 923 A.2d 473 (Pa Super. Ct. 2007), available at www.superior.court.state.pa.us/opinions/S15032_07.PDF. Other examples of complex families with three or more parents include a case in the District of Columbia where a court allowed two siblings to be legally adopted by their aunt and uncle without extinguishing the parental rights of their father, thereby creating a situation where the children had three legal parents. Petition of J.B & W.B., Superior Court of the District of Columbia, Family Court, Domestic Relations Branch, Apr. 27, 2012, available at https://www.dropbox.com/s/7m2u3qslewq7800/DC%20Three%20Parent%20Adoption%20Opinion%20REDACTED.pdf?dl=0.

95 Complaint for Declaratory Judgment and Injunctive Relief, *Lazaro v. Orr*, available at http://www.metroweekly.com/poliglot/ACLU-Illinois-Lazaro.pdf; "Client Profiles: Freedom to Marry in Illinois," American Civil Liberties Union, http://www.aclu.org/lgbt-rights/client-profiles-freedom-marry-illinois#3.

96 Kelsey Whipple, "Masterpiece Cakeshop Refuses to Bake a Wedding Cake for Gay Couple," *Denver Westwood* (blog), July 20, 2012, http://blogs.westword.com/cafesociety/2012/07/masterpiece_cakeshop_refuses_to_bake_a_wedding_cake_for_gay_couple.php; Michael Jones, "Canadian Flower Shop Says No Flowers for Gay Weddings," *Change.org*, Mar. 17, 2011, http://www.change.org/petitions/ask-new-brunswick-human-rights-commission-to-investigate-anti-gay-discrimination-from-florist; Chris Minor, "Same-Sex Couple Banned from Renting Moline Reception Hall," *WQAD.com*, June 21, 2012, http://wqad.com/2012/06/21/38890/.

97 See *Langbehn v. Jackson Memorial Hospital*, available at http://www.lambdalegal.org/in-court/cases/langbehn-v-jackson-memorial; "Fresno Hospital Bars Lesbian from Visiting Partner and Giving Advice about Her Treatment," American Civil

Liberties Union, accessed Feb. 23, 2013, http://www.aclu.org/lgbt-rights_hiv-aids/
fresno-hospital-bars-lesbian-visiting-partner-and-giving-advice-about-her-treat.

98 42 CFR Parts 482 and 485 effective January 18th, 2011 ("A hospital [that takes
Medicare or Medicaid payments] must have written policies and procedures
regarding the visitation rights of patients, including those setting forth any
clinically necessary or reasonable restriction or limitation that the hospital may
need to place on such rights and the reasons for the clinical restriction or
limitation. A hospital must meet the following requirements: (1) Inform each
patient (or support person, where appropriate) of his or her visitation rights,
including any clinical restriction or limitation on such rights, when he or she is
informed of his or her other rights under this section. (2) Inform each patient (or
support person, where appropriate) of the right, subject to his or her consent, to
receive the visitors whom he or she designates, including, but not limited to, a
spouse, a domestic partner (including a same-sex domestic partner), another
family member, or a friend, and his or her right to withdraw or deny such consent
at any time. (3) Not restrict, limit, or otherwise deny visitation privileges on the
basis of race, color, national origin, religion, sex, gender identity, sexual orientation, or disability. (4) Ensure that all visitors enjoy full and equal visitation
privileges consistent with patient preferences"), available at http://www.lambdale-
gal.org/in-court/legal-docs/exec_us_20101117_hhs-changes-to-visitation-rights.
See also "Alternatives to Marriage Project, Hospital Rights," *Unmarried Equality*,
http://www.unmarried.org/hospital-rights.html.

99 "Civil Unions in Illinois—How'd They Get It Right?" *Columbia Law School
Gender & Sexuality Law Blog*, http://blogs.law.columbia.edu/genderandsexuality-
lawblog/2011/02/07/civil-unions-in-illinois-howd-they-get-it-right/.

100 Jackie Goldberg, "Going Past Domestic Partnership: The Same-Sex Unions Law I
Wrote Was Never Supposed to Be an Excuse Not to Legalize Marriage for All," *Los
Angeles Times*, Aug. 9, 2007.

101 Paula L. Ettelbrick, "Since When Is Marriage a Path to Liberation," *Out/Look*, Fall
1989; Paula L. Ettelbrick, "Domestic Partnerships, Civil Unions or Marriage: One
Size Does Not Fit All," *Albany Law Review* 64 (2001), p. 905.

102 Paula L. Ettelbrick and Julie Shapiro, "Are We on the Path to Liberation Now?:
Same-Sex Marriage at Home and Abroad," *Seattle Journal for Social Justice* 2
(2004), p. 475.

103 "Judges Take Tough Tone at Gay Marriage Hearing," *New York Times*, Aug. 26,
2014.

104 See, e.g., Raynard Jackson, "What Republicans Can Learn from Being Gay,"
Black Enterprise, June 11, 2012, http://www.blackenterprise.com/news/
opinion-what-republicans-could-learn-from-being-gay/ ("A 'right' indicates
something you are entitled to—by birth, by God, by law, by social norms, etc.
Therefore, I would like my gay friends to explain to me the origin of their
rights. I believe they have rights as an American citizen, but not because they

are gay. . . . Civil Rights for Blacks was never about acceptance, but rather enforcement of the U.S. Constitution. The Constitution had already guaranteed us the very rights we were fighting for—right to vote, right to live anywhere, right to due process, etc. We were not seeking to create a special class of rights based on 'choices' we voluntarily made (we were born Black—we did not choose to be Black). We did not choose to come to America nor did we choose to be slaves. So, our Civil Rights movement was about enforcement of the rights we were already guaranteed by the U.S. Constitution. Therefore, in my opinion, there can be no equating Blacks and Civil Rights with gays and special rights!").

105 See Robert Mnookin and Lewis Kornhauser, "Bargaining in the Shadow of Law: The Case of Divorce," *Yale Law Journal* 88 (1979); Ariela R. Dubler, "In the Shadow of Marriage: Single Women and the Legal Construction of the Family and the State," *Yale Law Journal* 112 (2003).

106 Katherine Franke, "The Politics of Same-Sex Marriage Politics," *Columbia Journal of Gender and Law* 15 (2006), p. 236.

107 Chapter 3 of Michael Warner's *The Trouble with Normal: Sex, Politics and Ethics of Queer Life* (Cambridge, MA: Harvard University Press, 1999), pp. 81–148, offered one of the first of such arguments.

108 Brief for American Psychological Association and New Jersey Psychological Association as Amici Curiae in Support of Plaintiffs-Appellants at 51–52, *Lewis v. Harris*, 875 A.2d 259 (N.J. Super. Ct. 2005) (No. A-2244–03T5), available at http://www.lambdalegal.org/binarydata/LAMBDA_PDF/pdf/320.pdf. William Eskridge made a similar argument in "The Relational Case for Same-Sex Marriage," in Mary Lyndon Shanley, ed., *Just Marriage* (New York: Oxford University Press, 2004), p. 60 ("To put the matter more positively, by denying gay men and lesbians the right to marry, the state is foregoing an opportunity to reinforce the stability of the two-parent household for the children of those relationships").

109 See, e.g., Declaration of Maggie Gallagher in Support of CCF's Motion for Summary Judgment, *Thomasson v. Newsom*, No. 04–428794 (Super. Ct. S.F. Mar. 11, 2004).

110 Jordan Green, "Racialized Remark About Marriage Amendment Attributed to State Senator's Wife," *Yes! Weekly* (blog), May 1, 2012, http://yesweeklyblog.blogspot.com/2012/05/racialized-remark-about-marriage.html.

111 Dan Savage, "Black Homophobia," *The Stranger*, Nov. 5, 2008, http://slog.thestranger.com/2008/11/black_homophobia.

112 Raymond Leo Roker, "Stop Blaming California's Black Voters for Prop 8," *Huffington Post*, Dec. 7, 2008, http://www.huffingtonpost.com/raymond-leon-roker/stop-blaming-californias_b_142018.html.

113 Leo Bersani, *Homos* (Cambridge, MA: Harvard University Press, 1995).

CHAPTER 3. BOOTS NEXT TO THE BED

1 *Means v. State*, 99 Ga. 205 (1896), Record Number A-20270, Georgia State Archives.

2 Obituary of E.F. Edwards, *Georgia Enterprise*, May 30, 1902, available at http://files.usgwarchives.net/ga/newton/obits/e/edwards21050b.txt; Edwards House, Historic Architecture of Georgia, http://dbs.galib.uga.edu/cgi-bin/meta.cgi?userid=galileo&dbs=larc&ini=larc_galileo.ini&action=retrieve&id=hb00324&format=contact; Brief History of the Troup Artillery, http://www.jackmasters.net/troup/rosteh.html.

3 Edward L. Pierce, "The Contrabands at Fortress Monroe," *Atlantic Monthly*, Nov. 1861.

4 John Eaton, *Grant, Lincoln and the Freedmen: Reminiscences of the Civil War* (New York: Longmans, Green, and Co., 1907), p. 2.

5 Letter from Henry Rowntree to Contraband Relief Commission, Jefferson Davis Mansion, Apr. 13, 1864, RG 105, Entry 2150, p. 10–11, NA. Rowntree's work documenting the state of the freed men and women is notable as he was employed both by the Contraband Relief Society of Cincinnati and the Society of Friends—private relief and missionary organizations that worked hand in hand with the nascent public relief agencies to rebuild the South after the war. See also James E. Yeatman, Western Sanitary Commission, "A Report on the Condition of the Freedmen of the Mississippi" (1864) (containing a report dated Dec. 17, 1863, describing the destitute conditions of freedmen throughout Mississippi).

6 Preliminary Report, p. 12.

7 American Freedmen's Inquiry Commission, "Final Report of the American Freedmen's Inquiry Commission to the Secretary of War," May 15, 1864, S. Exec. Doc. No. 38–53, 107 n.1 (1st Sess. 1864) (hereinafter Final Report).

8 The Bureau of Refugees, Freedmen, and Abandoned Lands, more commonly referred to as the Freedmen's Bureau, was a federal agency established in March 1865 to coordinate the relief effort that aided the transition of formerly enslaved people to freedom.

9 Report by Chaplain Warren, May 18, 1864, in Report of John Eaton, General Superintendent of Freedmen, Department of Tennessee, Apr. 29, 1863, RG 94, M 619, roll 200, at p. 89–90, NA (hereinafter Eaton Report).

10 Eaton Report, pp. 89–90. Gutman reports that "the earliest 'contraband marriage' for which a record exists occurred during the first week of September in 1861." Gutman, *Black Family in Slavery and Freedom*, p. 412.

11 Eaton Report, pp. 89–90.

12 Pile Testimony.

13 Michael Grossberg, *Governing the Hearth: Law and the Family in the Nineteenth-Century America* (Chapel Hill: University of North Carolina Press, 1985), p. 133.

14 Laura Edwards, "The Marriage Covenant Is at the Foundation of All Our Rights: The Politics of Slave Marriages in North Carolina after Emancipation," *Law and*

History Review 14 (1996), p. 93 (quoting Alfred M. Waddell, a Confederate army officer and newspaper editor, and a member of the commission that designed the North Carolina Black Codes). See also Stampp, *The Peculiar Institution*, p. 12.

15 Regarding the "possession of several wives and also several husbands," see Report for the Month of September, 1867, for the Sub District of Greenville, Mississippi, Sept. 30, 1867, RG 105, M 826, roll 30, frame 455, NA; Report of the Sub District for Montgomery, Alabama, for the Month ending Aug. 31, 1865, Sept. 1, 1865, RG 105, M 809, roll 18, frames 566–67, NA.

16 Report for the month of August 1867, from Lt. George Waller, Sub Assistant Commissioner (Aug. 31, 1867), RG 105, M 826, roll 30, frame 225, NA.

17 Report of the Condition of the Sub Division, Woodville, Mississippi, Oct. 31, 1867, RG 105, M 826, roll 30, NA. See also Report of Events Pertaining to Bureau of Refugees, Freedmen, and Abandoned Lands, Sub District of Wordville, Mississippi, for the Month ending Sept., 1867, RG 105, M 826, roll 30, frame 486, NA; Report for the Month of Aug., 1867 from Lieutenant George Waller, Sub Assistant Commissioner, Aug. 31, 1867, ibid, frame 225.

18 Report of the Condition of the Freedpeople and Operations of the Bureau throughout the District for the Month of Jan., 1868, Jan. 31, 1868, RG 105, M 1027, roll 27, frames 323–24, NA.

19 Narrative Report for the Month of Aug., 1867, for the Sub District of Grenada, Mississippi, RG 105, M 826, roll 30, frame 232, NA.

20 Report from the Sub District of East Pascagoula, Mississippi, for the Month of Aug., 1867, Aug. 31, 1867, RG 105, M 823, roll 30, NA. See also Report for the Sub District of Rosedale, Mississippi, for the Month of Oct., 1867, Nov. 14, 1867, RG 105, M 826, roll 30, frame 1002, NA; Narrative Report for the Month of Oct., 1867 for the Sub District of Yazoo City, Mississippi, RG 105, M 826, roll 30, frames 784–85, NA; Report of the Condition of the Sub Division, Woodville, Mississippi, Oct. 31, 1867, RG 105, M 826, roll 30, NA; Narrative Report for the Sub District of Tupelo, Mississippi, for the month ending Aug., 1867, Aug. 31, 1867, RG 105, M 826, roll 30, frame 221, NA; Report of the Sub District for Montgomery, Alabama, for the Month ending Aug. 31, 1865, Sept. 1, 1865, RG 105; M 809, roll 18, frames 566–67, NA; Testimony taken in Kentucky, Tennessee, and Missouri before the American Freedman's Inquiry Commission, Nov. and Dec. 1863, RG 94, M 619–201, frame 140.

21 See Report of Events Pertaining to Bureau of Refugees, Freedmen, and Abandoned Lands, Sub District of Wordville, Mississippi, for the Month ending Sept., 1867, RG 105;, M 826, roll 30, frame 486, NA.

22 Report upon the Conduct of Affairs Concerning Freedmen in Mississippi for the Quarter Ending Sept. 30, 1868, Oct. 14, 1868, RG 105, M 826, roll 3, frame 1077, NA.

23 Brevet Major General Alvan C. Gillem to Major General O.O. Howard, July 15, 1867, RG 105, M 826, roll 30, NA.

24 Ibid.

25 Ibid.

26 Ibid.

27 Narrative Report for the Sub District of Grenada, Mississippi, for the Month of August 1867, RG 105, M 826, roll 30, frame 232, NA; Narrative Report for the Sub District of Grenada, Mississippi for the Month of Sept., 1867, Sept. 30, 1867, RG 105, M 826, roll 30, frame 426, NA.

28 Report of the Operations of the Bureau of Refugees, Freedmen and Abandoned Lands for the State of Mississippi for Month of Oct. 1867, Nov. 28, 1867, RG 105, M 826, roll 3, frames 17–18, NA. See also Preliminary Report, Report of the Operations of the Bureau in the State of Mississippi for the Quarter ending June 30, 1868, July 14, 1868, p. 10, RG 105, M 826, roll 3, frames 959–60, NA.

29 Civil Rights Act of Nov. 25, 1865, ch. 4, § 2, 1865 Miss. Laws 82, 82.

30 See, e.g., Act of Mar. 9, 1866, tit. 31, § 5, 1866 Ga. Laws 239, 240 (prescribing and regulating the relation of husband and wife between persons of color); Act of Mar. 10, 1866, ch. 40, §§ 1–5, 1866 N.C. Sess. Laws 99–101 (concerning negroes and persons of color or of mixed blood); Act of 1865, 1865 S.C. Acts 291, 292 (establishing and regulating the domestic relations of persons of color, and amending the law in relation to paupers and vagrancy); Act of Feb. 27, 1865, ch. 18, § 2, 1865 Va. Acts 85 (legalizing marriages of colored persons now cohabitating as husband and wife), in June Purcell Guild, *Black Laws of Virginia: A Summary of the Legislative Acts of Virginia Concerning Negroes from Earliest Times to the Present* (Westminster, MD: Willow Bend Books, 1996), p. 33. See also *Laws Relating to Freedmen*, Compiled by Command of Major General O.O. Howard, Commissioner; Bureau of Refugees, Freedmen and Abandoned Lands; S. Exec. Doc. No. 39–6, 179 (a collection of Black Codes assembled by the head of the Freedman's Bureau and submitted to Congress in 1866–67).

31 Act of Jan. 11, 1866, ch. 1469, § 1, 1865 Fla. Laws. 31.

32 North Carolina entitled the county clerk to charge the newlyweds a fee of 25¢ for the task of filing a certificate of marriage. See Act of Mar. 10, 1866, ch. 40, § 5, 1866 N.C. Sess. Laws 101. In 1866, 25¢ was an amount of money that put nuptial legitimacy well outside the reach of most African Americans. Recall that war widows were expected to support themselves and their children on $8 a month.

33 See, e.g., Act of Dec. 14, 1866, ch. 1552, § 1, 1866 Fla. Laws 22.

34 See Act of Mar. 10, 1866, ch. 40, § 6, 1866 N.C. Sess. Laws 101.

35 Narrative Report for the Sub District of Tupelo, Mississippi for the Month of Sept. 1867, Sept. 30, 1867, RG 105, M 826, roll 30, NA

36 James William Massie, *America: The Origin of Her Present Conflict, Her Prospect for the Slave, and Her Claim for Anti-Slavery Sympathy: Incidents of Travel During a Tour in the Summer of 1863, Throughout the United States, from the Eastern Boundaries of Main to Mississippi, Volume 3* (London: John Snow, 1864), p. 182.

37 Affidavit of Christianna Poole, in Pension File of Robert Poole, Dec. 8, 1890, Certificate 286,824, BPCWLPF, WCS, RG 15, NA.

38 See Gutman, *Black Family in Slavery and Freedom*, pp. 417–25; Litwack, *Been in the Storm So Long*, pp. 241–42.

39 Act of Mar. 9, 1866, tit. 31, § 5, 1866 Ga. Laws 240 (prescribing and regulating the relation of husband and wife between persons of color).

40 Act of 1865, 1865 S.C. Acts 291, 292 (establishing and regulating the domestic relations of persons of color, and amending the law in relation to paupers and vagrancy).

41 Litwack, *Been in the Storm So Long*, p. 242; see also Gutman, *Black Family in Slavery and Freedom*, p. 420.

42 Letter from Samuel Thomas to His Excellency B. G. Humphrey, Feb. 26, 1866, RG 105, M 826, roll 1, NA.

43 *Means v. State*, 99 Ga. 205 (1896).

44 Annual Report of the Operations of the Bureau of Refugees, Freedmen and Abandoned Lands for the State of Mississippi for the Year Ending Oct. 14, 1868, Dec. 12, 1868, RG 105; M 826, roll 3, frame 1183, NA.

45 *Brown v. State*, 52 Ala. 338, 340 (1875).

46 Fortunately for Mr. Williams the judge heeded the jury's recommendation that he receive a very light sentence for the crime. *Williams v. Georgia*, 67 Ga. 260 (1881).

47 Act of 1866, c. 40.

48 *State v. Melton*, 26 S.E. 933 (N.C. 1897).

49 *King v. Georgia*, 40 Ga. 244, 247–48 (1869).

50 *Kirk v. Georgia*, 65 Ga. 159 (1880).

51 *McConico v. State*, 49 Ala. 6, 6 (1873).

52 Narrative Report for the Sub District of Tupelo, Mississippi, for the Month Ending Aug., 1867, Aug. 31, 1867, RG 105, M 826, roll 30, frame 221, NA; Narrative Report for the Sub District of Tupelo, Mississippi, for the Month Ending Oct., 1867, Oct. 31, 186, ibid. at frame 812.

53 Act of June 6, 1866, ch. 106, § 11, 14 Stat. 56 (1866); Act of Aug. 7, 1882, ch. 438, § 2 (amending 57 U.S. Rev. Stat. § 4702); Pension File of Eli Johnson; Record Group 15; Application 253,796, BPCWLPF, WCS, RG 15, NA; Letter from Henry H. Molers, Special Examiner, to Hon. John C. Black, Commissioner of Pensions, in Pension File of Edward Johnson, Feb. 18, 1888, ibid.

54 Glenda Riley, *Divorce: An American Tradition* (New York: Oxford University Press, 1991), pp. 70–71; J. Nelson Frierson, "Divorce in South Carolina," *North Carolina Law Review* 9 (1931), p. 265.

55 Jennifer Roback, "Southern Labor Law in the Jim Crow Era: Exploitative or Competitive?" *University of Chicago Law Review* 51 (1984), pp. 1161–62 (for the term "labor-market cartel"); Eric Foner, *Reconstruction: America's Unfinished Revolution* (New York: Harper & Row, 1988), pp. 199–201.

56 Act of Nov. 29, 1865, ch. 23, § 5, 1865 Miss. Laws 165, 167.

57 Roback, "Southern Labor Law in the Jim Crow Era," p. 1170. See generally Ray S. Baker, *Following the Color Line* (New York: Harper & Row, 1964), pp. 95–97; Mary Church Terrell, "Peonage in the United States: The Convict Lease System and the Chain Gangs," *Nineteenth Century* 62 (1907), p. 308; William Cohen, "Negro Involuntary Servitude in the South, 1865–1940: A Preliminary Analysis," in Donald G. Nieman, ed., *Black Southerners and the Law, 1865–1900* (New York: Routledge, 1994), pp. 35, 59; Tessa M. Gorman, "Back on the Chain Gang: Why the Eighth Amendment and the History of Slavery Proscribe the Resurgence of Chain Gangs," *California Law Review* 85 (1997), p. 441; Matthew J. Mancini, "Race, Economics and the Abandonment of Convict Leasing," *Journal of Negro History* 63 (1978), pp. 339–40; Nancy A. Ozimek, "Reinstitution of the Chain Gang: A Historical and Constitutional Analysis," *Boston University Public Interest Law Journal* 6 (1997), pp. 753, 758–59; Emily S. Sanford, "The Propriety and Constitutionality of Chain Gangs," *Georgia State University Law Review* 13 (1997), p. 1155; Benno C. Schmidt, "Principle and Prejudice: The Supreme Court and Race in the Progressive Era. Part 2: The Peonage Cases," *Columbia Law Review* 82 (1982), pp. 646, 651. See F. Green, "Some Aspects of the Convict Lease System in the Southern States," *Essays in Southern History* 31 (1949), p. 121.

58 George Brown Tindall, *The Emergence of the New South, 1913–1945* (Baton Rouge: Louisiana State University Press, 1967), p. 213; Roback, "Southern Labor Law in the Jim Crow Era," pp. 1170–75.

59 Report for September, 1867, Sub District of Greenville, Mississippi, Sept. 30, 1867, RG 105, M 826, roll 30, frame 455, NA.

60 Narrative Report of Sub District of Macon, Mississippi for the Month of Oct., 1867, Nov. 9, 1867, RG 105, M 826–30, frame 775, NA.

61 Cal. Fam. Code § 297.5(a) (West 2006).

62 Cal. Fam. Code § 299.3 (West 2006).

63 Cal. Bill Analysis, AB 2580, S. Judiciary Comm., 2003–04, Reg. Sess. (June 22, 2004), (Comm. Rep.) available at WESTLAW (capitalization altered).

64 See, e.g., Kaiponanea T. Matsumura, "Reaching Backward While Looking Forward: The Retroactive Effect of California's Domestic Partner Rights and Responsibilities Act," *UCLA Law Review* 54 (2006), p. 185; Robert F. Kidd and Frederick C. Hertz, "Partnered in Debt: The Impacts of California's New Registered Domestic Partner Law on Creditors' Remedies and Debtors' Rights, under California Law and under Federal Bankruptcy Law," *San Diego Law Review* 40 (2003), pp. 427, 430.

65 Massachusetts General Laws, chapter 272 § 14: "A married person who has sexual intercourse with a person not his spouse or an unmarried person who has sexual intercourse with a married person shall be guilty of adultery and shall be punished by imprisonment in the state prison for not more than three years or in jail for not more than two years or by a fine of not more than five hundred dollars."

66 Jenny Jarvie, "Life Sentence for Adultery? Could Be," *San Francisco Chronicle*, Jan. 24, 2007.

67 In the Matter of David G. Blanchflower and Sian E. Blanchflower, 150 N.H. 226 (2003), available at http://www.courts.state.nh.us/supreme/opinions/2003/blanc150.htm.

68 New Hampshire House Bill 1125, http://legiscan.com/NH/text/HB1125/id/902575; House Bill 1218, http://legiscan.com/NH/bill/HB1218/2014.

69 Andra Varin, "Fla. Lawmaker Wants to Repeal Adultery Law," *Newsmax*, Aug. 31, 2011, http://www.newsmax.com/TheWire/Florida-adultery-law-repeal/2011/08/31/id/409316; "Michigan Senate Seeks to Repeal Adultery as Felony," *Oakland Press Law Blogger*, Apr. 19, 2009, http://oplawblog.blogspot.com/2009/04/michigan-senate-seeks-to-abolish.html.

70 Title 16, chapter 9, section 9 of the Georgia code of criminal conduct: "A married person commits the offense of adultery when he voluntarily has sexual intercourse with a person other than his spouse and, upon conviction thereof, shall be punished as for a misdemeanor."

71 Blake Spears and Lanz Lowend, "Beyond Monogamy: Lessons from Long-Term Male Couples in Non-Monogamous Relationships," *Electronic Journal of Human Sexuality* 123 (2010), available at http://thecouplesstudy.com/wp-content/uploads/BeyondMonogamy_1_01.pdf; Scott James, "Many Successful Gay Marriages Share an Open Secret," *New York Times*, Jan. 29, 2010, p. A17, available at http://www.nytimes.com/2010/01/29/us/29sfmetro.html.

72 Katherine Franke, "Marriage Is a Mixed Blessing," *New York Times*, June 23, 2011.

73 18 V.S.A. § 5160(f).

74 *Rosengarten v. Downes*, 71 Conn.App. 372, cert. granted, 261 Conn. 936 (2002); *Oehler v. Olson*, 2005 WL 758038 (Conn.Super. 2005).

75 *Dickerson v. Thompson*, 897 N.Y.S.2d 298 (3 Dept. 2010); *Parker v. Waronker*, 918 N.Y.S.2d 822 (Sup.Ct. 2010); *Anonymous v. Anonymous*, Sup. Ct., Monroe County, May 13, 2011, Bellini, J. (index No. 2010/14286); *Anonymous v. Anonymous*, Sup. Ct., Erie County, May 3, 2011, Nowak, J. (index No. SF2011–900220); *Anonymous v. Anonymous*, Sup. Ct., New York County, Mar. 21, 2011, Evans, J.; *J.R.H. v. P.R.M.*, Sup. Ct., Tompkins County, Dec. 21, 2010, Mulvey, J. (index No. 2010–0859); *Parker v. Waronker*, 30 Misc.3d 917, 918 N.Y.S.2d 822 (Sup. Ct. 2010); *Anonymous v. Anonymous*, Sup. Ct., Tompkins County, June 15, 2010, Mulvey, J. (index No. 2010–0493). See also *B.S. v. F.B.*, Sup. Ct., Westchester County, Mar. 3, 2010, Walker, J. (index No. 19624/09).

76 For a full discussion of this catch-22, see Courtney G. Joslin, "Modernizing Divorce Jurisdiction: Same-Sex Couples and Minimum Contacts," *Boston University Law Review* 91 (2011), p. 1669.

77 American Law Institute, Principles of the Law of Family Dissolution: Analysis and Recommendations § 6 (2000) ("Domestic Partners").

78 Ibid.

79 See, e.g., Grace Ganz Blumberg, "Cohabitation without Marriage: A Different Perspective," *UCLA Law Review* 28 (1981), p. 1125; Grace Ganz Blumberg, "The Regularization of Nonmarital Cohabitation: Rights and Responsibilities in the American Welfare State," *Notre Dame Law Review* 76 (2001), p. 1265; Nancy D. Polikoff, "Making Marriage Matter Less: The ALI Domestic Partner Principles Are One Step in the Right Direction," *University of Chicago Legal Forum* 2004 (2004), p. 353.

80 See Elizabeth Scott, "Domestic Partnerships, Implied Contracts, and Law Reform" in Robin Fretwell Wilson, ed., *Reconceiving the Family: Critique of the American Law Institute's Principles of the Law of Family Dissolution* (New York: Cambridge University Press, 2006), p. 331; Marsha Garrison, "Is Consent Necessary? An Evaluation of the Emerging Law of Cohabitant Obligation," *UCLA Law Review* 52 (2005), pp. 815, 846.

81 "Domestic Partnership Registration," Office of the City Clerk, City of New York, http://www.cityclerk.nyc.gov/html/marriage/domestic_partnership_reg.shtml.

82 Tara Siegel Barnard, "As Same-Sex Marriage Becomes Legal, Some Choices May Be Lost," *New York Times*, July 9, 2011, available at http://www.nytimes.com/2011/07/09/business/some-companies-want-gays-to-wed-to-get-health-benefits.html.

83 Columbia University Benefits, "New Rules for Same-Sex Marriages," Sept. 26, 2013, http://web.law.columbia.edu/sites/default/files/microsites/gender-sexuality/New%20Rules%20for%20Same-Sex%20Marriages.pdf.

84 Our brief to the provost outlining these arguments is here: http://web.law.columbia.edu/sites/default/files/microsites/gender-sexuality/Coatsworth%20DP%20Memo.pdf.

CHAPTER 4. AM I MY BROTHER'S KEEPER?

1 Affidavit of Matilda Damage, Jan. 5, 1866, Old Courthouse Museum, Vicksburg Mississippi.

2 For further information on Yerger's background, see Percy Lee Rainwater, *Mississippi: Storm Center of Succession, 1856–1861* (New York: Da Capo, 1938), pp. 207–9; James W. Garner, "Book Review," *Journal of Southern History* 4 (1938), pp. 250, 253; Letter of James W. Davis, Solicitor, Bureau of Refugees, Freedmen, and Abandoned Lands, Jan. 8, 1866, RG 105, M 826, roll 13, NA. For further information on Marmaduke Shannon's background, see Christopher Waldrep, *Roots of Disorder: Race and Criminal Justice in the American South, 1817–80* (Champaign: University of Illinois Press, 1998), p. 96.

3 Indictment of Issac Shaffer and Maria Wright, Warren Criminal Court, May 20, 1868, Old Courthouse Museum, Vicksburg, Mississippi; *Nolle Prosequi*, Warren County Criminal Court Minute Book, 1867–1869, November Term 1868, Warren County Courthouse, Vicksburg, Mississippi.

4 Indictment of Oliver Garrett and Sallie Simpson, Warren Circuit Court, Dec. Term, 1868, Old Courthouse Museum, Vicksburg, Mississippi; *Nolle Prosequi*, Feb. 9, 1870, Dec. Term 1869, Circuit Court Minute Book, Volume X, Dec. 13, 1869-Jan. 5, 1872, Warren County Courthouse, Vicksburg, Mississippi.

5 Indictment of Oscar Sanders and Liz Smothers, Dec. 10, 1870, Warren County Circuit Court, Old Courthouse Museum, Vicksburg, Mississippi; *Nolle Prosequi*, Apr. 22, 1871, Mar. Term 1870, Circuit Court Minute Book, Volume X, Dec. 13, 1869-Jan. 5, 1872, Warren County Courthouse, Vicksburg, Mississippi.

6 Indictment of Phillip Brazil and Eliza Ann Clark, Oct. 9, 1877, Warren County Circuit Court; Affidavit of Samuel Clark, Old Courthouse Museum, Vicksburg, Mississippi.

7 An Act to Regulate the Relation of Master and Apprentice, as relates to Freedmen, Free Negroes and Mulattoes, Nov. 22, 1865, Laws of the State of Mississippi.

8 Litwack, *Been in the Storm So Long*, p. 237.

9 Foner, *Reconstruction*, p. 201.

10 RG 105, M 826, roll 14, NA.

11 Letter of Thomas A. Magee, Probate Judge, Franklin County, Mississippi, dated July 15, 1866 to Captain Platt, RG 105, M 826, roll 14, NA.

12 Letter of Agent Nelson G. Gill to Colonel R.S. Donaldson, Subcommissioner, Bureau of Refugees, Freedmen and Abandoned Lands, Jackson, Mississippi, Mar. 22, 1866, RG 105, M 826, roll 14, NA.

13 Monthly Report for Pass Christian, Mississippi for May 1866 from First Lieutenant John D. Moore to Major General T.J. Wood, May 31, 1866, RG 105, M 826, roll 15, NA.

14 Captain Preston noted that the records did not record the race of ten of the eleven defendants, but given the kind of sentence they received, it is reasonable to assume that they were all black. Report of A. W. Preston to Lieutenant Stuart Eldridge, Bureau of Refugees, Freedmen and Abandoned Lands, Office of the Assistant Commissioner for the State of Mississippi, Feb. 16, 1866, RG, 105, M 826, roll 15, frames 531-2, NA; Warren County Mississippi Criminal Court Docket Book, Old Courthouse Museum, Vicksburg, Mississippi.

15 Foner, *Reconstruction*, pp. 199-200.

16 Kenneth A. Stampp, *The Era of Reconstruction, 1865-1877* (New York: Vintage, 1967), p. 79; An Act to Confer Civil Rights on Freedmen, and for Other Purposes, Nov. 25, 1865; An Act to Amend the Vagrant Laws of the State, Nov. 24, 1865; and An Act to Punish Certain Offences Therein Named, and for Other Purposes, Nov. 29, 1865, all in Laws of the State of Mississippi, Passed at a Regular Session of the Mississippi Legislature, Held in the City of Jackson, Oct., Nov. and Dec., 1865 (Jackson, Miss., 1866), 82-86, 90-93, 165-67; Letter from Samuel Thomas to Major General T.J. Wood, Mar. 12, 1866, RG 105, M 826, roll 1, NA.

17 U.S. Census Bureau, Ninth Census of Population 1870, Granville County, North Carolina, National Archives and Records Administration, Washington, DC; U.S.

Census Bureau, Tenth Census of Population 1880, Granville County, North Carolina, National Archives and Records Administration, Washington, DC.

18 See Foner, *Reconstruction*, p. 86; Jones, *Labor of Love*, p. 59.

19 U.S. Census Bureau, Ninth Census of Population 1870, Granville County, North Carolina, RG 29, M 593, Roll 1139, p. 267, Image 538, NA. U.S. Census Bureau, Tenth Census of Population 1880, Granville County, North Carolina; T9_965; Family History Film 1254965; Page: 475.2000; Enumeration District: 104; Image: 0014; National Archives and Records Administration, Washington, DC.

20 Indictment of Willis Chandler and Charry Downey, Special Term, 1875; Granville County Criminal Action Papers 1873–1875; 1875 Folder; North Carolina State Archives, Raleigh, NC.

21 "In all cases where men and women, both or one of them were lately slaves and are now emancipated, now cohabit together in the relation of husband and wife, the parties shall be deemed to have been lawfully married as man and wife at the time of the commencement of such cohabitation, although they may not have been married in due form of law. And all persons whose cohabitation is hereby ratified into a state of marriage shall go before the clerk of the court of pleas and quarter sessions of the county in which they reside, at his office, or before some justice of the peace, and acknowledge the fact of such cohabitation, and the time of its commencement, and the clerk shall enter the same in a book kept for that purpose." Act of Mar. 10, 1866, ch. 40, §§ 1–5, 1866 N.C. Sess. Laws 99–101.

22 Indictments of Berry and Bett Downey, Stephen Downey and Margaret Downey, Frank Pointer and Ereline Wilkenson, Rich Overby and Julie Downey, Charles Winston and Mary Hester, Jim Royster and Meely Overby, and Seth Royster and Mesan Royster, Special Term, 1875, Granville County Criminal Action Papers 1873–1875, 1875 folder, North Carolina State Archives, Raleigh, N.C.

23 N.C. Gen. Stat. § 14-184: "If any man and woman, not being married to each other, shall lewdly and lasciviously associate, bed and cohabit together, they shall be guilty of a Class 2 misdemeanor." Florida, Michigan, North Dakota, Mississippi, Virginia, and West Virginia also have laws on the books today making unmarried cohabitation a crime. "National Briefing Plains: North Dakota: Vote To Repeal Cohabitation Law," *New York Times*, Mar. 2, 2007.

24 Public Statutes of North Carolina, Bastard Children, chapter 12, section 1 (1855), revised in 1873, chapter 9, section 1.

25 Chapter 5, sections 1 and 5, of the Revised Statutes of the State of North Carolina passed by the General Assembly at the Session of 1836–37 (Raleigh, NC: Turner and Hughes, 1837).

26 Second Annual Report of the Bureau of Labor Statistics of the State of North Carolina for the Year 1888, volume 2 (Raleigh, NC: Daniels, 1888), pp. 212–13.

27 Ibid., p. 213.

28 McCollough and Smith to Howard, May 6, 1866, RG 105, M843, reel 8, NA.

29 *Raleigh Standard*, Oct. 5, 1887. See generally Edwards, *Gendered Strife and Confusion*, pp. 45–49; Karen L. Zipf, *Labor of Innocents: Forced Apprenticeship in North Carolina, 1715–1919* (Baton Rouge, LA: LSU Press, 2005).

30 *In Re Ambrose*, 61 N.C. 91, 96 (1867).

31 The American Missionary Association, for instance, raised substantial funds during the postwar period to support their work educating newly freed people. Teaching sexual morality was one of their principal efforts. See *History of the American Missionary Association: with illustrative facts and anecdotes* (New York: American Missionary Association, 1891), p. 46; Joe M. Richardson, *Christian Reconstruction: The American Missionary Association and Southern Blacks, 1861–1890* (Tuscaloosa: University of Alabama Press, 2009), pp. 240–41.

32 Saidiya Hartman, *Lose Your Mother: A Journey along the Atlantic Slave Route* (New York: Farrar, Straus and Giroux, 2007), p. 103.

33 Frederick Douglass, *My Bondage and My Freedom* (New York: Miller, Orton & Mulligan 1855).

34 Testimony of Henry G. Judd before the American Freedmen's Inquiry Commission, M 619, roll 200, NA.

35 *Nanny Bacon v. Titus Bacon*, Apr. 29, 1868, 1868 Proceedings of the Provost Court, Beaufort District, S.C., Case # 376, RG 393, Entry 4257, NA.

36 Dale Carpenter's book, *Flagrant Conduct: The Story of Lawrence v. Texas* (New York: W.W. Norton, 2012), recounts this story.

37 U.S. Department of Health and Human Services, Issue Brief: Addressing Racial Disproportionality in Child Welfare, Child Welfare Information Gateway (2011), available at http://www.childwelfare.gov/pubs/issue_briefs/racial_disproportion-ality/racial_disproportionality.pdf; Adoption and Foster Care Analysis and Reporting System (AFCARS) FY 2010 data (Oct. 1, 2009, through Sept. 30, 2010).

38 U.S. Department of Health and Human Services, Children's Bureau, Child Welfare Outcomes 2006–2009, Report to Congress (ACYF, ACF) of the (2009), available at http://www.acf.hhs.gov/programs/cb/pubs/cwo06-09/cwo06-09.pdf; V. Fajardo, H. Swope, and L. Zikratova, "The Decline in the Number of Children in Foster Care: Emerging Trends in AFCARS and NCANDS Data," Presentation at the Children's Bureau's 13th National Child Welfare Data and Technology Conference, Making IT Work, Hyatt Regency Hotel, Bethesda, Maryland, July 19, 2010; Dorothy Roberts, "Racial Geography of Child Welfare," available at http://www.oregon.gov/dhs/children/beyondfc/pages/news/2010-0927.aspx.

39 Wendy G. Lane, David M. Rubin, Ragin Monteith, and Cindy W. Christian, "Racial Differences in the Evaluation of Pediatric Fractures for Physical Abuse," *Journal of American Medical Association* 288 (2002), pp. 1603–9.

40 U.S. Department of Health and Human Services, Children's Bureau, National Study of Protective, Preventive, and Reunification Services Delivered to Children and Their Families, Executive Summary, Finding 4 (1997), p. 3.

41 *Nicholson v. Williams*, 203 F.Supp.2d 153, 248 (E.D.N.Y. 2002).

42 Dorothy Roberts, *Shattered Bonds: The Color of Child Welfare* (New York: Basic Civitas Books, 2002), p. 25; Susan L. Brooks and Dorothy E. Roberts, "Social Justice and Family Court Reform," *Family Court Review* 40 (2002), p. 453.

43 *Baskin v. Bogan*, 766 F.3d 648, 663 (7th Cir. 2014), *cert. den.*, 135 S.Ct. 316 (2014), citing Gary Gates, "Same-Sex Couples in Wisconsin: A Demo-graphic Survey" (Williams Institute, UCLA School of Law, Aug. 2014), http://williamsinstitute.law. ucla.edu/wp-content/uploads/WI-same-sex-couples-demo-aug-2014.pdf; Gary Gates, "Same-Sex Couples in Indiana: A Demographic Summary" (Williams Institute, UCLA School of Law, 2014), http://williamsinstitute.law.ucla.edu/ wp-content/uploads/IN-same-sex-couples-demo-aug-2014.pdf.

44 *Baskin v. Bogan*, 766 F.3d 648, 662 (7th Cir. 2014), *cert. den.*, 135 S.Ct. 316 (2014).

45 *Baskin v. Bogan*, at 663.

46 Rachel H. Farr and Charlotte J. Patterson, "Transracial Adoption by Lesbian, Gay, and Heterosexual Couples: Who Completes Transracial Adoptions and With What Results?," *Adoption Quarterly* 12 (2009), p. 195.

CHAPTER 5. THE AFTERLIFE OF RACISM AND HOMOPHOBIA

1 While Prop 8 was found by a federal judge in 2010 to violate the constitutional rights of gay people (*Perry v. Schwarzenegger*, 704 F.Supp.2d 921 (N.D.Cal. 2010)), its passage via popular vote in 2008 illustrates a troubling fact surrounding many of the victories for marriage equality: in many cases the courts (both state and federal) were out ahead of the majority of the people on the question of same-sex couples' entitlement to marriage rights. As such, the case for same-sex marriage illustrates well the "counter-majoritarian difficulty" inherent in a social movement that relies heavily on courts to bring about change that the majority of the people have not yet embraced. Alexander Bickel, *The Least Dangerous Branch: The Supreme Court and the Bar of Politics* (New Haven, CT: Yale University Press, 1986), pp. 16–22.

2 "Defining Marriage: State Defense of Marriage Laws and Same-Sex Marriage," *National Conference of State Legislatures*, http://www.ncsl.org/research/human-services/same-sex-marriage-overview.aspx; Moritz College of Law, "Research Guides: Same-Sex Marriage Laws," http://moritzlaw.osu.edu/library/samesexmar-riagelaws.php.

3 "Southern Baptist President Fred Luter Links Gay Marriage to North Korean Threats," *On Top Magazine*, Apr. 1, 2013, http://www.ontopmag.com/article.aspx?id=14839&MediaType=1&Category=26#.

4 "Anti-Gay Pastor Claims Michael Sam May Marry 9-Year-Old Boy," *Richard Fowler Show* (YouTube), http://www.youtube.com/watch?v=U-ET9p-haBs.

5 Andy Towle, "MS Lawmaker Andy Gipson Says Gays Spread Disease, Suggest They Should Be Put to Death," *Towleroad* (blog), May 18, 2012, http://www.towleroad.com/2012/05/ms-lawmaker-andy-gipson-says-gays-spread-disease-suggest-they-should-be-put-to-death.html.

6 See Adam Nagourney, "Gays Targeted in a California Initiative," *New York Times*, Mar. 24, 2015.

7 S.C. Code Ann. §§ 20–1–10 & 15 (Law. Co-op. Supp. 2004).

8 Tobias Barrington Wolff, "Interest Analysis in Interjurisdictional Marriage Disputes," *University of Pennsylvania Law Review* 153 (2005), p. 2215.

9 David Murray, "Church Discusses Gay Parishoners," *Great Falls Tribune*, Sept. 21, 2014; David Murray, "Gay Montana Couple Responds to Controversy," *Great Falls Tribune*, Sept. 25, 2014; Frank Bruni, "'I Do' Means You're Done," *New York Times*, Sept. 23, 2014.

10 Wolff, "Interest Analysis," p. 2227.

11 *Scott v. State*, 39 Ga. 321, 326 (1869).

12 *State v. Gibson*, 36 Ind. 389, 405 (Ind. 1871) (declaring right "to follow the law of races established by the Creator himself" to uphold constitutionality of conviction of a black man who married a white woman); *Green v. State*, 58 Ala. 190, 195 (Ala. 1877) (upholding conviction for interracial marriage, reasoning god "has made the two races distinct").

13 *Loving v. Virginia*, 388 U.S. 1, 3 (1967) (quoting trial court).

14 Rev. Rul. 71–447, 1971–2 C.B. 230; *Bob Jones University v. United States*, 461 U.S. 574 (1983).

15 *Newman v. Piggie Park Enters., Inc.*, 256 F. Supp. 941, 945 (D.S.C. 1966), aff'd in relevant part and rev'd in part on other grounds, 377 F.2d 433 (4th Cir. 1967), aff'd and modified on other grounds, 390 U.S. 400 (1968).

16 *Miller v. Jenkins*, 912 A.2d 951 (2006), 637 S.E.2d 330 (2006), 661 S.E.2d 822 (2008), 78 S.E.2d 268 (2009) 12 A.3d 768 (2010), 131 S.Ct. 568 (2010).

17 Sheryl Gay Stolberg, "Republicans Sign Brief in Support of Gay Marriage," *New York Times*, Feb. 26, 2013; Cary Franklin, "Marrying Liberty and Equality: The New Jurisprudence of Gay Rights," *Virginia Law Review* 100 (2014), pp. 820–23.

18 Brief for Kenneth B. Mehlman et al. as Amici Curiae Supporting Respondents at 2–3, *Hollingsworth v. Perry*, 133 S. Ct. 2652 (2013) (No. 12–144).

19 Sheryl Gay Stolberg, "Obama's Views on Gay Marriage 'Evolving,'" *New York Times*, June 18, 2011.

20 *Hollingsworth v. Perry*, Brief for Respondents on Writ of Certiorari to the United States Court of Appeals for the Ninth Circuit, available at http://www.afer.org/wp-content/uploads/2013/02/2013-02-21-Plaintiffs-Brief.pdf. The ACLU attorney challenging Oregon's ban on same-sex marriage similarly invoked "a badge of inferiority" as the injury of exclusion from marriage. "Oregon's Marriage Equality Lawsuit: Attorneys Argue Marriage Ban Is Unconstitutional," *Love: Oregon United for Marriage*, Apr. 23, 2014, http://www.oregonunitedformarriage.org/oregons-marriage-equality-lawsuit-attorneys-argue-marriage-ban-is-unconstitutional/.

21 Letter from Dale Carpenter et al. to Illinois Legislature on Same-Sex Marriage, Oct. 23, 2013, available at http://blogs.chicagotribune.com/files/five-law-professors-against-changing-sb-10.pdf.

22 Langston Hughes, "Silhouette," in *Selected Poems of Langston Hughes* (New York: Vintage, 1990), p. 171.

23 Frantz Fanon, *Black Skin, White Masks* (London: Pluto Press, 1986), p. 91.

24 Ibid., p. 95.

25 *Perry v. Schwarzenegger*, Pretrial Proceedings and Trial Evidence Credibility Determinations Findings of Fact Conclusions of Law Order, 704 F.Supp.2d 921, 974, 980 (N.D.Cal. 2010).

26 *Varnum v. Brien*, Ruling on Plaintiffs' and Defendant's Motions for Summary Judgment, 2007 WL 2468667 (Iowa Dist.) (Trial Order)(2007).

27 Devon Carbado similarly argues that "the gay rights advocates' representative gay man, the person they presented as the icon of gay victimization, was white." The strategy was to present a "but for" gay man—"a man, who, but for his sexual orientation, was just like everybody else, that is, just like every other white heterosexual person." "Black Rights, Gay Rights, Civil Rights," *UCLA Law Review* 47 (2000), pp. 1467, 1472.

28 "Should Gay Marriage Be Legalized?," *Debate.org*, http://www.debate.org/opinions/should-gay-marriage-be-legalized.

29 Sarah Muller, "Dolly Parton: Gays 'Should Suffer Just Like Us Heterosexuals,'" *MSNBC.com*, May 1, 2014, http://www.msnbc.com/the-last-word/dolly-parton-gay-marriage-support.

30 Adam Liptak, "Seeking a Same-Sex Marriage Case Fit for History," *New York Times*, Sept. 22, 2014, p. A19.

31 A notable exception is the Gay and Lesbian Advocates and Defenders, whose executive director is a man of color, Janson Wu.

32 Kenyon Farrow, "Is Gay Marriage Anti-Black?," June 14, 2005, http://kenyonfarrow.com/2005/06/14/is-gay-marriage-anti-black/.

33 "Slavery had a disastrous effect upon African-American families, yet sadly a child born into slavery in 1860 was more likely to be raised by his mother and father in a two-parent household than was an African-American baby born after the election of the USA's first African-American president" ("Marriage Vow").

CHAPTER 6. WHAT MARRIAGE EQUALITY TEACHES US ABOUT GENDER AND SEX

1 Catherine Hall, *Civilising Subjects: Metropole and Colony in the English Imagination 1830–1867* (Chicago: University of Chicago Press, 2002), p. 189.

2 Patricia Dixon, "Marriage among African Americans: What Does the Research Reveal?," *Journal of African American Studies* 13 (2009), p. 29.

3 Banks, *Is Marriage for White People?*

4 See the Williams Institute's estimates of the number of same-sex couples that have married: "LGB Families and Relationships: Analyses of the 2013 National Health Interview Survey," Sept. 2014, http://williamsinstitute.law.ucla.edu/wp-content/uploads/lgb-families-nhis-sep-2014.pdf.

5 See NJ ST 37:2–33: "A premarital or pre-civil union agreement shall be in writing, with a statement of assets annexed thereto, signed by both parties, and it is enforceable without consideration."

6 Ariela Dubler has updated Mnookin and Kornhauser's work on the shadow of marriage in ways that might inform the equities of the illustrative cases I offer in this essay. See Robert Mnookin and Lewis Kornhauser, "Bargaining in the Shadow of Law: The Case of Divorce," *Yale Law Journal* 88 (1979); Ariela R. Dubler, "In the Shadow of Marriage: Single Women and the Legal Construction of the Family and the State," *Yale Law Journal* 112 (2003).

7 See Eve Kosofsky Sedgwick, "Gosh, Boy George, You Must be Awfully Secure in Your Masculinity!," in Maurice Berger, Brian Wallis, and Simon Watson, eds., *Constructing Masculinity* 11 (New York: Routledge, 1995), p. 16.

8 See, e.g., Lenore Weitzman, *The Divorce Revolution: The Unexpected Social and Economic Consequences for Women and Children in America* (New York: Free Press, 1985) (noting that divorced women and children experience a 73% decline in standard of living post-divorce); Terry Arendell, *Mothers And Divorce: Legal, Economic and Social Dimensions* (Berkeley: University of California Press,1986); Saul Hoffman and John Holmes, "Husbands, Wives and Divorce," in Greg J. Duncan and James N. Morgan, eds., *Five Thousand American Families—Patterns of Economic Progress* (Ann Arbor, MI: Institute for Social Research, 1976); Leslie Morgan, *After Marriage Ends: Economic Consequences for Midlife Women* (Newbury Park, CA: Sage Publications, 1991); Randall D. Day and Stephen J. Bahr, "Income Changes Following Divorce and Remarriage," *Journal of Divorce* 9 (1986); Thomas J. Espenshade, "The Economic Consequences of Divorce," *Journal of Marriage and Family* 41 (1979); Marsha Garrison, "Good Intentions Gone Awry: How New York's Equitable Distribution Law Affected Divorce Outcomes," *Brooklyn Law Review* 57 (1991); James B. Mclindon, "Separate but Unequal: The Economic Disaster of Divorce for Women and Children," *Family Legal Quarterly* 21 (1987).

9 Cynthia Lee Starnes, *The Marriage Buyout: The Troubled Trajectory of U.S. Alimony Law* (New York: NYU Press, 2014), p. 147. June Carbone and Naomi Cahn offer a thoughtful critique of this model in "Whither/Wither Alimony?," *Texas Law Review* 93 (2015), p. 925.

10 News Release, Bureau of Labor Statistics, U.S. Dept. of Labor, Employment Characteristics of Families—2013, p. 2, available at http://www.bls.gov/news.release/pdf/famee.pdf, archived at http://perma.cc/43N9- 8A6A (showing that approximately 65% of married mothers worked outside the home in 2013).

11 See, e.g., Dena Hassouneh and Nancy Glass, "The Influence of Gender Role Stereotyping on Women's Experiences of Female Same-Sex Intimate Partner Violence," *Violence against Women* 14 (2008).

12 Katherine Franke, "The Domesticated Liberty of *Lawrence v. Texas*," *Columbia Law Review* 104 (2004), p. 1408.

13 Of course there are plenty of heterosexual married couples that do not have children, as the advocates argue as well.

14 See *Baskin v. Bogan*, 766 F.3d 648, 663 (7th Cir. 2014), *cert. den.*, 135 S.Ct. 316 (2014), discussed in chapter 4.

15 David Scott, *Refashioning Futures: Criticism after Postcoloniality* (Princeton, NJ: Princeton University Press, 1999), p. 87.

16 Groups such as Queers for Economic Justice, the Sylvia Rivera Law Project, and the Alternatives to Marriage Project, among others, have taken up this hard work but have not been as well funded as have the mainstream LGBT organizations that have focused on marriage, employment discrimination, and parenting. Dean Spade and Andrea Ritchie have written thoughtfully on the need to have issues of race and class figure more prominently in the gay rights agenda. See Dean Spade, *Normal Life: Administrative Violence, Critical Trans Politics and the Limits of Law* (Cambridge, MA: South End Press, 2011); Joey L. Mogul, Andrea J. Ritchie, and Kay Whitlock, *Queer (In)Justice: The Criminalization of LGBT People in the United States* (Boston: Beacon Press, 2011).

APPENDIX

1 See the amendment adding a broad religious exemption to the New York marriage equality bill at http://www.governor.ny.gov/assets/GPB_24_MARRIAGE_EQUALITY_BILL.pdf, and Utah's Antidiscrimination and Religious Freedom law at http://le.utah.gov/~2015/bills/static/SB0296.html.

2 See the work of the Public Rights/Private Conscience Project at http://web.law.columbia.edu/gender-sexuality/public-rights-private-conscience-project.

INDEX

ABOUT THE AUTHOR

Katherine Franke is Sulzbacher Professor of Law and Director of the Center for Gender and Sexuality Law at Columbia University. She is among the nation's leading scholars working at the intersections of feminist, queer, and critical race theory. In addition to her academic work, she is Chair of the Board of Directors of the Center for Constitutional Rights.